Signature Pedagogies in International Relations

EDITED BY

JAN LÜDERT

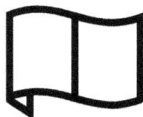

E-INTERNATIONAL RELATIONS PUBLISHING

E-International Relations
www.E-IR.info
Bristol, England
2021

ISBN 978-1-910814-58-1

Production: Michael Tang
Cover Image: Omelchenko/Nik Merkulov/Shutterstock

A catalogue record for this book is available from the British Library.

E-IR Edited Collections

Series Editor: Stephen McGlinchey
Books Editor: Bill Kakenmaster
Editorial assistance: Edoardo Pieroni and Tusharika Deka

E-IR's Edited Collections are open access scholarly books presented in a format that preferences brevity and accessibility while retaining academic conventions. Each book is available in print and digital versions, and is published under a Creative Commons license. As E-International Relations is committed to open access in the fullest sense, free electronic versions of all of our books, including this one, are available on our website.

Find out more at: http://www.e-ir.info/publications

About E-International Relations

E-International Relations (E-IR) is the world's leading open access website for students and scholars of international politics, reaching over three million readers per year. In addition to our books, our daily publications feature expert articles, reviews and interviews – as well as student learning resources. The website is run by a non-profit organisation based in Bristol, England and staffed by an all-volunteer team of students and scholars.

http://www.e-ir.info

Abstract

This volume builds on recent Scholarship of Teaching and Learning (SoTL) research to showcase a wide range of International Relations (IR) teaching and learning frameworks. Contributors explore their signature pedagogies (SPs) relevant to the study and practice of teaching IR by detailing how pedagogical practices and their underlying assumptions influence how we teach and impart knowledge. Authors from across the world and different institutional backgrounds critically engage with their teaching approaches by exploring the following questions: What concrete and practical acts of teaching and learning IR do we employ? What implicit and explicit assumptions do we impart to students about the world of politics? What values and beliefs about professional attitudes and dispositions do we foster and in preparing students for a wide range of possible careers? Authors, as such, provide IR educators, students, and practitioners' pedagogical insights and practical ways for developing their own teaching and learning approaches.

–

Jan Lüdert is an Associate Professor at City University of Seattle where he serves as Director of Curriculum and Instruction. He is a current Research Associate with the German Research Fund 'Dynamics of Security' project at Philipps Marburg University. Jan is an alumnus of the World Affairs Council Fellows and Liu Institute for Global Issues Scholar programs. He earned his Ph.D. at the department of Political Science at the University of British Columbia, Vancouver. Jan is a committed, passionate and award-winning educator as recognized by the prestigious Killam Teaching Award as well as Blackboard's Exemplary Course Program Award. His interests include International Relations Theory, Intergovernmental Organizations, Non-State Actors, Transnational and Cyberspace Politics, Global Norms, Human Rights, Security Studies, Teaching, Learning & Technology.

Acknowledgements

A number of people and institutions contributed to the realization of this volume. At the University of British Columbia (UBC) in Vancouver, Canada, I thank Joseph Topornycky and my colleagues at the Centre for Teaching, Learning, and Technology for introducing me to the scholarship on signature pedagogies. At UBC, I am also indebted to Julie Walchli and Sunaina Assanand for providing me with the space and funding to research signature pedagogies in the social sciences for a Teaching Learning Enhancement Fund (TLEF) project titled 'Educational and Career Outcomes for UBC Arts Students: Towards a new Paradigm.' I also thank Michael Griffin for entrusting me with leading research for a related TLEF on fostering citizenship skills in undergraduate education titled 'Cultivating citizenship skills through teaching and learning in the humanities.' For their encouragement to embrace my passion for teaching IR, my gratitude extends to, amongst others, Katharina Coleman, John Dryzek, Katherine Morton, Paul Keal, Richard Price, Allen Sens, and Christian Reus-Smit. At City University of Seattle, I want to thank my colleagues Scott Carnz, Joel Domingo, Mary Mara, and Gregory Price. I must thank participants and discussants at International Studies Association conferences for feedback on this project: Mark A. Boyer, the late Amy Eckert, Jamie Frueh, Gigi Gokcek, Eric K. Leonard, Jenny H. Peterson, Cameron G. Thies, Amy Skonieczny and Brent J. Steele. My gratitude goes to the authors of this volume for their commitment to teaching and learning, their patience and hard work. Finally, I owe my wife Cara and child Juno Cedar thanks for their loving support towards completing this project.

Jan Lüdert

Contributors

David Andersen-Rodgers is a Professor of Political Science at California State University, California. He is the co-author (with Kerry F. Crawford) of *Human Security: Theory and Action*. His teaching and research focus broadly on issues of peace and conflict with a particular focus on the effects of war on non-combatants.

Shane Joshua Barter is an Associate Professor of Comparative Politics at Soka University of America. He worked for Asian Human Rights NGOs (Forum Asia), the Carter Center, the Canadian Government, and the European Union, and is the former Director of the Pacific Basin Research Center. His research and teaching interests relate to politics in Southeast Asia, armed conflict, state and society, democratization, religious politics, and territorial autonomy.

Patricia Capelini Borelli is a PhD candidate in International Relations at the interinstitutional Graduate Program 'San Tiago Dantas' (UNESP, UNICAMP, PUC-SP). She holds a Master's degree (2016) in Strategic Studies from Universidade Federal Fluminense (UFF) and a Bachelor's degree (2012) both in International Relations and Economics from Faculdades de Campinas. Her areas of study are: International Security; International Political Economy; Defense Economics; Foreign Policy. She is a Professor of International Relations at Faculdades de Campinas (FACAMP) and Academic Coordinator of FACAMP's Model United Nations. She co-organized WFUNA International Model United Nations Brazil (2018).

Xira Ruiz-Campillo is a Professor of International Relations in the Faculty of Political Sciences at Complutense University of Madrid. She holds a PhD in International Relations. She has been a visiting fellow at the Urban Institute of the University of Sheffield and has professional experience in the Spanish Ministry of Defense and in the UNCHR. Her research interests focus on climate diplomacy in the European Union and the role of cities in the fight against climate change. Besides, her interests in improving the quality of teaching have led her to participate in several congresses and research projects on innovation in education.

Antonio Moreno Cantano is an Associate Professor in the Department of International Relations and Global History at the Complutense University of Madrid (Spain). He belongs to the History and Video Games research group at the University of Murcia. He holds a PhD in Contemporary History from the University of Alcalá de Henares. He combines his university teaching work with social science classes in an institute. His latest research focuses on the use of new sources for the study of international reality, especially digital games and graphic novels.

Daniel Clausen is a graduate of Florida International University's PhD program in International Relations. His research has been published in *Asian Politics and Policy*, *Electronic Journal of Contemporary Japanese Studies*, and *Diplomatic Courier*, among other publications. His teaching experience includes over nine years of experience as a TESOL instructor. He has also written several novels and short story collections. He teaches full-time at an English school in Japan and part-time at Nagasaki International University.

Mathew Davies is Senior Lecturer and Head of the Department of International Relations at the Coral Bell School of Asia Pacific Affairs, ANU College of Asia and the Pacific, the Australian National University. He is the author of *Ritual and Region: The Invention of ASEAN* (CUP 2018) and *Realising Rights* (Routledge 2014).

Kattya Cascante Hernández is an Associate Professor at Complutense University of Madrid. She is a current Research Associate with the University Institute for Development and Cooperation. She is a professor in the International Relations degree and International Cooperation MBA. Kattya earned her PhD at the department of International Relations and Global History at the Complutense University of Madrid. She is a committed international cooperation professional and has worked in development organizations in Latin American, African and Asian development regions.

Roberta Silva Machado holds a PhD in Political Science (University of Campinas) and a PhD in Law (University of Seville); a Master's degree in International Law and International Relations (University of Seville); and a Bachelor's degree in International Relations. She was a Visiting Scholar at University of Seville (2015). Her areas of interest are human rights, the United Nations system, and international criminal tribunals. She is currently a Professor of International Relations at Faculdades de Campinas (FACAMP) and Academic Coordinator of FACAMP Model United Nations (FAMUN). She co-organized WFUNA International Model United Nations Brazil (2017–2018).

Lisa MacLeod is an Associate Professor of International Studies at Soka University of America. She teaches Introduction to International Relations, Introduction to Human Rights, International Law, the UN and World Politics, and Peace and Conflict Resolution. She received her PhD from the University of Denver's Graduate School of International Studies.

Talita de Mello Pinotti is a PhD student in Social Sciences at the State University of Campinas and holds a Master's degree in Political Science from the Federal University of Rio Grande do Sul. Her research interests include: UN studies, China and global governance, and Chinese foreign policy. She is currently a Professor of International Relations at Faculdades de Campinas (FACAMP), Director of its Study and Research Center on IR, and Academic Coordinator of the FACAMP Model United Nations since 2015. She co-organized WIMUN Brazil with WFUNA (2017–2018). In 2014, she was an intern at the Permanent Mission of Brazil to the UN (NY).

Patrícia Nogueira Rinaldi holds a PhD and Master's degree in Political Science from the State University of Campinas, and a Bachelor's degree in International Relations from Faculdades de Campinas (FACAMP). She was a visiting scholar at the Ralph Bunche Institute for International Studies, CUNY (2015). Her areas of study are the UN development system and the Global South. She is a Professor of IR at FACAMP, Director of its Center of Studies and Research in IR, and is the Academic Coordinator of FACAMP's Model UN. She co-organized WFUNA International Model United Nations Brazil (2017–2018).

Jenny H. Peterson is an Associate Professor of Teaching at the Department of Political Science at the University of British Columbia. She is broadly interested in the politics of international aid with her past work analyzing process of liberal peacebuilding and critiques thereof. Finding much of this critical work homogenizing of a diverse range of processes she has recently begun exploring conceptual and empirical deviations from the liberal model. Engaging with debates on agonism, resistance, hybridity, and political space she is now exploring diversity and innovation, both local and international, in peace/justice movements. She has conducted research and led student fieldtrips in Kosovo, Sri Lanka, and Ghana. Her teaching interests include International Relations, comparative politics, humanitarian studies, and peace studies. Based in Political Science, she will also be teaching at UBC's new Vantage College.

Xiaoye She is an Assistant Professor of Political Science at California State University San Marcos (CSUSM). Her area of expertise is in comparative and international political economy with a focus on the Asia-Pacific region. Her most recent research examines subnational variations in Chinese welfare capitalism, as well as China's emerging role in Asian development finance. She teaches a variety of courses in International Relations, comparative politics, political economy, and research methods, with strong emphasis on active and problem-based learning pedagogies, such as team-based learning, case studies, and simulations.

William J. Shelling II is a Master's student at the School of Public Policy and Global Affairs at the University of British Columbia.

Archie W. Simpson has been a teaching fellow in Politics and International Relations at a number of British universities. This includes teaching at St. Andrews, Aberdeen, Stirling, Nottingham, and most recently the University of Bath. He is a founding member of the Centre for Small State Studies at the University of Iceland, and a member of the international editorial board of the journal *Small States and Territories*.

Erzsébet Strausz is an Assistant Professor in the Department of International Relations at Central European University. She holds a PhD from Aberystwyth University and her research focuses on post-structuralist theory, critical security studies, critical pedagogy, as well as creative, experimental, and narrative research methods. She was awarded the British International Studies Association's Excellence in Teaching International Studies Prize in 2017 while she was teaching at the University of Warwick and more recently was one of the recipients of the CEU Distinguished Teaching Award. Her research monograph *Writing the Self and Transforming Knowledge in International Relations: Towards a Politics of Liminality* was nominated by Routledge for the Sussex International Theory Prize in 2019. With Shine Choi and Anna Selmeczi, she is co-editor of the edited volume *Critical Methods for the Study of World Politics: Creativity and Transformation*.

Ismail Erkam Sula is an Assistant Professor of International Relations, Faculty of Political Science, Ankara Yıldırım Beyazıt University. He specializes in the study of foreign policy, International Relations theory, and research methodology in social sciences. He teaches various courses at both graduate and undergraduate levels and utilizes a variety of teaching techniques focusing on "student active learning." He writes and uses various simulations to teach challenging topics of International Relations.

Tamara A. Trownsell is an Associate Professor of International Relations at the Universidad San Francisco de Quito, Ecuador. Earlier field research in development, conservation, and culture led to her interest in Andean philosophy, which she now uses to explore the implications of the typically embraced ontological suppositions about existence on knowledge production.

Contents

1. SIGNATURE PEDAGOGIES IN INTERNATIONAL RELATIONS
   Jan Lüdert   1

2. TEACHING INTERNATIONAL RELATIONS AS A LIBERAL ART
   Lisa MacLeod   16

3. SIGNATURE PEDAGOGIES AND INTERNATIONAL RELATIONS
   THEORY: FROM THOUGHTLESSNESS TO CITIZENSHIP
   Mathew Davies   28

4. SHALL WE DESTROY THE TEACHER? WHAT ENGLISH
   LANGUAGE TEACHERS CAN TEACH IR ABOUT PEDAGOGY
   Daniel Clausen   39

5. FOSTERING ONTOLOGICAL AGILITY: A PEDAGOGICAL
   IMPERATIVE
   Tamara A. Trownsell   54

6. MARKS THAT MATTER: SLOW LETTERS TO AUTHORS AND
   SELVES
   Erzsébet Strausz   69

7. TRAVEL LEARNING CLUSTERS AS SIGNATURE PEDAGOGIES
   Shane Joshua Barter   84

8. STUDENT LED ADVOCACY AND THE "SCHOLARS IN PRISON"
   PROJECT: EXPERIENTIAL LEARNING AND CRITICAL
   KNOWLEDGE(S) IN INTERNATIONAL RELATIONS
   William J. Shelling II and Jenny H. Peterson   97

9. KILLING YOUR STUDENTS: SIGNATURE PEDAGOGIES AND
   THE USE OF VIOLENCE IN IN-CLASS SIMULATIONS
   David Andersen-Rodgers   112

10. SUPERVISING IR DISSERTATIONS: USING PERSONAL
    ANECDOTES TO REFLECT A STRATEGY FOR SUPERVISION
    Archie W. Simpson   121

11. TEACHING AND LEARNING INTERNATIONAL RELATIONS
PROFESSIONAL SKILLS THROUGH SIMULATIONS
Patricia Capelini Borelli, Patrícia Nogueira Rinaldi,
Roberta Silva Machado and Talita de Mello Pinotti   133

12. TEACHING IR THROUGH SHORT ITERATED SIMULATIONS: A
SEQUENCED APPROACH FOR IR COURSES
Xiaoye She   147

13. TEACHING INTERNATIONAL RELATIONS IN THE
UNDERGRADUATE CLASSROOM: THE USE OF METAPHORS,
SIMULATIONS, AND GAMES
Ismail Erkam Sula   165

14. ENHANCING CREATIVITY AND COMMUNICATION SKILLS
THROUGH IR SIGNATURE PEDAGOGIES
Xira Ruiz-Campillo, Kattya Cascante Hernández
and Antonio Moreno Cantano   180

NOTE ON INDEXING   196

1

Signature Pedagogies in International Relations

JAN LÜDERT

This edited volume builds on recent Scholarship of Teaching and Learning (SoTL) research to showcase a range of teaching and learning approaches in International Relations (IR). A critical contribution arising from SoTL has been that effective IR teaching varies across academic disciplines and departments (Haynie, Chick, and Gurung 2009; Haynie, Chick, and Gurung 2012). Of course, teaching strategies travel across higher education institutions and are shared throughout the academy; as all educators need to lesson-plan, present relevant content in a structured and engaging manner, while actively including students in the learning process (Frueh et al. 2020; Vlcek and Bower 2020). Apart from the confluence of relevant disciplinary content, the pedagogical approach and instructional repertoire, as well as the program objectives in which a course is couched; an effective instructor will draw on common teaching strategies shared across the discipline while bringing a unique style of instruction to the discipline.

This chapter introduces the reader to the signature pedagogy framework and its relevance to teaching and learning International Relations. It establishes that IR as a discipline, although carrying the semblance of a singular pedagogy like other social sciences, is more usefully understood as a place of plurality; hence the volume's title: 'Signature Pedagogies in International Relations.' Second, it details how pedagogical practices and their underlying assumptions influence how we teach and impart knowledge, and offers a synthesis on the diverse contributions of the volume. This collection of signature pedagogies, more broadly, intends to present a wide range of active learning strategies and offer critical reflections on IR teaching as a moral and ethical endeavor through which students come to appreciate eclectic theorizing, encounter global affairs via layering central concepts, and gain transferable skills for a wide range of possible careers. By sharing techniques and reflections, authors in this book provide pedagogical insights for IR educators, students, and practitioners, as well as practical ways for developing their own approaches to learning about the world of politics. As such, this volume offers a unique collection bringing together IR educators from across the world and various university settings.

Contributors take as their starting point that IR is a practical form of education. At the most basic level, and irrespective of theoretical persuasion, IR is animated by the question of 'how we should act' (Reus-Smit and Snidal 2008, 7). Yet an IR education is, strictly speaking, neither professional nor vocational in orientation, but introduces students to different theoretical and methodological perspectives with the intent of illuminating global issues that demand action (e.g., promoting peaceful coexistence between nations or addressing transboundary challenges, such as climate change). By discussing aspects of their own IR signature pedagogies and detailing specific teaching models, the authors in this volume explore the following questions:

1. What concrete and practical acts of teaching and learning IR do we employ?
2. What implicit and explicit assumptions do we impart to students about the world of politics?
3. What values and beliefs about professional attitudes and dispositions do we foster in preparing students for a wide range of possible careers?

Leading on from this, we encourage others in the field to consider how their own teaching, and especially its underlying assumptions, influence how we impart knowledge to the next cadre of IR graduates.

Mapping Shulman's Signature Pedagogy Framework onto International Relations

Lee S. Shulman, emeritus professor at the Stanford Graduate School of Education, first proposed the conceptual framework for developing signature pedagogies in 2005.[1] Shulman advanced that education, irrespective of discipline, constitutes professional preparation and that conceptualizing

---

[1]   Shulman (2005a, 2005b), in his seminal work, did not focus on the social sciences. He developed the signature pedagogies framework for professions such as law, medicine, nursing, and engineering. This volume picks up on the work by Gurung, Chick, & Haynie (2009) who adapted Shulman's framework for other disciplines and by taking the assumption that IR educators prepare students for various roles in the larger field of International Relations.

signature pedagogies (SPs) helps reveal the methods of instruction common in an academic discipline. SPs, as such, are pervasive and cut across individual courses and institutions. An SP's central function is to build *habits of mind* in students, which lead them to act and think like experts and professionals. SPs, in other words, socialize students into academic disciplines and act as steppingstones for their careers. Signature pedagogies matter precisely because they

> implicitly define what counts as knowledge in a field and how things become known. They define how knowledge is analyzed, criticized, accepted or discarded. They define the functions of expertise in a field, the locus of authority, and the privileges of rank and standing (Shulman 2005b, 54).

In other words, SPs are less concerned with what content we teach, focusing instead on how we teach and impart knowledge. SPs, in essence, are types of teaching that organize the fundamental ways of preparing future practitioners and are used by educators to transfer skills of how *to think*, *perform*, and *act*. Moreover, signature pedagogies are integral to an instructor's pedagogical content knowledge (Shulman 1986). Such focus clarifies the intersection between educators' subject matter expertise (or disciplinary content knowledge) and their pedagogical knowledge (the instructional strategies used to impart content knowledge). Although SPs, as the foundation of pedagogical content knowledge, remain discipline-specific, they, as Shulman (2005a) noted, share three common dimensions.

First, they have a *surface structure*, which includes the concrete acts of teaching and learning. Surface structure involves the practical and operational parts of teaching: how lessons are planned and organized, and how teaching and learning praxis are enacted within a particular discipline (e.g., lectures, seminars, flipped classrooms, case studies, simulations). Indeed, Daniel Clausen in Chapter 3 challenges us to consider ways to decrease our reliance on lecturing, and instead establish the IR classroom as a place where students speak more and the IR teacher speaks less. A call most, if not all, authors, in this collection share. Archie W. Simpson, in Chapter 10, for example, pays heed to the overlooked aspect of supervising undergraduate dissertations (or honors theses), which prepare students to become research-active, engage them in analytical and critical thinking, and encourage originality as future IR scholars or practitioners. Xiaoye She, in Chapter 12, provides the reader with an overview on the use of simulations as an integral part of IR signature pedagogies. She employs a series of small, in-class simulation in combinations with games, case studies, and discussion groups to create recursive and active learning sequences.

Second, SPs are based on a *deep structure* of assumptions about how best to impart a certain canon of knowledge (e.g., Socratic method, applied and participatory learning, problem-based learning, service learning, negotiated curricula). Shane Joshua Barter, in Chapter 7, here analyzes 'Learning Cluster' courses that take students abroad (e.g., Indonesia, Malaysia, Singapore) to encounter international studies as a form of experiential education. His unique teaching, in fact, disrupts more common IR surface and deep structures away from the comforts and confines of the classroom to the complexities of international studies on the ground. In Chapter 8, authors William J. Shelling and Jenny H. Peterson share insights on experiential learning in a human rights course in partnership with the Scholars at Risk Network, which aims to free wrongfully imprisoned scholars around the world. In their case, students apply human rights advocacy strategies while being sensitized to the central function of academic freedom. In Chapter 13, Ismail Eerkam Sula presents three active learning techniques as part of his SP; namely, strategy games, crisis simulations, and the use of storification. With the latter being particularly innovative, employing a tale of two villages: 'Rationalia' and 'Reflectia' to engage students in theoretical debates on rationalist and interpretivist IR methodologies. In Chapter 14, by Xira Ruiz-Campillo, Katty Cacante Hernández, and Antonio Moreno Cantano, the authors underscore that fostering students' creativity and innovation is essential for IR graduates to meet twenty-first century challenges arising from technological advances, social change, and global transformations. They offer readers an explication of the pedagogical use of policy memos, graphic novels, and virtual posters.

Third, SPs have an *implicit structure,* which is related to the moral values and beliefs about professional attitudes, conduct, and disposition. Implicit structures include the normative and moral aspects of teaching and learning in a specific discipline, including ontological beliefs, ethical values, and methodological and pragmatic attitudes (e.g., speaking truth to power, reporting facts, parsimonious theorizing, the nature of objectivity, which actors count, the connection between the 'is' and 'ought' in IR). As Lisa MacLeod underscores in Chapter 2, an IR education seeks to help students gain liberal arts skills that apply beyond academia. In the end, a degree in IR equips students with transferable skills and, most importantly, an analytical, critical, and enquiring mind. Mathew Davies establishes in Chapter 3 how an IR degree promotes global citizenship skills, which his teaching approach revolves around fostering students' thoughtfulness as understood by Hannah Arendt. Erzsébet Strausz, in Chapter 6, shares a method of students not simply reading IR scholars but engaging instead in 'letter-writing' to them. With this effort, Strausz intends to transform students' experiences of disconnection into dialogue. By writing to IR authors (real and imagined), student-teacher relationships are transfigured, novice-expert positions open up, enabling learners to realize their agency as part of the discipline. In Chapter 9, David Andersen-Rodgers, challenges readers to consider the ethics of teaching the use of violence in in-class simulations and especially with respect to effects on students engaging in questions of life and death not merely from a strategic but, as he emphasizes, a moral position. Patricia Capelini Borelli, Patrícia Nogueira Rinaldi, Roberta Silva Machado, and Talita de Mello Pinotti, in Chapter 11, illustrate the deep integration of a Model United Nations simulation project as practice for students' professional formation. Through these simulations, students learn to negotiate, find consensus, and persuade in real-world multilateral and multi-stakeholder scenarios.

With this synthesis in mind, it is important to note that signature pedagogies also share a set of common temporal features. First, they embody and demarcate teaching frameworks that are *pervasive* and *routinized.* They, fully or in part, carry over generations of educators. A memorable example in my own socialization is when a leading constructivist professor asked us during the very first graduate seminar what our orientation on human nature was: Do we think individuals are inherently 'good' (the liberal view), 'bad' (the realist view), or that good and bad are 'socially constructed' (constructivist view). This simple technique left an indelible mark on me. I have since used it as a point of departure for introducing students to IR theories and to encourage valuing theoretical plurality. Pervasive practices and routines, of course, are not without problems when stagnant and lacking innovation; yet remain useful because they enable a focus on complex subject matters, which, in turn, develop *habits of mind* around various affective, cognitive, and psychomotor learning (Lüdert and Stewart 2017). Indeed, as the authors make clear, institutions of higher learning continue employing classic forms of lecturing while increasingly incorporating new technologies (e.g., learning management systems, graphic novels, virtual posters, use of clickers) and active learning strategies (e.g., experiential learning, travel clusters, problem-based learning, team projects, and simulations). Second, SPs involve capturing and measuring student performance; while emphasizing their role as visible, active, and accountable learners. SPs are, in the end, pedagogies of uncertainty; rendering the classroom a space that may be unpredictable and surprising. This latter aspect, as the authors of this volume illustrate, entails that IR subject matters involve learning to navigate complexities that defy simple solutions as well as ethical dilemmas, including the realities of violence and the persistence of global inequalities. This type of learning content that is so central to IR undoubtedly raises the emotional stakes for both the instructor and learner, leading to the need for teachers to foster curiosity while decreasing anxiety and with the goal of enhancing students' learning outcomes. A focus Tamara A. Trownsell takes up in her chapter, which encourages us to prepare students to be both ontologically resilient and versatile.

To take stock, SPs hold value across higher education institutions and departments. When consciously formulated and employed they, as this volume advances, promise to help IR educators tailor active, collaborative, and transformative learning strategies. As a result of examining and formulating our teaching, we improve the means by which student learning takes place. By gaining insights into how our teaching methods are couched in our disciplines, we can devise learning activities and outcomes that are a) suitable to our field and assessment strategies and b) prepare students for their varied future career paths inside and outside the ivory tower. Of course, as noted by Murphy and Reidy (2006), there is a distinction to be made between professions and academic disciplines. International Relations degrees neither prescribe a single career path nor intend to train students for a specific profession. By exploring IR signature pedagogies, we aim to offer a guide to students interested in taking ownership over their studies while preparing novice students to emerge as the next generations of experts (whether as future scholars, policymakers, or other practitioners in diverse sectors).[2]

Valuing Innovation and Plurality in IR Teaching

As scholars with busy research agendas and full teaching loads, we tend to overlook that IR is a practical form of education. At the most basic level and irrespective of theoretical persuasion, IR is, as mentioned, a practical discourse animated by understanding global political phenomena. Because an IR degree prepares students for a range of possible careers, we purposefully focus our instruction on IR's key concept, theories, methods, and perspectives with the goal of helping students competently analyze global issues.[3] By beginning to formulate their own IR signature pedagogies, the authors in this volume take stock of how teaching IR is neither monolithic nor stagnant, but a space of innovation and plurality (Hagmann and Biersteker, 2014).

While IR educators employ different strategies, it seems manifest, nonetheless, that we typically model our teaching on the concrete act of organizing syllabi and lectures around canonical texts. Indeed, is there an introductory class to IR that does not talk about Waltz and anarchy, about E.H Carr and the twenty-year crisis, about Kant and the democratic peace? The answer is likely no and introductory textbooks, although increasingly paying

---

[2]   Even though an IR education, like other social sciences, does not train students for specific careers, it remains important to prepare students at all levels for multiple career pathways, in and outside of academy.

[3]   As Garrett points out the social sciences are seen as academic rather than vocational or professional (1999:312).

attention to diverse theories, typically follow a framework that sequences IR theories temporally from realism, to liberalism, and then to critical approaches. Implicit in these ways of teaching is that we foster a set of assumptions that relate to the praxis of what happens in the world of politics and how we make sense of that world through theoretical approaches, their ontological presuppositions, and methods for discovery or confirmation. These assumptions include, among other things, that there are certain actors in International Relations, which we treat as central: states. We assume that these states behave in a certain way and foster a certain type of relation with each other and vis-à-vis other actors. In fact, we frequently center classroom debates by mapping theoretical assumptions onto particular cases studies concerned with the relevance of states: the Concert of Europe, the Cold War, Globalization, and Decolonization to name a few.

Yet again such habits of teaching IR are in flux as most authors in the volume attest. This is most evident as we introduce students to other types of actors that are both interesting and important. It is here, with subsequent chapters detailing, that much is happening in our discipline that requires us to evaluate and reflect on the beliefs we have about International Relations as a practical discourse and field of inquiry. This is why there is broad consensus amongst the contributors to incorporate not only discussions of states, but broaden students' view in light of other interesting actors in the realm of world politics: non-state actors, International Organizations, epistemic communities, citizen and interest groups, corporate as well as criminal, and others. In this way, students are equipped to engage with the material not only in light of empirical realities, but to reflect on the 'state' of our theories and their utility through, for example, simulations and mock negotiations. Widening perspectives on IR actors changes the classroom climate away from passive regurgitation of state-centrism toward providing students with a view that not all important actors are states, and instead signals that purposeful agency is situated within other actors, including individuals like themselves.

By broadening IR signature pedagogies along these lines of inquiry, our students begin to engage with the implicit structure of learning about global affairs. It is here that the authors have taken cues from students who keep pushing us to review our teaching as an iterative process of continuous improvement (and which inevitably involves a level of risk taking). For instance, IR's reliance on the traditional lecture format, seminars, and tutorials appear outdated, especially in the face of technological innovations. In fact, we all notice a shift in the ways students use technology in the classroom. With that realization, we can all agree how we, as instructors, ought to pay attention to changing processes of learning.[4] Especially since Covid-19 and

---

[4]   My personal teaching style is based on backward design principles that first identify

the requirement to teach online, we are likely to further integrate flipped classroom modalities, varied technologies, and media into our courses (Goldgeier and Mezzera 2020). In fact, these kinds of changes to the surface structure of our instruction should be embraced as they afford students the ability to take greater ownership over their research projects and the production of online as well as graphic and video artifacts. This correspondingly has the budding benefit of developing student information literacy by providing opportunities to implement communication, technical, and research skills (Lüdert 2017).

Aside from deepening cognitive learning, authors in subsequent chapters underscore the importance of perspective-taking techniques to develop students' affective empathy. Here, contributors discuss ways of how our instruction goes beyond preparing students to be proficient in consuming news about World Politics but are enabled to present and write about politics and policies as informed, thoughtful global citizens. In this sense, contributors discuss how specific teaching approaches are intended to prepare students for actual work in International Organizations, Non-Governmental Organizations, government agencies, and other careers. Indeed, several authors design their courses to achieve larger learning goals surrounding transferable skills, aptitudes and dispositions relevant for IR careers and beyond.

On the flip side, authors question the reliance on lecturing students and detail how they create space for peer engagement and participatory learning instead. As the chapters on simulations highlight, for instance, students work on applied, emblematic, and illustrative case studies in Intergovernmental Organizations (IGO) simulations or mock climate change conferences. These types of experiential and active learning approaches shift our roles away from all-knowing lecturers to facilitators of learning. The benefits of this shift in our role are wide-ranging. They provide space to walk around the class, answer individual questions, listen carefully to group discussions, and gain an overall better understanding of students' comprehension and comfort with the material. In fact, these types of direct conversations with students deepen our engagement, as opposed to answering only a few questions in a large lecture setting.

---

desired learning results, from which appropriate forms of measuring students' performance are developed via sequenced learning activities (Wiggins & McTighe, 2011). In terms of individual lesson planning, I embrace a structured teaching model – known as the BOPPPS model – which breaks lesson plans into six distinct components. Structuring classes around lesson planning models allows for greater consistency while fostering accountability for instructors and students. See for an overview: https://wiki.ubc.ca/Documentation:Mini-Lessons_Basics_BOPPPS_Model_for_Planning_Lessons.

Teaching IR as a Practical Discourse and Field of Inquiry

The study of IR is a practical discourse and field of inquiry that centers on conceptions of the 'is' and the 'ought.' Students of IR have always been animated to investigate the global politics empirically, while concurrently being asked to consider the normative dimensions undergirding phenomena of international significance or finding possible solutions to them. As E.H Carr put forth in the *Twenty Years' Crisis*,

> Utopia and reality are [...] the two facets of political science. Sound political thought and sound political life will be found only where both have their place (Carr 1946, 10).

As IR educators, we ask our students to grapple with contending ideas and competing theories or; to put it differently: we require students to assess the relative merits of IR 'isms.' The cacophony of theories—from realism, liberalism, constructivism to critical theory and post-modernism—are reflect-ive of IR's breadth and theoretical diversity. Irrespective of our own theoretical persuasions, we do intend to pass on to students the ability to draw competently on these 'isms.' Building students skills on identifying the use of IR 'isms' (by politicians, in the news, or scholarship) or drawing on them in their own research is key to drive students' understanding of IR as a practical discourse and field of inquiry. Through teaching IR 'isms,' we essentially help students realize how theory-building takes place in relation to both empirical and normative questions about the international landscape. We clarify for students that IR theorizing rests on assumptions about what matters empirically as well as normatively (e.g., states are central actors, agents are rational utility maximizers, norms constitute interests and identities, human rights are universal) and help them to differentiate how IR theories are informed by specific and/or overlapping ontological and epistemological assumptions. As the authors make clear, we all seek to foster in students a stance of eclectic theorizing. We underscore that IR 'isms' answer some big and important questions, and that no single approach that answers all questions exists. With such an understanding, we expand students' insights and IR knowledge base. Indeed, through plurality, we accommodate adher-ence to diverse research traditions and by facilitating fruitful conversations across and outside the boundaries of the academe (Sil and Katzenstein 2010).

We achieve this by enabling students to think critically and logically about central IR concepts, knowledge practices and dispositions. One useful tool I like to put forward is to explore and layer IR's threshold concepts through the two faces of empirical and normative IR theorizing. Threshold concepts (TCs) are foundational or core concepts, which once grasped by students, transform their perception of a subject matter, discipline, or field of study. Meyer and Land (2003) first popularized threshold concepts in relation to troublesome knowledge, or those ideas, concepts, theories, mechanisms, that at first appear difficult to grasp, strange, or counterintuitive.[5] They conceptualize threshold concepts as,

> akin to a portal, opening up a new and previously inaccessible way of thinking about something. It represents a transformed way of understanding, or interpreting, or viewing something without which the learner cannot progress. As a consequence of comprehending a threshold there may thus be a transformed internal view of subject matter, subject landscape, or even world view. This transformation may be sudden, or it may be protracted over a considerable period of time, with the transition to understanding proving troublesome (Meyer and Land 2003b, 1).

Threshold concepts have four common characteristics. First, they are irreversible, as perspective change and transformation resulting from the acquisition of a TC are often accompanied by an *aha* moment: a breakthrough that is not forgotten or can be unlearned only through considerable effort. This can be observed, for instance, when students contend with the historically contingent and socially constructed nature of the assumption of sovereign states. Second, TCs are integrative, by clarifying and exposing to students previously obscure and hidden connections within a discipline or subject matter. An illustrative example here would be the transition students undergo when grasping theoretical assumptions underlying foundational concepts with wider everyday meaning, such as anarchy, order, and hierarchy. Third, TCs are bounded insofar as any conceptual space carries borders, which demarcate new conceptual areas of comprehension. Finally, and as mentioned, they are troublesome, because students move 'from a common sense understanding to an understanding which may conflict with perceptions that have previously seemed self-evidently true' (Davies and Brant 2006, 114).

The claim here is that there is a discernable connection between TCs and SPs. Threshold concepts are specific to disciplinary teaching contexts insofar as they transform how students think in a particular discipline, and how they perceive, apprehend, or experience particular phenomena within that discipline. TCs are deeply embedded in SPs because as conceptual gateways a

---

[5]   Examples include threshold concepts such as 'Personhood' in Philosophy; 'Gravity' in Physics; 'Depreciation' in Accounting; 'Legal Narrative' in Law; 'Limit' in Mathematics or 'Power' in Political Science. See Meyer, Land & Baillie, 2010, p. ix

given threshold concept is

> ritualized, inert, conceptually difficult, alien or tacit, because it
> requires adopting an unfamiliar discourse, or perhaps because
> the learner remains 'defended' and does not wish to change or
> let go of their customary way of seeing things (Meyer, Land &
> Baillie, 2010, ix).

By making IR's foundational concepts tangible for students through exploring substantive problems, key issues and exemplary case studies in original, creative ways, drawing on various theoretical traditions and eclectic scholarship (e.g., war and peace, cooperation and governance, justice and [in]equality) we ultimately help students to emerge as critical thinkers, future practitioners, or scholars. This is different from structuring IR courses as a set of competing and segmented theories—a classical pedagogic approach risking excessive compartmentalization with students—instead of building their knowledge base. Instead of teaching via compartmentalizing IR theories, I contend that it is more productive to help students illuminate connections, similarities, and differences between IR theories and research traditions, their assumptions, and explanatory reach. Appreciating IR through an eclectic set of theories or as a *toolbox* or as *lenses*, as subsequent chapters underscore, supports students in illuminating complex interactions among processes and mechanisms that bear on a given problem, helps them recognize related aspects in a similar issue area, and ultimately moves students toward richer explanations and interpretations of global issues. Helping students recognize the dynamics and complexities of real-world problems and the practical effects for solving these through the eclectic lens of various IR theories, in turn, assists them in appreciating the importance of empirical and normative dimensions inherent in the study of IR on their own terms.

While there are a wide variety of big and important IR concepts to comprehend, those listed below seem central in supporting students' transformation and progression from novice to expert.[6] With that caveat in mind, it is helpful to introduce threshold concepts in clusters or groups of questions so students can delve deeper into (inter)relationships of 'isms' and perspectives on the 'is' and 'ought' of IR. In fact, threshold concepts are vehicles for structuring IR curricula away from sequencing them along with standalone 'isms.' They, as outlined below, help students emerge with richer and deeper affective and cognitive connections about IR as a practical discourse and field of inquiry:

---

[6]   To be clear this is my own approach/focus and various authors in this volume advance signature pedagogies that challenge the explication here. I welcome their perspectives as it pushes me (and I hope others) to reflect on improving teaching and learning IR.

- Units and levels of analysis; or who matters and has effects in IR? (e.g., exploring state centrism, states as unitary actors, individuals as utility maximizers, domestic/international politics, non-state actors, IGOs, epistemic communities, etc.)
- System, Structure, Society; or how should we comprehend the nature of IR? (e.g., from the study of 'International Relations' or toward the study of 'global society,' perspective taking 'view from below and from above')
- Hierarchy, Order, Anarchy, Hegemony, Governance; or how we narrate the story of IR?
- Agency and Structure; or what determines individual behavior: social structures or human agency?
- Ideational and material dimensions; or what are (social) facts and which of them count as evidence?
- Authority, Power and Legitimacy; or how is influence yielded and projected? (e.g., compulsory, structural, institutional, productive)
- Value and ethical commitment; or what matters (most) and to whom? (e.g., national interest, individual freedom, international cooperation, responsibility towards others, inclusivity/self-reflexivity)
- Change and Continuity; or what is our orientation towards stasis or evolution? (e.g., agnostic, skeptical, optimistic, past awareness, present focus, future orientation, etc.)

In essence, IR signature pedagogies include a focus on both traditional lectures and active learning techniques, including, but not limited to, seminars, discussions, simulations, and case studies, and can be advanced by layering threshold concepts relevant to studying international, regional, and local phenomena.

Conclusion

This volume's introductory chapter examined how SoTL research related to Shulman's signature pedagogy framework improves teaching and learning IR. Understanding the 'how' we are teaching International Relations—as the authors in this volume demonstrate in subsequent chapters—enables us to teach beyond content, formulate learning outcomes and assessment strategies suitable to our field, and articulate to our students how learning IR maps onto their career aspirations. The central takeaway here is that, by formulating our SPs, we can better assess whether and how well we are preparing students to be the next generation of scholars, experts, policymakers, or practitioners. Examining IR signature pedagogies primarily offers a framework to focus our individual teaching strategies and, in extension, advances our collective understanding of effective pathways for learning in our discipline. As subsequent chapters make clear, we must continuously adjust and refine our teaching practice to be more effective by seeking students' feedback and reflecting on our teaching praxis. By deploying IR signature pedagogies, we support individual learners' growth and motivate them to be prepared for their careers as well as to emerge as informed global citizens and changemakers. By drawing on a variety of learning techniques, we help students connect, center, collaborate, and reflect on their learning, and by bringing a practical and ethical focus to IR teaching, we contribute to student development beyond the university setting—as practitioners in their chosen field. A charge, I trust, we can all embrace.

I would like to thank Lisa MacLeod, Jenny H. Peterson and Tamara A Trownsell for their comments.

References

Davies, Peter, and Jacek Brant. 2006. *Business, economics and enterprise: teaching school subjects 11–19*. Psychology Press.

Frueh, Jamie, ed. 2019. *Pedagogical Journeys Through World Politics*. New York: Springer.

Frueh, Jamie, Paul F. Diehl, Xiaoting Li, Gigi Gokcek, Jack Kalpakian, William Vlcek, Adam Bower, Raúl Salgado Espinoza, Santiago Carranco, Jacqui de Matos-Ala, Navnita Chadha Behera, Amitav Acharya. 2020. "The Introductory Course in International Relations: Regional Variations." *International Studies Perspectives*. 1–34.

Goldgeier, J. and C. I. Mezzera. 2020. "How to Rethink the Teaching of International Relations". *Foreign Policy,* 12 June. https://foreignpolicy. com/2020/06/12/how-to-rethink-the-teaching-of-international-relations

Hagmann, J. and T. J. Biersteker. 2014. "Beyond the Published Discipline: Toward a Critical Pedagogy of International Studies". *European Journal of International Relations* 20, no. 2, 291–315.

Haynie, Aeron, Nancy L. Chick, and Regan A. R. Gurung. 2009. "From Generic to Signature Pedagogies: Teaching Disciplinary Understandings." In *Exploring Signature Pedagogies: Approaches to Teaching Disciplinary Habits of Mind*, edited by Aeron Haynie, Nancy L. Chick, and Regan A. R. Gurung. Vol. 1st ed. Sterling, Va: Stylus Publishing.

Haynie, Aeron, Nancy L. Chick, and Regan A. R. Gurung. 2012. "Signature Pedagogies in Liberal Arts and Beyond." In *Exploring More Signature Pedagogies: Approaches to Teaching Disciplinary Habits of Mind*, edited by Nancy L. Chick, Aeron Haynie, and Regan A. R. Gurung, 1–12. Sterling, UNITED STATES: Stylus Publishing, LLC.

Jenkins, Daniel M. 2012 "Exploring Signature Pedagogies in Undergraduate Leadership Education." *Journal of Leadership Education* 11, no. 1.

Land, Ray, Jan HF Meyer, and Caroline Baillie. 2010. *Editors' preface: threshold concepts and transformational learning*. Vol. 42. Sense; Brill.

Lüdert, Jan and Katriona Stewart. 2017. *Nurturing Cognitive and Affective Empathy: The Benefits of Perspective-Taking*. E-International Relations, 19 November. Accessed 03 December 2020. https://www.e-ir.info/2017/11/19/nurturing-cognitive-and-affective-empathy-the-benefits-of-perspective-taking

Lüdert, J. 2016. Signature Pedagogies in International Relations, E-International Relations. 19 November. Accessed 03 December 2020. https://www.e-ir.info/2016/06/18/signature-pedagogies-in-international-relations

Lüdert, J. 2016. Implementing a Flipped Classroom: Student Generated Wikis and Videos, 18 July. E-International Relations https://www.e-ir.info/2016/07/18/implementing-a-flipped-classroom-student-generated-wikis-and-videos

Lüdert, J. 2016. Drawing on Universal Design Principles in Interdisciplinary Teaching, E-International Relations. 19 November. Accessed 03 December 2020. https://www.e-ir.info/2016/09/21/drawing-on-universal-design-principles-in-interdisciplinary-teaching/

Meyer, Jan, and Ray Land. 2003. *Threshold concepts and troublesome knowledge: Linkages to ways of thinking and practising within the disciplines*. Edinburgh: University of Edinburgh.

Meyer, Jan HF. 2008. *Threshold concepts within the disciplines*. Sense Publishers.

Meyer, Jan HF, and Ray Land. 2005. "Threshold concepts and troublesome knowledge (2): Epistemological considerations and a conceptual framework for teaching and learning." *Higher education* 49, no. 3: 373–388.

Murphy, Mary C., and Theresa Reidy. 2006. "Exploring political science's signature pedagogy." *Academic Exchange Quarterly* 10, no. 4: 1–7.

Reus-Smit, Christian, and Duncan Snidal, eds. 2008. *The Oxford Handbook of International Relations*. Oxford: Oxford University Press.

Shulman, L. 2005a. "The Signature Pedagogies of the Professions of Law, Medicine, Engineering, and the Clergy: Potential Lessons for the Education of Teachers". Talk delivered at the Math Science Partnerships (MSP) Workshop: 'Teacher Education for Effective Teaching and Learning', hosted by the National Research Council's Center for Education, 6–8 February.

Shulman, L. S. 2005b. "Signature Pedagogies in the Professions". *Daedalus* 134, no. 3, 52–59.

Sil, Rudra, and Peter J. Katzenstein. 2010. "Analytic eclecticism in the study of world politics: Reconfiguring problems and mechanisms across research traditions." *Perspectives on Politics* 8, no. 2: 411–431.

Wiggins, Grant P., Grant Wiggins, and Jay McTighe. 2005. *Understanding by design*. VA: Ascd.

2

Teaching International Relations as a Liberal Art

LISA MACLEOD

Shulman's original application of the signature pedagogy (SP) concept focused on professional education and the ways in which students develop the knowledge, skills, and attitudes necessary to be accepted as a competent practitioner in their chosen field. Although Shulman did not address the relationship between SPs in professional training and those that might exist at the undergraduate or other pre-professional level, he confidently asserted that SPs 'operate at all levels of education' (2005, 53) and that 'education in the liberal arts and sciences can profit from careful consideration of the pedagogies of the professions' (2005, 58).

Two edited books — *From Generic to Signature Pedagogies: Teaching Disciplinary Understandings* (Haynie, Chick, and Gurung 2009) and *Signature Pedagogies in Liberal Arts and Beyond* (Haynie, Chick, and Gurung 2012) — build on Shulman's foundation. In these volumes, the SP concept is considered in the context of undergraduate education. With the knowledge that undergraduates frequently do not become practitioners of their undergraduate major, liberal arts educators,

> pride themselves in training their students to be critical thinkers, strong writers, and adept in quantitative skills, essential, but generic skills that aren't unique to specific disciplines. Most [disciplines in the liberal arts and sciences (LAS)] ... have core content areas they expect their students to master in addition to the aforementioned skills, so the primary focus of LAS programs is to convey such content and skills. (Haynie, Chick, and Gurung 2009, 3)

This dual purpose — helping students develop disciplinary content knowledge and generalist skills of critical thinking and communication — has informed my approach to teaching International Relations at a small liberal arts college. I know that most of my students will not become diplomats or international civil servants, nor are they likely to join the next generation of International Relations scholars. The best service I can provide my students is to use their interest in International Relations to help them build the 'liberal arts skills' that, in the words of Jan Lüdert, 'serve as stepping-stones ... for a wide range of possible careers' (Lüdert 2020).

The Liberal Arts

The debate over what constitutes the liberal arts, and what *should* constitute the liberal arts, has ancient roots. What has remained largely consistent is the purpose of a liberal arts education. In the Western tradition, it emerged as a means of training *free men* to participate in public life as political and cultural leaders. Despite a shared general understanding of the purpose of education, there has always been some disagreement over the substantive content and skills that best produced this result (Kimball 2010). As the liberal arts have evolved, the skills of critical thinking, persuasive communication, and capacity for self-directed learning have remained at its core.

One aspect of the liberal arts education that is often under-appreciated is its moral ethic of civic engagement and active citizenship. The revitalization of the ethical core of the liberal arts education has allowed it to survive criticism that it was an elitist bastion for the Eurocentric study of the writings of dead, white men. As Martha Nussbaum argues, the critique of traditional sources of authority is at the core of the Socratic tradition that "insists on teaching students to think for themselves" (Nussbaum 2010, 16). Liberal education should be "committed to the activation of each student's independent mind and to the production of a community that can genuinely reason together about a problem, not simply trade claims and counterclaims" (Nussbaum 2010, 19). Liberal arts education serves a larger social purpose; "[t]o unmask prejudice and to secure justice" (Nussbaum 2010, 533). The deep structure of a liberal arts education has never been the pursuit of knowledge solely for knowledge's sake.

The skills and habits of mind, combined with the ethic of civic engagement, have allowed the liberal arts to survive the culture wars and continue as the touchstone for undergraduate education. It is not because the Ancient Greeks discovered 'Truth.' They embraced a process of questioning, thinking, and argumentation that was driven by a social purpose. Because it is not rooted in any particular set of 'great books,' a tradition that originated in one place and time has responded to criticism with new inputs. The call for greater representation of non-Western and non-male voices has contributed to the emergence of the global liberal arts. As students, faculty, and curricular content have become more diverse, the larger purpose of liberal arts education—its *deep structure*—has remained true to its roots. The creation of liberal arts programs throughout the world testifies to the broad appeal of Global Liberal Arts ("Liberal Arts Alliance" n.d.; "Alliance of Asian Liberal Arts Universities|AALAU" n.d.). Students are trained to become lifelong learners, independent and critical thinkers, and skilled communicators so that they can effectively participate in civic life. Contemporary liberal arts education—in the words of my own institution's mission statement—is designed 'to foster a steady stream of global citizens committed to living a contributive life' (Soka University of America, Mission Statement). One cannot help but hear the echoes of Shulman's view that signature pedagogies teach students 'to think, to perform, and to act with integrity' (2005, 52) and Reus-Smit's and Snidal's contention that International Relations (IR) is fundamentally about understanding 'how we should act' (2008, 7).

Teaching Introduction to International Relations to Aspiring Global Citizens

When deciding what content and skills to teach in my own 'Introduction to International Relations' course, I try to balance teaching content and liberal arts skills, particularly those that are likely to apply beyond an academic environment. A quick survey of the many available textbooks reveals the discipline's surface structure with limited variation in content and organization. The real challenge of teaching International Relations as a liberal art has been deciding how to pare down content to ensure adequate opportunities to practice liberal arts skills. Nonetheless, I feel an obligation to students to cover a fair bit of the content shared across most introduction to International Relations textbooks so that they are well prepared for more advanced undergraduate International Relations courses and meet disciplinary expectations for those who pursue graduate education.

Decisions about pedagogical choices have been much less straightforward. This is one indication that International Relations does not yet have a signature pedagogy; at least not one that provides a widely shared learning experience across instructors and institutions. Rather, my experience as an undergraduate IR major and my early career teaching experience was with *expedient* pedagogy characterized by 'one-way transmission of ideas and information … in which instructors race to cover the [discipline's] "canon"' (Maier, McGoldrick, and Simkins 2012, 100). Although both signature and expedient pedagogies can be characterized as the conventional mode of disciplinary teaching, they are motivated by very different purposes. In Shulman's account, SPs are designed to provide training in the knowledge, skills, and habits of mind necessary to become a competent practitioner of a field. In the context of undergraduate liberal arts education, SPs aspire to establish a 'harmony of purpose, practice, and results in teaching and learning' (Ciccone 2009, xvi).

In contrast, an expedient pedagogy is much less focused on training students to think and act as disciplinary practitioners. Maier, McGoldrick, and Simkins (2012)—using survey data of economics instruction in American undergraduate programs (Becker and Watts 2001; Brosshardt and Watts 2008)—describe students as passive recipients of textbook-driven, lecture-based teaching. This description of the student-teacher relationship is very similar to Freire's banking (or narration) model of instruction.

> Narration (with the teacher as narrator) leads the students to memorize mechanically the narrated content. Worse yet, it [turns] them into "containers," into "receptacles" to be "filled" by [the] teacher. The more completely she fills the receptacles, the better a teacher she is. The more meekly the receptacle permit themselves to be filled, the better students they are (2008, 163).

Although I was unable to locate data on teaching practice in political science or International Relations, there is sufficient anecdotal evidence to suggest that, for the most part, undergraduate teaching in International Relations also uses an expedient pedagogy driven by "convenience, custom, and inertia" (Maier, McGoldrick, and Simkins 2012, 100).

Despite long-standing criticism from Scholarship on Teaching and Learning (SoTL), the American undergraduate education system strongly supports continued reliance on expedient pedagogy. Most college-level educators are not trained as teachers. Academics often begin their teaching careers with little pedagogical training or guidance. Thrown into the classroom as graduate teaching assistants, or as all but dissertation (ABD) or newly minted-PhD instructors, it is only natural that they recreate the lecture-based mode of teaching they most likely experienced as students. Even in teaching environments with small class sizes that should be most conducive to student-centered learning, expedient pedagogies creep in. So-called class discussion can quickly turn into an instructor-focused *semi-lecture*, emphasizing *correct answers* rather than Socratic dialogue supporting the development of critical thought processes.

My own path as an educator began with the advice to not "waste" too much time on undergraduates at the expense of my research. For too many in academia, teaching, especially undergraduate teaching, is viewed as a necessary evil rather than an endeavor worthy of the same creativity and dedication invested in research and writing. Pedagogy articles with titles such as 'Running Simulations without Ruining Your Life: Simple Ways to Incorporate Active Learning into Your Teaching' (Glazier 2011), make it easy to see why many instructors shy away from these teaching strategies. Those who have not achieved some degree of professional security in the form of tenure are often hesitant to make innovative teaching a professional priority. This is not to say that there are not excellent undergraduate teachers, many of whom are also innovative and productive researchers. Professional rewards, however, tend to place much higher value on writing and research than on teaching.

Further contributing to the durability of pedagogies of convenience in university teaching are broader economic trends. As with other career fields, "the Boomer Blockade" has contributed to a very competitive job market as senior positions are held by incumbents working well past the traditional age of retirement. At the same time, the number of tenure-track positions at American colleges and universities has steadily declined while the number of non-tenure-track and part-time instructor positions has risen (Millerd 2020). In 1979, 43% of faculty positions were non-tenure track; this percentage rose to 53% in 1989, and to 65% in 2016 (TIAA Institute 2018). When the rare tenure-track position does become available, the candidates' publication records often determine who will make the first cut. For those that successfully land a tenure-track position, tenure and promotion committees tend to prize publication over innovative teaching that improves student learning outcomes.

The relatively low status of pedagogy in IR is also evident in the work of the Teaching, Research, and International Policy Project (TRIP). If there were a research group within the discipline positioned to document IR's signature pedagogy, TRIP would be it. The TRIP Faculty Survey focuses on the linkages between academic research and policy. Questions about teaching are primarily related to content (e.g., theory, methodology, and epistemology). In TRIP's most recent faculty survey (2017), the only question related directly to teaching and pedagogy asks, "Is/Are your IR course(s) for undergraduates designed more to introduce students to scholarship in the IR discipline, or more to prepare students to be informed about foreign policy and international issues?" ("Faculty Survey | Teaching, Research, and Inter-national Policy (TRIP)" n.d.). This emphasis on content transmission in the absence of questions related to training students "to think," "to perform," or "to act with integrity" (Shulman 2005, 52) indicate that the SP concept is not yet incorporated into the survey. Despite this shortcoming, the TRIP Project plays an important role in creating awareness of the disconnect between the academic and policy worlds. To date, it has encouraged academics to "bridge the gap" through policy-relevant research. A natural extension of this initiative is the development of a graduate-level signature pedagogy to better prepare students for careers as IR practitioners and scholars. It is hard to imagine that such an initiative would not also positively impact pedagogical practices at the undergraduate level.

An Emerging International Relations SP?

The International Studies Association (ISA) has two sections focused on teaching International Relations: The International Education Section (IES) and the Active Learning in International Affairs Section (ALIAS). The IES promotes itself as "an essential forum for conversation about international studies and study abroad programs, including their curriculum, identity, assessment, and administration that is not available elsewhere" ("International Education (IEDUC) Section 2019 Annual Report," n.d.). Since 2005, the section's membership has rarely surpassed 100 members. As of 2019, it was the smallest ISA section. The future of this section is uncertain as it struggles with low membership numbers and declining active participation by section members ("International Education (IEDUC) Section 2019 Annual Report," n.d.).

In contrast, ALIAS and the American Political Science Association's (APSA) Political Science Education Section have both grown steadily. Case-based teaching was pioneered in IR in the 1980s. From 1990 to 1995, efforts to develop case-based and active-learning pedagogies were continued through Harvard University's Pew Faculty Fellowship program (Pettenger 2010). ALIAS became the institutional home for this work when it was established in 1996. Among its other initiatives, ALIAS has collaborated with Georgetown's Institute for the Study of Diplomacy (ISD) to support the development of resources for case-based teaching ("Institute for the Study of Diplomacy, Georgetown University, USA," n.d.; "Case Studies for Students" n.d.). Members of ALIAS contributed to *The New International Studies Classroom: Active Teaching, Active Learning,* which focuses on the case method, simulations and games, and technology in the classroom (Lantis, Kuzma, and Boehrer 2000). Similarly, APSA has sponsored an annual Teaching and Learning Conference since 2000; the first edition of the *Journal of Political Science Education* followed in 2005. Since 2018, APSA has held a teaching and learning conference in conjunction with its annual meeting. ALIAS held its first Innovative Pedagogy Conference in 2018.

That case-based and active learning pedagogies are framed as "new" and "innovative" is evidence of the prevalence of textbook and lecture-based pedagogies of convenience. Nonetheless, there are promising signs that active learning strategies, especially case-based learning, simulations, role-play, and games, are becoming part of the mainstream. Whereas, historically, the SoLT has been limited to journals focused on the highly specialized subfield of pedagogy, it has become more common to see essays devoted to teaching in International Relations in widely read disciplinary journals including *International Studies Perspectives* (Asal and Blake 2006; Bridge and Radford 2014; Ehrlander and Boylan 2018). The essays in *Pedagogical Journeys through World Politics* (Frueh 2020) are but the most recent contribution to the ongoing conversation about pedagogy in the discipline.

Although there are many reasons for the continued predominance of expedient pedagogy, this is not to say that signature pedagogies cannot emerge in IR. An active group of dedicated teacher-scholars is working to develop and share active-learning strategies informed by student learning outcomes. As the COVID-19 pandemic has forced all of us to rethink curriculum, course content and adjust to alternative teaching modalities, these teacher-scholars have provided significant support. ISA's ALIAS and IES, The ISA Innovative Pedagogy Conference Initiative, *International Studies Perspectives*, Paul Diehl, and Mark Boyer co-sponsored a day-long webinar in early August 2020. Georgetown's Institute for the Study of Diplomacy sponsored two webinars featuring Eric Leonard: 'The New Reality: Teaching International Affairs On-line' (August 2020) and 'Making the Case: Case Studies in Online Classrooms' (September 2020). These webinars addressed the short-term concerns of teaching during a pandemic and highlighted ways in which technology can support active learning strategies.

Pedagogies of convenience take hold when there is absence of incentives to do otherwise and when support for doing otherwise is not available. I believe that the forced experimentation with teaching strategies spurred by the pandemic will inform my teaching for years to come. The switch to remote teaching forced me to actively seek new teaching strategies. These webinars provided practical advice, allowing me to adapt and scale active learning exercises to my teaching environment and instructional goals. That so many of us are going through this process at the same time creates a wonderful opportunity for the disciplinary conversation needed to develop a signature pedagogy.

IR, Liberal Arts, and Wicked Problems

Active learning strategies are especially appropriate for the liberal arts.

Nussbaum (2010) reminds her reader that, rather than teaching students to be "passively reliant on the written word," books should "make the mind more subtle, more rigorous, [and] more active" (34). The active pursuit of knowledge takes place in a "messy, puzzling, and complicated" (35) world. Kolko's (2020) conception of "wicked problems" is quite similar,

> [Wicked problems are] a social or cultural problem that is difficult or impossible to solve for as many as four reasons; incomplete or contradictory knowledge, the number of people and opinions involved, the large economic burden, and the interconnected nature of those problems with *other* problems (10).

IR is one of many disciplines focused on "wicked problems." Training across the liberal arts provides students with the tools to seek, create, analyze, and communicate the knowledge necessary to find appropriate responses to the wicked problems of today and tomorrow.

My courses are shaped by a sense of obligation to students who do not aspire to careers in foreign affairs as much as to those that do. The surface and deep structures of IR present no conflict between disciplinary socialization and teaching the discipline as a liberal art. Both require that students appreciate the interconnectedness of a globalized world and practice skills necessary to become lifelong learners. Through formal academic writing and presentations, nonacademic writing (e.g., blogs, editorials, policy papers), and role-play simulations, students develop research, critical thinking, and communication skills. These assignments also ask students to engage the ethical and pragmatic concerns of implicit structure. Pandemic teaching has spurred me to learn much more about my institution's learning management software (LMS). It offers much more than drop box, email, and gradebook features. Discussion or chat features (or shared reading annotation software) can help students to better understand assigned readings, share ideas, and collaborate. If you are not fortunate enough to have a Center for Teaching and Learning at your home institution, Vanderbilt's Center for Teaching provides many easy to implement resources. "Flipping the classroom" (i.e., recording short lectures that students can view outside of class) creates time for these activities. Although the process may sound intimidating, it requires minimal technical expertise.

IR is especially well-suited to the use of role-play simulations as an active learning strategy. With the right preparatory and debriefing assignments, they can provide a rich learning experience beyond the day of the simulation. Statecraft Simulations (https://www.statecraftsims.com/) and the University of

Maryland's International Communication & Negotiation Simulations Project (ICONS Project) (https://icons.umd.edu/) offer excellent resources to help students and instructors navigate the process. It is not too difficult to create your own role-play experience. Dividing students into "country expert" teams is an easy way to create an "expert symposium." Collaborate with your library staff to ensure students know how to use library databases and access internet resources. Ask teams to give a briefing explaining their country's concerns and preferred outcomes. Ask them to analyze the domestic and international factors shaping likely events in the region. After this exercise in peer teaching and learning, students are well-prepared to write individual essays. In the process, they gain a greater understanding of regional issues and have an opportunity to practice liberal arts skills. Providing students with frequent opportunities to practice oral and verbal communication, problem-solving, and critical thinking and reading skills is an excellent antidote to expedient pedagogy.

When I talk to former students about their undergraduate education, they are much more likely to recall exercises designed to support their development as liberal artists than disciplinary knowledge. Some have pursued careers in diplomacy and international civil service. There are even a few in academia. Many more work in the public and private sectors, whether for local NGOs or multinational corporations. They have pursued careers in teaching, journalism, technology, law, consulting, and entrepreneurship. Teaching International Relations as a liberal art is about nurturing your students' love of learning and coaching them to become better critical thinkers and communicators. My students acquire both transferrable liberal arts skills and disciplinary content knowledge; they are well-prepared to pursue the path of their choosing. Creative problem-solving is needed to address some of today's most "wicked problems." IR content knowledge will likely play some role; liberal arts skills most certainly will.

With great appreciation to Daniela Soto for her research assistance on this project.

References

"About Us | Teaching, Research, and International Policy (TRIP)." n.d. Accessed September 26, 2020. https://trip.wm.edu/about-us

"Alliance of Asian Liberal Arts Universities|AALAU." n.d. Accessed September 22, 2020. https://www.aalau.org/

Asal, Victor, and Elizabeth L. Blake. 2006. "Creating Simulations for Political Science Education." *Journal of Political Science Education* 2 (1): 1–18. https://doi.org/10.1080/15512160500484119

Becker, William E., and Michael Watts. 2001. "Teaching Methods in U. S. Undergraduate Economics Courses." *The Journal of Economic Education* 32 (3): 269. https://doi.org/10.2307/1183384.

Bosshardt, William, and Michael Watts. 2008. "Undergraduate Students' Coursework in Economics." *The Journal of Economic Education* 39 (2): 198–205. https://doi.org/10.3200/JECE.39.2.198-205.

Bridge, Dave, and Simon Radford. 2014. "Teaching Diplomacy by Other Means: Using an Outside-of-Class Simulation to Teach International Relations Theory." *International Studies Perspectives* 15 (4): 423–37. https://doi.org/10.1111/insp.12017.

"Case Studies for Students." n.d. Institute for the Study of Diplomacy at Georgetown University. Accessed August 28, 2020. https://isd-georgetown-university.myshopify.com/collections/frontpage

Ciccone, Anthony A. 2009. "Forward." In *Exploring Signature Pedagogies: Approaches to Teaching Disciplinary Habits of Mind*, edited by Aeron Haynie, Nancy L. Chick, and Regan A. R. Gurung. Vol. 1st ed. Sterling, Va: Stylus Publishing. EBSCOhost.

Ehrlander, Mary F., and Brandon M. Boylan. 2018. "The Model Arctic Council: Educating Postsecondary Students on Arctic Issues and Governance through Simulation." *International Studies Perspectives* 19 (1): 83–101. https://doi.org/10.1093/isp/ekx005.

"Faculty Survey | Teaching, Research, and International Policy (TRIP)." n.d. Accessed September 26, 2020. https://trip.wm.edu/data/dashboard/faculty-survey

Freire, Paulo. 2008. "Pedagogy of the Oppressed (1970)." In *Contemporary Latin American Social and Political Thought: An Anthology*, edited by Ivan Marquez, 162–72. Latin American Perspectives in the Classroom. Lanham, Md: Rowman & Littlefield.

Frueh, Jamie, ed. 2020. *Pedagogical Journeys through World Politics*. Political Pedagogies. Cham: Springer International Publishing. https://doi.org/10.1007/978-3-030-20305-4.

Glazier, Rebecca A. 2011. "Running Simulations without Ruining Your Life: Simple Ways to Incorporate Active Learning into Your Teaching." *Journal of Political Science Education* 7 (4): 375–93. https://doi.org/10.1080/15512169.2 011.615188.

Haynie, Aeron, Nancy L. Chick, and Regan A. R. Gurung. 2009. "From Generic to Signature Pedagogies: Teaching Disciplinary Understandings." In *Exploring Signature Pedagogies : Approaches to Teaching Disciplinary Habits of Mind*, edited by Aeron Haynie, Nancy L. Chick, and Regan A. R. Gurung. Vol. 1st ed. Sterling, Va: Stylus Publishing. EBSCOhost.

Haynie, Aeron, Nancy L. Chick, and Regan A. R. Gurung. 2012. "Signature Pedagogies in Liberal Arts and Beyond." In *Exploring More Signature Pedagogies: Approaches to Teaching Disciplinary Habits of Mind*, edited by Nancy L. Chick, Aeron Haynie, and Regan A. R. Gurung, 1–12. Sterling, VA: Stylus Publishing. Proquest Ebook Central.

"Institute for the Study of Diplomacy, Georgetown University, USA." n.d. SAGE Knowledge. https://sk.sagepub.com/cases/content-partner/ georgetown-diplomacy

"International Education (IEDUC) Section 2019 Annual Report." n.d. International Studies Association. https://www.isanet.org/Portals/0/ Documents/EDUC/IEDUC%20Annual%20Report%202019. pdf?ver=2020-02-18-094651-743

Kimball, Bruce A. 2010. *The Liberal Arts Tradition: A Documentary History*. Lanham, MD: UPA. Proquest Ebook Central.

Kolko, Jon. 2020. "Wicked Problems: Problems Worth Solving (SSIR)." *Stanford Social Innovation Review*. March 6, 2020. https://ssir.org/books/ excerpts/entry/wicked_problems_problems_worth_solving

Lantis, Jeffrey S., Lynn M. Kuzma, and John Boehrer. 2000. *The New International Studies Classroom: Active Teaching, Active Learning*. Boulder, Co.: Lynne Rienner Publishers.

"Liberal Arts Alliance." n.d. Liberal Arts Alliance. Accessed September 22, 2020. https://liberalartsalliance.org/about-us/

Lüdert, Jan. 2020. "Call for Contributors on Signature Pedagogies in International Relations." *E-International Relations*. April 17, 2020. https://www.e-ir.info/2020/04/17/call-for-contributors-on-signature-pedagogies-in-international-relations/

Maier, Mark H., Kim Marie McGoldrick, and Scott P. Simkins. 2012. "Is There a Signature Pedagogy in Economics?" In *Exploring More Signature Pedagogies: Approaches to Teaching Disciplinary Habits of Mind*, edited by Nancy L. Chick, Aeron Haynie, and Regan A. R. Gurung, 97–111. Sterling, VA: Stylus Publishing. Proquest Ebook Central.

Millerd, Paul. 2020. "The Boomer Blockade: How One Generation Reshaped Work." *Boundless: Beyond The Default Path* (blog). January 24, 2020. https://think-boundless.com/the-boomer-blockade/

Nussbaum, Martha C. 2010. "A Classical Defense of Reform in Liberal Education (1997)." In *The Liberal Arts Tradition: A Documentary History*, edited by Bruce A. Kimball, 531-378 Lanham, MD: UPA. Proquest Ebook Central.

Pettenger, Mary. Memorandum to International Studies Association Governing Council. 2010. "Re-Charter of the Active Learning in International Affairs Section (ALIAS)," December 20, 2010. https://www.isanet.org/Portals/0/Documents/ALIAS/Recharter_ALIAS_Dec2010.pdf?ver=2013-06-09-115720-000

Reus-Smit, Christian, and Duncan Snidal. 2008. "Between Utopia and Reality: The Practical Discourses of International Relations." In *The Oxford Handbook of International Relations*. Oxford University Press, Oxford. https://doi.org/10.1093/oxfordhb/9780199219322.003.0001.

Shulman, Lee S. 2005. "Signature Pedagogies in the Professions." *Daedalus* 134 (3): 52–59. https://doi.org/10.1162/0011526054622015.

TIAA Institute. 2018. "The Changing Academic Workforce: Composition of the Faculty." New York, N.Y: Teachers Insurance and Annuity Association of America-College Retirement Equities Fund. https://www.tiaainstitute.org/sites/default/files/presentations/2018-11/TIAA_Changing_Academic_Workforce%20R1r.%2010-30-18.%20FINAL.pdf

3

Signature Pedagogies and International Relations Theory: From Thoughtlessness to Citizenship

MATHEW DAVIES

To think about signature pedagogies in the teaching of International Relations (IR) is to ask, who are the students we are teaching, and for what professional roles are we preparing them? We often think about future diplomats, politicians, and public servants, and these roles fill the pages of glossy brochures on programs, and then "alumni stories." This is certainly not wrong, but it is also the case that the scale of teaching IR at many universities, when compared to the fewer number of jobs available in these professions, suggests that we cannot be satisfied with simply training our students for professional roles they may never occupy. In this chapter, I discuss how I try to prepare students in my International Relations Theory (IRT) course to perform the role of "citizen." This need not supplant other professions and pedagogies, but is intended to be beneficial to all students who pass through the course (this framing of professions and performance comes from Shulman 2005b, 57).[1]

---

[1]   In this way, the chapter is compatible with, but ultimately separate from, recent arguments about ensuring pluralism in IR classes (Hagmann and Biersteker, 2014) and about articulating the values that should underpin political science—"*truthfulness ... agency ... inquiry ... and autonomy*" (Flinders and Pal, 2020, 274). The benefit and need for pluralization of education in IR has become an area of keen interest. Ettinger (2020) gives an excellent recent overview and links well to existing literature on the subject. See also, from a different perspective, Goldgeier and Mezzera (2020). It is worth noting, however, that pluralism is insufficient to achieve the thoughtfulness that Hannah Arendt suggests is important. Knowing more about something, and knowing

My particular concern is to reflect on the *implicit structure* of my teaching—that is, the beliefs about "attitudes, values, and dispositions" as they relate to thinking about citizenship if not necessarily as a profession, then at least as something that our students are going to be called to do (Shulman 2005b, 55). Ultimately, I am interested in promoting thoughtfulness here as understood by Hannah Arendt, who framed it not as universal knowledge or the unproblematic and easy occupation of "the right." The quintessence of thinking, as Arendt notes, "can only lie in the actual thinking process and not in any solid results or specific thoughts" (Arendt 1981, 191). The benefit of this thoughtfulness for Arendt is twofold. First, being thoughtful inoculates the thinker from the perils of thoughtlessness—an inability to reflect on the world and one's place in it, which leads to acceptance of the immoral actions of others not simply procedurally, but through the redefinition of one's own understanding of moral and political order. It was this redefinition that she saw in Adolf Eichmann at his trial in 1961, and it was his thoughtlessness that enabled the perpetration of Nazi evils. Second, to be thoughtful is to consummate your humanity. Thinking distinguishes us from "sleepwalkers" (Arendt 1981, 191). It enables us to transcend the physical world and, in doing so, explore the "world's realness and their own." In essence, thoughtfulness means to think about the ways we think and how we live and act in the world around us, and is intimately related to the necessities of citizenship—how we live and act in political and social groups. Arendt's ideas have, I now realize after some 15 years of teaching, pre-empted in a more sophisticated and coherent form some of the ways I have come to think about teaching, why I value it, and how I conduct it. In this chapter, I explain how generating some degree of thoughtfulness can be achieved in the classroom, and specifically how teaching IRT may be particularly well suited to this goal.

My signature pedagogy hopes to enable thoughtfulness through two stages. The first stage rests on destabilizing the factors that may lead to thoughtlessness—complacency, surety, and detachment—and how these issues are introduced by discussing both the incommensurability of perspectives within a theoretical field and one's own hypocritical response to the values that different theories proffer as significant (some values you will disdain but enact, others you will acclaim but not live up to). Here, I identify two particular approaches that help in this process—teaching incommensurability and hypocrisy (the surface structure in Shulman's account). The second stage involves helping students think through the consequences of incommensurability and hypocrisy in meaningful, rigorous, and honest ways. The values of humility, bravery, and agency come to the fore, and they balance the

---

that thing from multiple perspectives, is not the same as actively reflecting on the self—although as I note it is not a barrier to this either. To achieve thoughtfulness, one needs more than simple pedagogical pluralism, as it is not reducible to knowing more. It is about knowing differently and so suggests that alternate approaches are necessary.

importance of thoughtfulness as a personal and internal characteristic of a mature thinker with the necessities placed upon us through a citizenship that is embedded in the physical world, characterized as it is by failure and injustice, but also by the role of our own hope within it and about it.

Before turning to the substantive discussion, it is important to note that these discussions can be discomforting. Students should not be required to think in these ways or be put under any pressure to publicly respond to these issues—the process at all times has to be supportive, personal, and ultimately voluntary. I outline my 'destination' to students at the start of the course so they can reflect on the course and their learning within it in active ways. Whilst the discussion below outlines paths to thinking about thoughtfulness, they are options, not requirements. The course remains accessible and meaningful to students who want to get different things from it.

Destabilizing Thoughtlessness and Teaching Incommensurability and Hypocrisy

Facilitating thoughtfulness is best done indirectly – destabilizing *thoughtlessness* is key. This approach to teaching IRT has evolved piecemeal for quite some time as IRT has grappled with how to demonstrate its value. One response can be found in Reus-Smit and Snidal (2008). Their argument rests on the claim that all theories inevitably contain both empirical and normative dimensions—they outline how the world is (or at least the theoretician's claims about the nature of the actors and processes in the world), and how the world should be. At the confluence of these two inevitable modes of theorizing emerges an argument about the value of knowing about theory—that individual theories are ethical inasmuch as they are responses to the question, how should we act? Whilst individual theories may or may not provide answers that are appealing or emancipatory, they are all practical—the world is like this, and so you should do this as a result. There is considerable value, both in terms of appreciating the benefit of IRT and of thinking through the personal consequences of it. When teaching diplomats, I have used this approach to help explain how theories, whether individually or collectively, can be used to interrogate the motivations of interlocutors, and to frame how they may view the world and what they respond to. For students, the approach suggests a bridge between the arcane world of thinking and the more exciting world going on outside the classroom—these theories are not simply cloistered academics saying silly things (well, not *only* that), but are somehow related to the big questions of war, peace, diplomacy, and statecraft.

These arguments have helped move the teaching of IRT away from the unreflexive approaches that have long characterized teaching, and towards thoughtfulness. The issue is that whilst the "ethics of theories" approach opens up new ways to think about what IRT is and how to teach it, it ultimately does not destabilize thoughtlessness because it does not challenge the things that support thoughtlessness (at least in the way I have defined it above—complacency, surety, and detachment). Whilst the "ethics of theories" approach advances how we think about theories, it does not address how we think about our thinking about theories, and this "double move" is necessary. Let me explain. The biggest reason for thoughtlessness is the student's desire to choose right answers—let's call it the "I am" approach, as in "I am a realist." Students tend to love the "I am" approach for three reasons. First, it fits the need for easy characterization of an abstract subject—there are distinct entities called theories that stand for different things. Second, once the theories are distinguished from one another, it enables choices to be made between them on some absolute basis (theories identify sets of cause-action relations, which vary in accuracy).[2] Third, it enables students to conflate their individual choice of perspective with being right in some way. For some, the results are a sense of complacency (theories are discrete and knowable), surety (easy choices can be made), and detachment (these choices can be made independently of an assessment of ourselves).

Along with the ethics of individual theories and arguments about IRT as a practical discourse stands the ethics of a theoretical discipline such as IRT, and the thoughtfulness that this can promote. There are two surface structures—operational acts of teaching (Shulman 2005b, 54)—particular to this signature pedagogy that now become important—revealing the incommensurability of theories and the role of hypocrisy, both of which go towards destabilizing complacency, surety, and detachment. Incommensurability is introduced in two ways almost immediately to students in the opening class as part of the process of "assessing a theoretical discipline." The first involves a discussion of the origins and demise (or lack thereof) of IRT positions. Theories emerge for a range of interlocking reasons—changes in the real world, instability within the "received wisdoms" of the academy, importation of ideas from outside IR (either from other disciplines or because of shifts in the philosophy of science), and the incentives of individuals within bureaucratized institutions and disciplines (PhDs require innovation, for example, so there is always a motor of new thinking in the replication of the discipline). Conversely, once hatched, theories rarely, if ever, die (there are realists today,

---

[2]   This ties in with generalized assumptions of progress that students presume apply to the social sciences—new theories are better than old theories—which I discuss later. Interestingly, Katzenstein and Sil (2008) argue that analytical eclecticism is an escape from choosing. This is true, inasmuch as it advocates the use of multiple lenses, but it offers an escape from the need to think about how we choose, which is a dead-end in terms of the pedagogical approach being discussed.

just as there were in the 1950s, for example, who continue to produce important insights, despite significant innovation and change in the discipline). There is a fair degree of cynicism in this, which is not intended to devalue the work of theorists or their creations. Instead, it introduces students to the personal, political, and institutional contexts in which new knowledge is demanded and created, humanizing an otherwise abstract discipline and those who constitute it.

The generation of theories, and their open-ended life cycles and continuing value despite subsequent changes, problematizes simple and linear visions or progress, and disabuses students of particularly lazy ways of assessing the quality of theories (newer must be better than older, or the inverse, that older must be better as "realism has been around since Thucydides," whereupon we all sigh deeply). This suggests that there is something more than simple "improvement" (or debasement) in IRT over time, and so we have no easy option to distinguish between good and bad theories. From there, I introduce students to how we may adjudicate between theories (saying "it doesn't matter they are all the same" is a sure-fire path to assessment failure if nothing else).

I do this with a slide of two paintings of the Grand Canal in Venice—the *Entrance to the Grand Canal* by Canaletto and *The Grand Canal* by J. M. Turner. I use these paintings as an entry point to the consideration of theories, less as the science that some seek to portray it as, and more as an ultimately artistic endeavor (see the recent discussion in Ramel (2018) on the aesthetic turn in IR and teaching). I ask the students who painted these pictures. Sometimes they know, sometimes they do not. I ask them which they prefer, which elicits a range of answers that flow intuitively. I then ask which painting is correct, which brings silence and perplexity. This is the crucial moment of departure. Theories are aesthetic statements that emerge through the conversation between artist/theorist, the world they seek to depict, and us as active observers, and we can approach them through affective learning. We know, instinctively, that these paintings are not right or wrong, and we know, equally as automatically, that their "lack of rightness" does not mean they lack value or that we are powerless to choose between them. Instead, our acts of choice come down to personal preference, constructed out of a multitude of subjectivities and experiences of which we are only partially aware. Theories are paintings of the world—they blend conformity to conventions with the innovations that set individual artists apart. The key lesson is that we cannot choose between theories except subjectively, and we cannot determine right and wrong in any absolute sense. Claims to objective scientific status and particular visions of progress are partial and political (though that does not denude them of value, insight, and beauty that we can appreciate). Whilst every theoretical position establishes its own way of measuring value and progress, these do not come together in some grand unified theory of world politics; they always remain fragmented and in tension. The incommensurability of theories as theories—introduced in the first class and then returned to throughout the course—are not simply presented. Instead, the reasons for the emergence and shaping are disc- ussed, making students reflect on the limitations of their own choices about theories (and indeed, if so many intelligent women and men are unable to determine right and wrong, what is a theoretical discipline actually aiming for beyond simple correctness?).

If incommensurability is the entry point to progress towards some sort of thoughtfulness, then a second strategy helps drive forward that process— revealing our own (and others') hypocrisy. This is more personal, confronting, and delicate than the incommensurability of theories. Approaching hypocrisy must be done with care, because students should not be alienated from the process, even if they are hopefully confronted by it. Here, pedagogies of uncertainty (not knowing the nature of the student response) are important (see Shulman 2005a).

To manage uncertainty, I turn the process of realizing and confronting hypocrisy on myself. Consider a class on theories of international distributive justice, where we discuss the work of people like John Rawls and Charles Beitz, and how they can map out in ideal theory different ways to think about the world. We can see visions of justice, of equality, of redistribution. Many, perhaps all, of the people in the room will claim some sort of allegiance to these values. The question is, why do we not live in this world? If we can think it, why can we not enact it? Well, the students say, it is too difficult, those evil politicians, there are just so many obstacles between us and the realization of these values, if only they were not in the way. Here is the moment. I am, I tell them, a well-educated and hopefully smart person. I know that all these perspectives are desirable and morally defensible. Yet I continue to buy stupidly expensive things, using my personal resources to collect more shoes or another designer bag (at this point, I usually wave around something, a Prada briefcase that I bought for my birthday being a favorite teaching aide). I know these theories outline worlds that I find app- ealing, but I also know I do not live up to the consequences of that revelation. I live my life in a state of protracted hypocrisy, and perhaps, as I look around the room, you do as well. As such, the moment of vulnerability is centered on me, but the students are invited to share and reflect upon it in a space where they know I am the target of the criticism, not the bestower of critique. In this way, we problematize easy assumptions of our own goodness to force us to think about our position in the world and responses to the injustices that surround us, that we are aware of, and about which we do not do enough. Such approaches parallel the "pedagogy of discomfort" (Boler 1999) and the benefits that come from helping students to have an "ambiguous and flexible sense of self" (Boler 1999, 176). Ideal theory, then, is not only a critique of the world as it exists—it is a critique of me and of us for not realizing that world and instead being comfortable in a world of injustice. We are so quick to jump on the hypocrisy of others, but we must face and reckon with our own.

The consequences of incommensurability and hypocrisy are destabilizing and decentering. They remove easy certainties about progress, about choosing right answers, and about how we can engage with the world around us. We are decentered from our own metrics of right and wrong, and instead revealed to be as political, partisan, and partial as those with whom we engage and critique. Complacency, surety, and detachment are undermined, and new opportunities emerge to be considered about how we think about ourselves and others, both in terms of the world around us and in terms of how we see ourselves in that world.

The Consequences of Thoughtfulness: Humility, Bravery, and Agency in the Face of Failure

Revealing incommensurability and hypocrisy is deconstructive in that it breaks down barriers to thoughtfulness, laying the groundwork for considering what the response to thoughtfulness may be. Again, the signature pedagogy framework is useful as it focuses attention not simply on the detail of what we teach—the facts, theories, opinions, and debates—but the deeper processes that can underpin this conveying of information—the pedagogies of formation, and the way we can build identity and character, dispositions and values, through education. In this context, it is important to remember that part of our role as educators is to equip students with the skills necessary to exist and flourish in a world of doubt, injustice, impermanence, and complexity. It is not enough to simply tell them about the world, but how they may live in that world; whilst also noting it is not our place to denote any particular answer to that question so much as it is important that we provide a guide to how they can think of their own responses.[3] The aim is more modest than some sort of preparation for "transformative political action" (see discussion in Head 2020, 86) and instead focuses on the development of three themes that have particular value.

---

[3]   This is a response to the demand to "show the benefit" of education in such areas as the arts and social sciences that makes a lasting impression on me. Efforts to demonstrate the benefit of non-STEM degrees through quantitative measurement are vital, but they are not definitive. Universities do not simply explain the world; they prepare people to live in that world, a task that is not reducible to a mechanistic understanding of parts of that world or even bounded proficiencies in forms of action in it.

The first is humility—or, as I describe it—the importance of holding your ideas lightly. This is not the same as believing or caring about nothing, nor is it equivalent to arguing that all positions are of equal value. Instead, it is the recognition of the importance of not mistaking your subjective beliefs for universal and incontrovertible facts. This can be fostered through class discussions, a probing respect for positions expressed, and studiously ensuring that I as a teacher do not express preferences for positions either actively or in response to student comments and questions. It is also important to legitimate the range of reasons for the opinions that students express. Students often remark that they feel uncomfortable using their own life experiences and opinions to engage with theories, especially when those theories are written by the "big names" of the discipline. Showing how those big names are as subjective and partial as we are is an empowering act—that the reasons for the theories are as personal as the reasons for one's response to them, and that we are all equal thinkers in this regard. Ideally, the result is that humility leads to empathy for alternative perspectives and the basis of those perspectives. Empathy is not relativism, and it does not mean every approach should be agreed with equally, but it does mean a sense of awareness that the reasons we think and choose in the ways we do are similar to the reasons others think and choose in the ways they do.

The second value, emerging from the twin suggestions of humility and empathy, is that it takes bravery to think, in two respects. First, it requires the ability to hold simultaneously the benefit and discomfort of a belief in some sort of balance—the thesis and its negation—without falling victim to either the comfort of certainty or, comforting, perhaps in a different way, disinterest. Second, it suggests a constant restlessness, the requirement of uncertainty not only about what we think, but the ways in which we think. Student feedback shows that this benefits them, especially when reassured that the discomfort they feel in "not choosing" but "continually thinking" was shown to be part of the point of the class.[4]

The third is the consequence of the previous two—remembering agency. What we all do, individually and collectively, in public and in private, is significant. From talking to students, I know the concerns that we share when we look to the future and think about the world and its crises and dangers. The agency of students is a response to that heaviness, and the recognition of this agency is the best vaccination we have against the fear of what surrounds us. This agency is less about specific programs of action, and

---

[4]   Students have sometimes referred to this as a "real education" that they distinguish from simply learning more things. One personal communication noted that "you have given me through this course a real education—helping me to think not only about answers but how I think about getting to answers."

more about helping students remember they have choices to face and that it is within their power to think about outcomes and make meaningful decisions. It is worth noting that student responses to this varies. Some have let me know that they struggled with this in the course because it seemed removed from IRT, whilst others told me that this was the most positive thing that they took away from the course because they found it relevant to their lives and experiences.[5]

Concluding Thoughts

What is the point of teaching IRT? We have answers in terms of how it reproduces the discipline through training future academics, how it shapes the thinking of practitioners, and how it can influence our students (the published, practiced, taught distinction that Ettinger (2020) talks of, and which I touch on in a different way, see Davies 2017). In each of these dimensions, there are opportunities to "do better," and here I have focused on what "doing better" means for me in terms of education at this point in my career. It is not the educators' place, at least in something as groundless as theories, to tell students what to think, but it is important to shape not only how they think, but how they think about thinking and how that "double thinking" impacts on their location in the embodied world. It seems suitable, given we have focused on what I do in the classroom, to end this chapter as I end both my opening session on IRT in week one, and the entire seminar series at the end of week 12.

I usually start the final session with a simple question—what have you learned in this course? I then ask, what do you think I wanted you to learn in this course? Both questions bring out a range of entertaining answers. We end up, however, as follows. Inscribed on the Temple of Apollo at Delphi were at least two maxims, or at least we are told they were there. The first of these was "know thyself." Here is a restless injunction to subject the self to scrutiny, to contemplate the consequences of our thoughtlessness, our hypocrisy, and our embeddedness in the world. Like Arendt, knowing oneself is a process of reflection on our humanity, our moral imaginary, and our political nature. The second of these was "nothing to excess." Here we find a response to incommensurability, a lightness of perspective that does not require a lack of belief or action, but a recognition that belief and action are always based on subjectivities and incompleteness. The result of knowing yourself is not

---

[5]   I am grateful for conversations with Dr. Christopher Hobson on this point. He has talked about the importance of providing students with ways to think about being in the world and helping them to approach that world in constructive ways, especially in the context of COVID-19 and the disruptions to their education and life plans that the students are facing.

agnosticism or inaction; neither of those are brave. The result, instead, is the constant discomfort of knowing that your thoughts and actions are limited, wrong, and inescapably partisan, but that we must act despite these limitations, and our status as ethical agents comes not from surety, but from the absence of certainty coupled with the overwhelming necessity to do "something" in the face of a world where inaction is also morally wrong.

I return to Arendt to tie this together. If the call is for thoughtfulness, then we must overcome the smothering of thought caused by our own self-satisfaction. Critical thinking is no easy remedy, because Arendt focuses attention not on our engagement with the world, but on our engagement with ourselves *in* that world. To be thoughtful is to perceive and ponder the subjectivities that shape how we see and think about the world around us, and to be discomforted by those relationships; to ask questions not simply about why others are wrong, but to think about how we are wrong, and how that wrongness is the inescapable product of being a thinking moral agent in the world. We must perceive, encounter, and respond to the vulnerability of our thinking processes, the objects we think about, and the world in which we think (see discussion in Hobson 2017). For me, the response is a balance between decentering students from their own narratives and then developing within them the bravery to act in the face of this decentered status. The value of political science in general, and IRT as my own small field to both care about and care in, comes down to this—the creation of informed citizens who see the world with empathy, with humility, but with hope in their own agency. Instead of turning them into little proselytizers of partisan truths, it is incumbent upon us through our teaching to develop not only their critical faculties, but their human qualities. We have enough people in the world who know they are right. My job boils down to ensuring that they know they are wrong, and yet helping them care enough—and be brave enough—to act, despite this profoundly uncomfortable realization.

References

Arendt, H. 1981. *The Life of the Mind*. Boston, MA: Houghton Mifflin Harcourt.

Boler, M. 1999. *Feeling Power: Emotions and Education*. New York: Routledge.

Davies, M. 2017. "Academic Citizenships". *Australian Journal of International Affairs* 71, no. 1, 12–15.

Ettinger, A. 2020. "Scattered and Unsystematic: The Taught Discipline in the Intellectual Life of International Relations". *International Studies Perspectives* 21, no. 3, 338–361.

Flinders, M. and L. A. Pal. 2020. "The Moral Foundations of Public Engagement: Does Political Science, as a Discipline, Have an Ethics?" *Political Studies Review* 18, no. 2, 263–276.

Goldgeier, J. and C. I. Mezzera. 2020. "How to Rethink the Teaching of International Relations". *Foreign Policy,* 12 June. https://foreignpolicy. com/2020/06/12/how-to-rethink-the-teaching-of-international-relations/

Hagmann, J. and T. J. Biersteker. 2014. "Beyond the Published Discipline: Toward a Critical Pedagogy of International Studies". *European Journal of International Relations* 20, no. 2, 291–315.

Head, N. 2020. "A 'Pedagogy of Discomfort'? Experiential Learning and Conflict Analysis in Israel-Palestine". *International Studies Perspectives* 21, no. 1, 78–96.

Hobson, C. 2017. "Reckoning with Our Limits". *Australian Journal of International Affairs* 71, no. 1, 20–23.

Katzenstein, P. and R. Sil. 2008. "Eclectic Theorizing in the Study and Practice of International Relations". In *The Oxford Handbook of International Relations*, edited by C. Reus-Smit and D. Snidal, 109–130. Oxford: Oxford University Press.

Ramel, F. 2018. "Teaching International Relations through Arts: Some Lessons Learned". *International Studies Perspectives* 19, no. 4, 360–374.

Reus-Smit, C. and D. Snidal. 2008. "Between Utopia and Reality: The Practical Discourses of International Relations". In *The Oxford Handbook of International Relations,* edited by C. Reus-Smit and D. Snidal, 3–37. Oxford: Oxford University Press.

Shulman, L. 2005a. "The Signature Pedagogies of the Professions of Law, Medicine, Engineering, and the Clergy: Potential Lessons for the Education of Teachers". Talk delivered at the Math Science Partnerships (MSP) Workshop: 'Teacher Education for Effective Teaching and Learning', hosted by the National Research Council's Center for Education, 6–8 February.

Shulman, L. S. 2005b. "Signature Pedagogies in the Professions". *Daedalus* 134, no. 3, 52–59.

4

Shall We Destroy the Teacher? What English Language Teachers Can Teach IR about Pedagogy

DANIEL CLAUSEN

The discipline of International Relations (IR) is frequently one where a professor—often treated as a "master" or "virtuoso"—lectures and students listen. The teacher-centeredness of the IR classroom is often taken for granted. After all, the professor is the "star performer" who has mastered the nuances of the subject matter. When teachers do utilize active learning techniques, the activities are too often limited by class size or the teacher's inexperience using them. For this reason, the opportunities for students to find their voice within the discipline of IR are usually stunted. In contrast, the discipline of English language teaching has developed teaching approaches to limit "teacher talk time" and enhance the role of the student. An English language classroom "lecture" is more likely to feature elicitation, brainstorming, and speculation than an IR classroom. An English language classroom is a place where students are more likely to be moving, interacting, and speaking. The teacher's role is more likely to be a conductor than a performer, and if he or she performs this role well, increasingly the students may even begin to take over the role of conducting the class. Thus, the ultimate aim of an English language teacher is to have an ever-diminishing voice.

Both the idea that a teacher's role should be limited and that English language teaching can "teach IR a thing or two" will be explored in this chapter. In addition to the staples of active learning (role-plays, games, presentations, student polling, and debates), English language teaching offers an even deeper challenge to IR's pedagogical tenets. Should IR make sure the voice with the most authority and wisdom is heard? Or, should it maximize the opportunities for each student to find the version of their voice that has the most authority and wisdom?

The IR Teacher as Professional Talker

For those who imagine the classroom as a collaborative space full of rich conversation, experience, and activity, the IR classroom can sometimes be a depressing place. I speak as someone with an early background in the humanities. As an undergraduate major in English literature, my typical classrooms were places where class discussions and Socrative methods were taken for granted. After my undergraduate degree, I went to Japan as an English teacher. During my four years in this role, I progressively learned how to quiet my own voice so that students might find theirs. It is perhaps unsurprising, then, that when I started as a graduate student in International Relations, in classrooms and in conferences, I often found myself in noisy cacophonous spaces. What may have seemed normal for students with social science backgrounds seemed to me places full of obnoxious posturing, ego-driven monologues, and discussion monopolists. In short, it was a place full of teacher talk—and students practicing their own version of teacher talk.

Perhaps this is an oversimplification, a caricature of IR at its worst (or, perhaps its best). But even in its exaggerated form, it represents my experience of the classroom coming from a place of quiet students (Japan) in a profession where teachers are encouraged to be quiet and listen (English language teaching). Is the teacher-centered classroom a necessity in IR? Should one of its signature pedagogies continue to be the teacher-focused lecture? Or, perhaps, English language teachers can teach IR teachers how to embrace a better model, one that includes a greater role for simulations, debates, interactive lectures, and the negotiated curriculum. Little by little, the classroom can become a place where students speak more and the IR teacher speaks less. Perhaps English language teachers can teach IR how to destroy the teacher.

Teacher Talk: Modeling an Essential Professional Skill?

Shulman (2005) writes, "We all intuitively know what signature pedagogies are. These are the forms of instruction that leap to mind when we first think about the preparation of members of particular professions" (Shulman 2005, 52). The signature pedagogy I will explore has many names. I have heard it referred to as "pontificating," "punditry," and "expounding." In my own frustr-ated moments, I have referred to the culprit as the "discussion monopolist"—a label that could apply to assertive students as well as teachers. Positive labels might include "the maestro," "the master," or "the expert at his/her best." A generic label would simply be "lecture" or "talk." Because of my experiences prior to IR—both as an English major and as an English language teacher—and because this essay is sympathetic to the perspective of English language teachers, I will refer to this signature pedagogy as "teacher talk."

In defense of IR teacher talk, I would like to state that there are real-world implications involved in using and promoting this technique. Shulman writes that a signature pedagogy has three dimensions, "a *surface structure*, which consists of concrete, operational acts of teaching and learning... a *deep structure*, a set of assumptions about how best to impart a certain body of knowledge and know-how. And it has an *implicit structure*, a moral dimension that comprises a set of beliefs about professional attitudes, values, and dispositions" (Shulman 2005, 54-55). Focusing just for the moment on the "teacher talk" approach to IR, I think we would find a *deep structure* that takes the effectiveness of lectures for granted and an *implicit* structure that values expertise and authority. Thus, we may say that IR scholars, in their will to dominate a conversation, are actually performing an important function. They demonstrate how to marshal expertise and knowledge to make authoritative presentations. And in the places where IR scholars might function in the real world, these authoritative presentations are greatly valued.

In the real world, IR experts are often called on to give authoritative talks on important issues to decision-makers, some of whom might not be sympathetic to the message of the speaker (usually for political, bureaucratic, or ideological reasons). These arenas of talk can be highly competitive. Some might be negotiations over the allocation of scarce resources, such as money or attention. If a practitioner were to demonstrate excessive empathy—the kind that is often found in the humanities and arts—that empathy might be used against the speaker and his or her interests. Thus, turn-sharing, empathetic listening, or actively empowering other speakers might be the wrong model for students who will need to function in debates, budget and policy meetings, briefings, and other competitive settings where important and often contentious decisions are made. As Shulman (2005, 16) writes, "pedagogies must measure up to the standards not just of the academy, but also of the particular professions." Therefore, there may be good professional reasons why IR classrooms lack the kind of pedagogical approaches that are found in the humanities. There may also be good reasons why regard for hierarchy based on expertise needs to be protected. Perhaps in IR, as in the real world, one must earn the right to speak.

English Language Teaching: The Fine Art of Destroying a Teacher

And yet, one need not look far to find vehemence for the narrating teacher. The deep moral challenge to teacher talk is represented by such classics of education philosophy as Paulo Freire's (2005, 72) *Pedagogy of the Oppressed*, which challenges the "banking" system of education, where students are seen as empty vessels ready to collect the gifts bestowed on them by narrating teachers. In a similar vein, the education classic by David Kolb (1984), *Experiential Learning*, places student experience at the center of a cycle of learning. The "Kolb's Learning Cycle," as it is known, has students make sense of their experiences, form their theories, and actively experiment with them (Kolb 1984; Brock and Cameron 1999). In both of these classics of education, the student is treated as the center of the learning experience. The teacher acts as a partner, an assistant, or even a consultant, rather than as a boss or lead performer.

Though elements of IR share this aversion (especially outside the mainstream of IR), the revulsion is reflected even more in the realm of English language teaching. In English language teaching, when it comes to teacher talk, less is more. One should avoid essentializing English teaching techniques too much. The body of research and theory that informs English language teaching has gone through many changes. From the largely passive techniques of the early days (grammar-translation and audio-lingual approaches) to more experimental approaches (such as the silent way, suggestopedia, and total physical response) to communicative language approaches, to say nothing of the split between Applied Linguistics and practical teaching research (see Ariza et al. 2011, 63–74; Richards 2008). It is hard to generalize too much about the totality of English language teaching.

And yet one generalization, I believe, is not unfounded: active learning techniques are the norm in English language teaching. Whether they are task-based, competency-based, or communicative approaches, English language teachers are encouraged to get their students speaking through role-plays, discussions, projects, and tasks. The key insight behind all of these active approaches is that English is not just a body of knowledge to be taught, but a tool to get things done. The value of giving students time to use their English in meaningful contexts is so taken for granted that almost no English language teacher would dispute it. And yet, there is an even more radical approach to creating a communicative classroom. I have come to refer to this as the doctrine of "destroying the teacher." This approach is detailed in Alan McLean's (1980) short article "Destroying the Teacher: The Need for a Learner-Centered Teaching." In his article, McLean (1980, 16–17) proposes five principles for organizing a better English language classroom:

1. Reduction of coercion
2. Active learner involvement
3. Experience before interpretation
4. Avoidance of oversimplification
5. The value of silence

To these five principles generated by McLean, I would add two more suggested by David Nunan (2013, 60) in his body of research.

1. Encourage students to become teachers
2. Encourage students to become researchers

For various reasons, some of these principles might not apply to the IR classroom. For scholars with a focus on critical perspectives (for example, feminist, neo-Marxist, postcolonial, and postmodern approaches), the reduction of coercion and avoidance of oversimplification are often key aspects of the classroom. However, in mainstream IR, the ability to make complex phenomena simpler is often highly valued. Additionally, if students feel they are being coerced into studying things that are irrelevant to them, then they are free to take other classes. For practical reasons, experience before interpretation may not be possible. A short trip to the UN headquarters or an active combat zone is typically not feasible. Though, when we examine the active learning literature further, we will see that there are times when fieldwork is possible.

While all seven principles mentioned above can be useful for IR, two are particularly relevant: active learner involvement and the value of silence. Active learner involvement (a technique that also usually reduces coercion) can improve motivation and increase student autonomy. In an English language classroom, often the richness and fluency of a student's speech improves when they are discussing topics about which they are passionate. Allowing students to choose some of their own content increases their motivation. Involving students early and often also increases their autonomy and makes them rely less on the teacher.

Though active silence on the part of the teacher is a key component of English language instruction, from my experience, it is not enough. Not only must a teacher control his or her own ego, but he or she must strive to constrain the other egoists—the excessive-talkers-in-waiting—among the class. In my experience, this problem is significantly larger in an IR classroom, a place where egoists seemed to be attracted and where ego-driven discussion monopolists can sometimes be encouraged. When the egoists dominate, the class is usually deprived of the insights of the thoughtful introverts who have been developing their ideas through long periods of quiet reflection.

Active Learning: An IR Perspective

Thus far, I have discussed active learning and student-centered learning as if they were the sole domain of English language classrooms. However, the tradition of "destroying the teacher" is also alive and well in the political science and IR literatures, especially in the pages of *International Studies Perspectives,* which regularly devotes issues to the subject of pedagogy. In this IR, active learning not only includes presentations and discussions, but also role-plays, simulations, and experience-based learning. This version of IR also realizes the benefit that active learning brings to learner motivation (Mikalayeva 2016; Lüdert and Stewart 2017; Oros 2007; Simpson and Kaussler 2009).

Murphy and Reidy (2006) stand out as two early scholars who examined the signature pedagogy of political science and found teacher-centric approaches, such as lectures, wanting. Much as I am imploring IR scholars to learn from English language teachers, they implore teachers to borrow from the humanities and physical sciences. Lüdert and Stewart (2017), reflecting on their own classroom experiences, have found benefits to using debates, simulations, one-minute papers, creative presentations, and the creation of posters, flipcharts, and PowerPoint presentations, as well as using perspective-taking activities within the framework of a case study.

Games, role-plays, and simulations—the staples of English language teaching—are also frequently utilized by IR teachers. The tradition of using games and simulations has a long tradition (Arnold 2015; Asal 2005; Mikalayeva 2016; Newman and Twigg 2000; Simpson and Kaussler 2009). Though using games in the classroom can be time-consuming, Arnold (2015) finds that playing classic board games like *Diplomacy* can stimulate both enthusiasm for the subject matter and familiarity with its core concepts. Whether an instructor uses an established board game (Arnold 2015) or designs their own simulation (Newman and Twigg 2000), the use of games tends to make classroom experience richer and more memorable.

Of course, there is no teacher quite like experience. Incorporating real-world experience into IR lessons can be difficult, but not impossible. Kachuyevski and Jones (2011) have used short field studies abroad to help teach key concepts in minority rights and ethnic conflicts in the Ukraine. Others, such as Barber and Battistoni (1993) and Harris (2012), have made the case for incorporating service-learning into the curriculum. The recommendation that students serve their community adds an important element that is hard to duplicate in the classroom: real-world experience.

Digging Deeper: The Negotiated Curriculum

In addition to the active learning techniques discussed above, other ideas that can improve IR pedagogy include *learner-centered teaching, learner-needs surveys,* and the *negotiated curriculum.* Increasingly, English language programs are de-emphasizing a complete mastery of the English language (an unrealistic goal) and using learner-needs surveys to try to understand what aspects of the English language are most valuable to students (Nunan 2013, 16). This approach is frequently referred to as learner-centered teaching (as opposed to subject-matter-centered teaching). The approach is driven partly by pragmatism: it is impossible to teach the entire English language, and typically learners have a better knowledge of what aspects of the language are most useful in their lives.

A similar approach could be used in IR classes, even in levels as low as introductory courses. At the moment, student choices are usually restricted to a few key aspects of the course, such as what topics to write papers on or what books they might review. Learner-needs surveys could be used to make more fundamental changes to the curriculum, such as what assignments to include and whether to include topical elements, such as articles from respected newspapers and foreign policy periodicals. The following is an example of a question that might be included in a learner-needs survey.

> As a part of this course, you are required to do a project worth 20% of your grade. Which of the following projects would you prefer to undertake?
>
> 1.   Create and present a poster (15 minutes) on a key topic.
> 2.   Write a five-page paper on a key topic.
> 3.   Create a short ten-minute video on a key topic to present to the class.
> 4.   Write your own idea here: _____

At the core of this approach is the assumption that the curriculum needs to be negotiated and renegotiated with students (Nunan 2013, 57). Allowing students to continue to make meaningful choices about their curriculum throughout the semester helps keep their motivation high, and (in the vein of McLean's (1980) article) reduces coercion. Learner-needs surveys, too, might turn up surprising findings. Students, might, for example, value lectures over the active learning techniques described in this chapter. Whatever choices students make, the rigor of the course can be kept consistent by allowing students to choose from a menu of activities that represent approximately the same commitment of time and energy.

Digging Deeper: One Model for How to Destroy the Teacher

A common rejoinder from those who prefer narrative methods of instruction is that students are not ready to take on more active roles in the classroom. My reply is that "destroying the teacher" can be conceptualized as a process. The "destroyed teacher" is the product of a teacher successfully identifying where students are in their learning and guiding them to higher stages of learning autonomy. The following is my attempt to present McLean's idea of "destroy-ing the teacher" as a process with various levels.

Level 0 – The Narrative Approach

In this essay, I have identified this level as the one to be avoided. At this level, there is a clear hierarchy of who speaks. The teacher speaks and the student is the recipient of that speech, collecting what knowledge they can. This level is often negatively referred to as the "banking model" of education (see Freire 2005).

Level 1 – Moving Away from Narration

In this first step, the teacher moves away from teacher-talk in gradual steps. Students are encouraged to participate in lectures in limited ways. For example, they are urged to *speculate* about the meaning of key terms, and *Socratic questioning* and other *elicitation* methods are used to get students speaking. At this stage, the teacher points out student errors but encourages students to *self-correct* when possible.

Level 2 – Highly Structured Activities

At this stage, students are given activities to do in groups or pairs. Discussions, projects, role plays, and simulations are utilized more often. However, the teacher provides abundant structure in the form of outlines, prompts, examples, and desired outcomes. At this stage, following Nunan's (2013) guidance on the negotiated curriculum, students are also given more input over the curriculum, typically through A/B choices.

Level 3 – Activities Take Center Stage

At this stage, role-plays, simulations, games, presentations, group/pair work, and discussions are a regular part of the classroom. The activities have less structure than before and students have more freedom to choose their own desired outcomes. The teacher spends less time lecturing and more time providing feedback. At this stage, students regularly make decisions about the curriculum.

Level 4 – Peer Teaching and Student Research

At this stage, in addition to active learning methods, students regularly take over "teacher" roles, such as setting up activities, generating class content, and providing feedback. Students present more of their own research during class and engage in peer-teaching. At this stage, the teacher serves as a safety net or support system when students falter.

Level 5 – Students as Peers

Success! The students have reached a level where they now feel comfortable making informed decisions about the curriculum, can give feedback to their fellow students, and can teach each other meaningful content. The student has now become something close to a peer to the teacher.

The model above should not be seen as a program to be implemented in every teaching situation in every classroom, but rather as a rough guide. While the "students as peers" level may be unrealistic for first-year undergraduates, it is helpful to remember why this is a valued end-state. The model can be seen as a heuristic for how every classroom can become a more active space, regardless of a student's current level of learning autonomy. The key point is that except for level 0—which rejects the idea of the active student to begin with—there are methods at each level to make classrooms more active and engaging.

Shall We Always Destroy the Teacher? Reservations, Hesitations, and Open Questions

Having stated my case for a more active classroom, I now feel it appropriate to explore some of the lingering questions and my own reservations surrounding the idea of "destroying the teacher."

Safe or Unsafe Spaces?

Typically, in an English language classroom the teacher attempts to create a "safe space" where errors are okay or even encouraged. After all, how do you learn a language without making errors? In contrast, an IR classroom can often feel like an "unsafe space," where nonsensical utterances or ideology-based editorializing are discouraged. Even many role plays, such as those that involve international negotiations, are assumed to be competitive. Their value often comes from the sense of competition that would exist in the real world. Perhaps, then, it makes sense to maintain this sense of danger in the IR classroom. It may even be productive to import this sense of danger to the English language classroom when the stakes of misspoken language could have severe real-world consequences (for example, when role-playing an emergency call). My sense is that pragmatism should drive decisions regarding how much to make spaces of discourse safe or unsafe in the classroom. Perhaps the closer the student is to the professional world, the more he or she should be made to feel that (simulated) danger.

The Knowing/Doing Gap and its Relevance to IR

In melding the pedagogical conversations of IR and English language teaching, one of the hardest problems I have had to deal with is the knowing-versus-doing problem. In the field of English language teaching, the original impetus for the switch from passive forms of study (such as translation, grammar exercises, and listening exercises) to active learning approaches was a recognition that many graduates of English language programs knew quite a bit about English without being able to use it (Nunan 2013, 65–66). In IR, there has been a similar debate between how IR is studied and how IR is performed in the real world (see, for example, Weiss and Kuele, 2013). However, since researching IR can also be a form of "doing IR," it is questionable whether this gap exists in the same way it does for English language students. While it is clear that English, or any language, is of little use without the ability to use it in meaningful contexts, it is not clear that the same is true for IR. Knowing the subject matter of IR, even if one's opportunities for using this knowledge are limited, could still be seen as an important part of a well-rounded liberal education. At the very least, I would suggest that IR teachers should think about what meaningful skills—critical thinking, theory development, writing, presenting, debating—can be developed through their courses. Even if students of IR will only be doing IR in a limited way once they graduate, they should still be practicing skills they will be using throughout their life.

When Not to Destroy the Teacher?

My contention is that IR classrooms have more in common with English language classrooms than IR teachers realize. Much like English language students, I believe IR students at all levels want to be active participants in their own education, negotiating what is taught, engaging in what is said, and practicing what is learned. And, they typically want these roles to grow over time. And yet, there are times when the teacher should not be destroyed. The role of the teacher is important when motivation is at its highest. When students have ambitious goals and need all the help they can get to achieve them, they may not have the patience for slower Socratic methods. This is the same whether it is an English language student preparing for a rigorous test or an IR graduate student hoping to finish an ambitious research project. The student needs the teacher's expertise directly and in a hurry.

Ironically, the teacher also needs to be preserved and strengthened when motivation is at its lowest. In dire situations—usually when students have been coerced into class, such as student-athletes or non-majors who need a particular credit, or when there is simply a lack of student maturity—the teacher needs to be both the master of conversation and an autocrat. Unfortunately, active teaching methods in these environments usually just lead to students goofing off.

The Cost-Benefit Analysis of Active Learning Methods: The Dubious State of Statistical Evidence

Active teaching approaches can be costly in terms of preparation time, especially if a teacher is developing tools for the first time. Does this preparation time pay off in terms of learning and student satisfaction? Thus far, I have found very little statistical evidence to support this point. More interestingly, I have found a controversy surrounding a commonly quoted statistic that is used to support active learning methods. The statistic is associated with Edgar Dale's "Cone of Learning" and other variations of this model. It states that learners remember 10 percent of what they read, 20 percent of what they hear, 30 percent of what they see, 50 percent of what they hear and see, 70 percent of what they say and write, and 90 percent of what they say as they perform an authentic activity.[1] The statistic and its variants (since often the numbers and labels change depending who is citing whom), while intuitively appealing, seems to be the product of a kind of academic hearsay and circular referencing rather than any experimental study of learning. For those interested in unraveling the mystery behind these magical numbers, I recommend reading an investigation by Deepak Prem Subramony (2003) or conducting your own investigation. Regardless, scholars should be skeptical of those trying to use statistical evidence to suggest unambiguous confidence in the superiority of any one method or set of methods over another, active learning or otherwise.

---

[1]   This statistic has been encountered in a few articles reviewed for this essay and has been experienced by the author in several different contexts that span teaching seminars to casual conversations. I have refrained from citing authors or naming individuals in order to spare embarrassment or stir controversy.

Expand the Toolbox Slowly

Finally, there is no need to rush to embrace new methods. For those who are used to lectures, who have mastered their lecture notes, and can keep their students enthralled with speech, active teaching will not fix something that is not broken. And a rush to replace tried methods with the unfamiliar will most likely lead to catastrophe. My own experience has shown that—just like a lecture—the use of role-plays, games, and simulations improves with each iteration. Thus, teachers should not give up on active teaching methods too soon. In addition, teachers should focus their efforts on resources that can be re-used and improved over time. And so, I suggest the magical rule of 10 percent. Devote 10 percent of class time to experimenting with something new. Expand the methods that work well for you and throw out those that are holding you back. Ten percent is not revolutionary if only tried once; but done consistently, it will revolutionize your teaching.

The Deeper Challenge to IR

Now that I have revealed all my hesitations, let me return to English language teaching pedagogy—in particular, its deepest challenge to IR. The deepest challenge comes not from its use of active teaching methods (surface structure) or even the repeated mantras that inform its practices (the deep structure), such as its injunction to "destroy the teacher." Rather, its deepest challenge comes from its implicit structure, where the moral core of the discipline is found. At their core, English language teachers (and their IR active learning compatriots) believe that more people should be empowered to speak. They believe a teacher's authority comes from his or her ability to diminish the ego in the service of helping others find their voice.

In IR classrooms, where the discussion monopolist dominates, authority comes from the ability to marshal knowledge and expertise to make sure the most reasoned argument prevails. The deep and implicit structures of this approach are grounded in the real-world struggles IR practitioners face when they leave the classroom, and the value and prestige IR training should bestow on expert voices. Rather than try to reconcile these opposing views—opposing values are rarely so easily reconciled—I will instead appeal to the pragmatism of the professional talkers, since it is often pragmatism that informs their practice. Meager though these arguments might be, I urge you to ponder them deeply. (And, if you are so disposed, to debate them actively in class.)

The first argument: many of your students will be non-native speakers. It is possible that you too are a non-native speaker, teaching in a language strange from your own. Try to think of the delight your student will feel when they are encouraged to speak and rewarded for speaking, despite their imperfections. Think of the boost of motivation a student will feel when they speak out for the first time and are rewarded for their contribution.

The second argument: in this tumultuous 21st century, there is no guarantee that the monologuer or discussion monopolist will be the wisest person in the room. (Spoiler alert: often they are not.) There is no guarantee that students will always have access to wizened experts. In the age of social media, expertise is often confused with exposure, and authority comes from approval in the form of "likes," recirculated hashtags, and viewership numbers. That should give teachers added motivation to see the classroom not as a place for wonderful performances of expertise, but as a place to develop the student's critical faculties as a bulwark against an uncertain future. Certainly, exposure to the wizened voices of experts will be an important component, but not a sufficient one. Students will also need to overcome the habits of passivity. They will need to be encouraged to make choices, evaluate infor-mation, form their own opinions, and join conversations, all in a context where teachers provide feedback in a way that enhances their growing learning autonomy. In building this critical faculty, a healthy suspicion of those who would monopolize discussions or try to dominate others in speech—whether they have advanced degrees or not—may also be the most useful tool a student takes out of the classroom.

References

Ariza, Eileen, Yahya, Noorchaya, Zainuddin, Hanizah, Morales-Jones, Carmen, and Gerena, Linda. 2011. *Fundamentals Of Teaching English To Speakers Of Other Languages In K-12 Mainstream Classrooms*, 3rd ed. Kendall Hunt Publishing Co.

Arnold, Richard. 2015. "Where's the Diplomacy in Diplomacy? Using a Classic Board Game in "Introduction to International Relations." *PS: Political Science & Politics,* 48 (1): 162–65.

Asal, Victor. 2005. "Playing Games with International Relations". *International Studies Perspectives,* 6 (3): 359–73.

Barber, Benjamin and Battistoni, Richard. 1993. "A Season of Service: Introducing Service Learning into the Liberal Arts Curriculum". *PS: Political Science & Politics,* 26(2): 235–240.

Brock, Kathy, and Cameron, Beverly. 1999. "Enlivening Political Science Courses with Kolb's Learning Preference Model". *PS: Political Science and Politics, 32*(2): 251–256.

Freire, Paulo. 2005. *Pedagogy of the Oppressed*. Translated by Myra Bergman Ramos. (Originally published 1970). New York, Continuum.

Harris, Clodagh. 2012. "Expanding Political Science's Signature Pedagogy: The Case for Service Learning". *Eur Polit Sci,* 11: 175–185.

Kachuyevski, Angela and Jones, Sandra. F. 2011. "Bringing Theory to Life Through Field Study". *International Studies Perspectives,* 12 (4): 447–456.

Kolb, David. 1984. *Experiential Learning: Experience as the Source of Learning and Development.* Englewood Cliffs, NJ: Prentice-Hall.

Lüdert, Jan. and Stewart, Katriona. 2017. "Structuring a Mixed-Methods Course". *E-International Relations,* November 7. https://www.e-ir. info/2017/11/07/structuring-a-mixed-methods-course/

McLean, Alan. C. 1980. "Destroying the Teacher: the Need for a Learner-centred Teaching". *English Teaching Forum*, 28 (3): 16-19. https:// americanenglish.state.gov/files/ae/resource_files/mclean_the_need_for_ learner-centered_teaching.pdf

Mikalayeva, Luidmila. 2016. "Motivation, Ownership, and the Role of the Instructor in Active Learning". *International Studies Perspectives*, Volume 17 (2): 214–229.

Murphy, Mary. C. and Reidy, Theresa. 2006. "Exploring Political Science's Signature Pedagogy". *Academic Exchange Quarterly,* 10:4 (Winter). http:// www.rapidintellect.com/AEQweb/7mar3562z6.htm

Newman, William W. and Twigg, Judyth L. 2000. "Active Engagement of the Intro IR Student: A Simulation Approach". *PS: Political Science & Politics,* 33 (4): 835–42.

Nunan, David. 2013. *Learner-Centered English Language Education: The Selected Works of David Nunan.* New York and London: Routledge.

Oros, Andrew. 2007. "Let's Debate: Active Learning Encourages Student Participation and Critical Thinking". *Journal of Political Science Education,* 3 (3): 293–311.

Richards, Jack C. 2008. "Growing Up with TESOL". *English Teaching Forum*, 46 (1): 2-11.

Shulman, Lee S. 2005. "Signature pedagogies in the professions". *Daedalus*, 134(3): 52-59.

Simpson, Archie W and Kaussler, Bernie. 2009. "IR Teaching Reloaded: Using Films and Simulations in the Teaching of International Relations". *International Studies Perspectives,* 10 (4): 413–427.

Subramony, Deepak Prem. 2003. "Dale's Cone revisited: Critically examining the misapplication of a nebulous theory to guide practice". *Educational technology,* 7(8): 25-30.

Weiss, Thomas G and Kuele, Giovanna. 2013. "Theory vs. Practice, Myth or Reality?" *E-International Relations* (May 23). http://www.e-ir.info/2013/05/23/theory-vs-practice-myth-or-reality

5

Fostering Ontological Agility: A Pedagogical Imperative

TAMARA A. TROWNSELL

"Our task as social scientists is to account for the multiplicity of ways in which the political world around us is viewed and experienced."
—Somdeep Sen (2020)

"Students of international politics are led to act on imageries of Africa, Islam, the Balkans, China, and any other seemingly 'exotic' or 'distant' region or topic, without an awareness of the ways in which these imageries have been intimately colored by Western authors and their respective histories, trajectories, values, and world views. Instead of speaking *with* others about political issues, students of world politics are essentially induced to speak *about* others and their political topics."
—Jonas Hagmann (2015, 3)

How are we supposed to learn how to carry out the task condoned by Sen if we are busily reproducing the scenario described by Hagmann? Speaking *with* others requires more than just language acquisition and an openness to converse. Besides acknowledging ontological pluralism, Sen's plea prods us to build the capacity to fittingly traverse worlds constituted through distinct, fundamental existential suppositions. This chapter asserts that IR students must become savvy in applying a diverse ontological toolset to engage with lifeways based on incommensurate, fundamental existential assumptions. As a pedagogical goal, however, fostering ontological agility is not feasible in a single semester because it requires denaturalizing our most fundamental existential assumptions, learning how to apply others, and becoming nimble at doing so. Among undergraduate students it is possible to fulfill the following preliminary steps necessary for generating ontological competence while also reaching a given International Relations (IR) theory course's regular set of learning objectives: (a) teach a pluralized understanding of ontology, (b) make students, through the metaphor of "fishbowls," conversant with intersubjectively co-constituted timespacescapes that together constitute a pluriverse of worlds, and (c) build student tolerance to existential discomfort.

In this book, Jan Lüdert aims to identify the "surface," "deep," and "implicit structures" of what Shulman (2005, 54) calls a signature pedagogy (Lüdert 2016). He asked us to discuss the "concrete and practical acts of teaching and learning IR," the "implicit and explicit assumptions" that "we impart to students about the world of politics," and the "values and beliefs" we hold while preparing students for a wide range of possible careers. This chapter, in response, reviews pertinent elements on all three levels of "existential calisthenics," a signature pedagogical program that prepares students to become ontologically agile.

It is prudent to forewarn that while the transversal meta-objective for all of my courses described here is not incompatible with the purpose of signature pedagogies—"to transfer skills [to students] of how *to think*, *to perform* and *to act with integrity* in their professional work" (Shulman 2005, 52)—the pedagogical strategy of fostering ontological agility may not align well with the proposal to define a concerted set of pedagogical sensibilities in the IR classroom. This essay starts with the premise that "the fundamental ways in which future practitioners [have been getting] educated for their new professions" (Shulman 2005, 52) in IR have been ontologically myopic and thus impair us from engaging fruitfully with differently co-constituted timespacescapes. Alternatively, if we are not trying to standardize "pedagogical content knowledge" but are instead inculcating a sensitivity toward and willingness to maintain the space for a plethora of voices (Lüdert, this volume), then the following could represent *one* way of preparing students to engage more effectively with multiplicity and difference. With the precept that this project in no way seeks to become an overarching, singular strategy, the first half of the chapter explores the central assumptions, values, and beliefs that drive the impulse to foster ontological pluralism and agility, before reviewing some concrete pedagogical strategies in the second.

Disciplinary Myopia: A Pedagogical Call to Action

As a discipline, IR is unique in that it aspires to engage, understand, and even at times explain *world* politics, but it cultivates a parochial attitude toward Others who contribute to those politics equally, yet who act based on very disparate fundamental existential assumptions (Chakrabarty, 2000; Agathangelou and Ling 2004; Shani 2008; Tickner and Wæver 2009; Acharya and Buzan 2010; Nayak and Selbin 2010; Shilliam 2015).[1] Critiques have been mountingly launched over the past 40 years that the discipline has been historically incapable of engaging other forms of being and knowing in ways that do not involve further exacerbating epistemic violence.[2] For a discipline that seeks to decrease conflict and/or increase peace worldwide, this claim is bitterly ironic.

Wemheuer-Vogelaar and her colleagues (2020, 17) conclude, upon concisely reviewing the non-, post-, and beyond Western debates, that diversifying the discipline does not only involve research: "The IR research community's efforts to create a more inclusive discipline can only be permanent if [the global IR] debate is taken to the classroom." I could not agree more, but there are ontological reasons why the discipline suffers from parochialism. So, before we bring historically silenced voices that depart from distinct, fundamental existential commitments into the discipline, it must first become ontologically plural.

In more traditional IR settings, we typically learn and teach approaches that reaffirm examining multiplicity through a singular ontological register. This register—one that encompasses *both* dualist *and* monist approaches in the discipline and that informs its various methodological strategies—is monopolized by the assumption of separation as the primordial condition of existence. That is, even the most heated disciplinary debates on ontology that seek to legitimize other ontological schemes beyond those with positivist underpinnings[3] still hold onto an underlying commitment to separation *prior to*

---

[1]   Manuela Picq (2013, 445) has described it thus: 'Critics accuse IR of two significant, interrelated sins. The first is an ingrained hegemony. IR has long been accused of US-centrism, as when Stanley Hoffmann (1977) described it as an American social science. ... Related to this first critique is the charge that IR is out of touch with many important issues in the world because of its narrow disciplinary approach. Scholarly dominance implies a certain conceptual parochialism, with inevitable epistemological implications. The study of International Relations, it turns out, is often not all that *worldly*.' I emphasize here that this dominance stems from a particular shared configuration of fundamental existential assumptions.

[2]   The feminist, queer, post-colonial, decolonial, indigenous, post-Western, post-human, and green IR literatures have shown the systematic way in which various "different Others" have been marginalized. Historically affected human clusters include indigenous groups, political/ethnic minorities, enslaved groups, trafficked groups, refugees, people with disabilities, and persons of distinct genders, sexual orientations, religions, etc., whereas in the nonhuman realm, ecosystems, minerals, climate patterns, flora, and fauna have been regularly and systematically excluded from consideration in the discipline. For a succinct review of the ethnocentric biases extant in what Shilliam (2015, 13) calls the "colonial science" of IR, see Capan (2016). Regarding anthropocentric biases, see Chandler, Müller and Rothe (2021).

[3]   Some classic ontological arguments include Walker (1992), Patomäki and Wight (2000), and Jackson (2011).

any commitment to interconnection, be it the anthropocentrism of post-structuralism or the continued insistence on differentiating between subjects and objects and human and non-human (even if enmeshed and co-constitutive) in the new materialisms. The predominant, separation-based register makes us blind to other possible ontological configurations through its reductionist nature and therefore incapable of grasping the robust nature of concepts borne through incommensurate, fundamental existential commitments.

This leads to two issues that the following pedagogical strategy seeks to mitigate. First, ontological reductionism begets exclusion, capture, and domination. In IR, ontological blind spots and silences translate into forms of epistemic violence in the classroom and into literature and policy that reinforce exclusionary practices. Second, having too narrow a set of existential tools, especially one produced through a reductionist register, is overly risky when facing today's accelerated environmental, social, political, and technological complexity. Having only one ontological scheme with which to operate means that most people are easily overwhelmed and become susceptible to forms of extremism, fundamentalism, and/or violence in response.

We can no longer afford to remain "unknowingly" faithful to separation as the only primordial condition of existence solely because its use is so pre-dominant and lens so reductionist that we cannot even recognize, much less respect, other assumptions that constitute other co-created worlds.[4] Here is where academia and the IR discipline could play a crucial mitigating role in our ability to survive as a species by proactively instructing people to become comfortable with shifting ontological schemes so that they could become versatile in and adaptable to new circumstances. However, the *pedagogical imperative* to prepare students to engage with the multiplicity of distinct forms of being/thinking/doing that give shape to world politics implies an overhaul within the discipline itself first. As scholars and professors in the discipline, we would need to become excruciatingly aware of the link between our particular configuration of fundamental existential assumptions and their impact on how we "world." Next we would need to acknowledge that more than one possible primordial condition of existence exists and then hone ontological agility ourselves by learning how to also embrace interconnection *prior to* any presupposition of separation.

---

4   With the post-positivist turn has come a flourishing of previously silenced voices, which have been absolutely crucial for opening up the discipline. Yet these voices still are divided along categorical lines even if sometimes treated intersectionally. Here, I am *not* referring to a particular *kind* of voice; I am referring to how the fundamental existential commitments collectively shared in certain worlds beget fruits that are ontologically incommensurate with those borne through other ontological registers.

Having access to and knowing how to use a plural ontological register offers several benefits. First, it allows us to acknowledge that each person holds dear a particular configuration of existential assumptions that filters how they make sense of the world and according to which they direct their vital life force to co-create. From there, we can identify how molds deriving from other fundamental existential commitments provide radically distinct panoramas with their own affordances and limitations. The contrasts provided through these mirrors then enable recognizing how our own existential assumptions crucially limit and shape *in specific and regular ways* what we see as an issue and the range of potential strategies that we can imagine in response. By showing how distinct primordial existential assumptions translate into disparate lifeways that are neither commensurate nor easily grasped through a non-synonymous ontological register, we make the space available to understand that there are distinct ways of doing things and that none is the single answer to all. This is a crucial step for cultivating empathy, the significance of which "has been largely neglected in the field of IR... in a teaching or classroom setting" (Arian 2020, 23). One important advantage has become evident through my teaching context. Since 2005, I have worked at two universities in Ecuador as a white woman, originating from and educated in the United States. In addition to showing me first-hand why the claims at the beginning are both real and disconcerting, my embodied experience in a context of deeply torn social fabric and a constantly replaying *chuchaki colonial*, or colonial hangover, has shown me how fostering ontological pluralism can help rebuild socio-cultural-historical self-esteem in post-colonial contexts.

Navnita Chadha Behera (2020, 25–27) reinforces the principle of ontological pluralism in her own post-colonial IR classroom in India by "traveling back in time" with her students. There, she covers both "the history (read the European history that forms the bedrock of the meta narratives and theories of IR) and theirs (read local histories)" (26) to "make students aware that the universe for thinking through the knowledge categories is not singular but plural" (27). By juxtaposing IR "textbook formulations against our collectively shared 'pasts' and 'present lived experiences,'" Behera demonstrates "how some of these knowledge categories, which the disciplinary practices of IR take for granted, came to be constituted in the first place—historically, socially, and politically." Students "also learn that if they choose to include a 'non-dualistic mode of thinking,' as suggested by the Indian traditions, for understanding the world cast in a 'dualistic,' 'either-or,' 'oppositional mode of thinking,' difference may no longer or necessarily be an a priori source of friction and threat." Behera's example demonstrates how we can both engender learning through difference and underscore the pivotal importance of lifeways that have undergone colonization.

Because I have seen how well this training works in encouraging students to examine any set of circumstances from a variety of angles and in bolstering their capacity for empathy and innovation, I have developed methods to intentionally trigger the denaturalization process while at the same time supporting students as they move through their emotional reactions throughout the semester and beyond. Below, I present some basic pedagogical tools for building ontological competence among undergraduate IR students, including the fishbowl metaphor, modes of engagement, method of contrast, and guided existential discomfort.

Existential Calisthenics: A Pedagogical Program for Fostering Ontological Agility

Let's face it, most human beings, undergraduate students included, like being able to count on certain parameters of their given modus operandi. While most are paying a fee to learn, they are not usually requesting to have their existential boat completely rocked. Yet getting out of IR's vicious cycle of continually reproducing ontological parochialism requires just that. Unfortunately, the benefits of engaging in *existential* calisthenics are not as obvious as the physical version, although both can be painful particularly at first. This means that students cannot imagine where you are taking them or why. It is hard for them to see that they are consistently embracing certain fundamental existential assumptions, that this configuration of assumptions intimately affects how they participate in their own ontological fishbowl (that is, how and what they imagine, perceive, interpret, strategize about, and act upon), and that making those assumptions and not others is actually a choice. Moreover, because the collectively co-constituted timespacescape, or *fishbowl*, in which they operate is so naturalized, they have no apparent reason to contemplate others as inhabiting differently constituted worlds especially when the only thing apparently separating them is air. After all, others *seem* to be doing the same things—being human, finding food and shelter, relating, reproducing, etc. It is difficult to realize that what seem to be the "parallel fruits" of another way of life—even if recognized as distinct cultural artifacts—are actually borne through a radically distinct logic based on other fundamental existential assumptions.

Initially, then, my job is to show that many ways of understanding existence are available and that it is possible to discern the contours of the fishbowl they inhabit through contrast with others. Once they cognitively understand that beings from other fishbowls do not necessarily follow the same logic that they take for granted, it is then possible to propose that the lens they have learned to use might not be fully equipped to understand ideas or artifacts coming out of other fishbowls. At this point, in my "Contemporary IR Theories" course, for example, I would bring in the post-Western literature to contemplate collectively what it might mean for an academic discipline that focuses on *world* politics to not be able to perceive, let alone understand, other lifeways that are radically distinct from our own.

Actively "provincializing" the predominant ontological register of the IR discipline and broader educational system in general should be accompanied by significant reminders. First, students have no reason to feel bad or guilty for how they have been raised. Furthermore, my job is not to teach them that one particular approach to life is good and another bad. This didactic exercise is about recognizing multiplicity. In the end, they get to embrace the theoretical current that most resonates with them. For the time being, though, they study many disparate theoretical perspectives to learn how certain existential assumptions afford some imaginable possibilities and disallow others, and how each implies radically distinct strategies for engaging existence.

In parallel fashion, I introduce the tool of existential *modes of engagement*. Fear is the predominantly applied mode in IR, and it can be illustrated easily through the *Leviathan*, where Hobbes (1996, 26–30, 38) articulates explicitly how he encounters the different Other through fear. Since how we approach difference starts at the ontological level, it is critical to illustrate how certain fundamental existential assumptions encourage the rejection of difference and the subsequent drive to annihilate it, while others encourage its embrace and an openness to sit in tension with it. The latter induces us to use curiosity, through which we can ask lots of questions without determining beforehand whether an encountered Other will be good or bad and calls us to be very present to find out what we can learn from the difference. After prodding students to conjure other modes of engagement, I encourage them to identify their most frequently employed mode and to explore how they feel when they intentionally use other modes. While at first this exercise may seem irrelevant to the study of IR, it is a pivotal preliminary step in nudging students to experiment at the existential level so that they become ever-more aware of how their fundamental existential *assumptions* shape how they engage with all that is.

The content normally taught and reproduced within the IR discipline constitutes the fodder for my work. Besides demonstrating how each theorization relies on a particular ontological architecture, I help students locate patterns emerging out of historically shared configurations of ontological commitments so that they may begin to conceive of how these configurations exert worlding effects. In one example, I show how embracing separation as the primordial condition of existence generates a common logic that plays out in distinct ways in both English School and Marxist theorizing

(Bull 2002; Linklater 1996; Cox 1996). Both utilize linear notions of time and "teleological measuring sticks," or arbitrary social constructions conceived as vertical arrows extending between two (never-to-be-reached) imagined conditions with the one at the top deemed superior and at the bottom the inferior one to be avoided (Trownsell 2013, 290–318). In both literatures, we also find a universal(ized) end goal of transforming the system to something better conceived in cosmopolitan (and, therefore, ethnocentric) terms. I focus students' attention on how, despite the very distinct problematics that motivated Bull's and Marx and Engels' work, each respective argument and corresponding strategies are faithful to a particular shared set of existential assumptions.

In cases like this, it is difficult to fully grasp what I am talking about without a contrasting backdrop. After all, I am trying to get them to recognize the contours of the naturalized fishbowl in which they have been indoctrinated and the nature of the particular water in which they swim. Consequently, to make evident how each theory becomes possible through a particular logic afforded by distinct configurations of existential assumptions and not others, I use the *method of contrast* to reflect examples back and forth. The circle that I open with the study of international society and further sketch when we get to the Communist International can be closed through the contrast provided by queer theory, where it becomes evident that the "teleological measuring stick" is only *one way* of reading and responding to complementary opposites.

To teach students that multiple ontological readings exist and that they have radically different implications depending on the particular configuration of existential assumptions used to perceive and understand them, I clarify the link between a fundamental assumption and its corresponding logic. For instance, I show how heteronormativity is the fruit of embracing separation due to the focus it generates on physical bodies as separable categories, which leads us to want to talk about gender and sexuality in terms of men and women as embodied entities. The ontological panorama afforded by separation also encourages a logic of either-or, which drives the need to evaluate things or situations in terms of better-worse so as to know how to select among alternatives. We can see, then, how this logic drives the marginalization and violence targeted at those who do not abide by the heteronormative metanarrative. In contrast, when interconnection is embr- aced, the either-or logic is not even existentially possible, nor is the focus on "in-corp-orated" characteristics. Instead, all beings are manifestations of the dynamic interplay between *both* feminine *and* masculine energetic impulses. That is, each body is constituted through both masculine and feminine elements. In addition to teaching Weber's (2014, 598) queer logic of the and/ or, I use examples from robustly relational Andean philosophy, a contextually important contrast, to distinguish between the implications of reading binaries as dualities/dualisms through the lens of separation and as parity-based relations through interconnection (Lajo 2004, 81–85).

This method of contrast with other ways of seeing a seemingly similar situation is critical for recognizing one's own fishbowl or way of being in the world. This process though, as we can imagine in the case of denaturalizing heteronormativity for someone who has never been taught to question it, is not without its emotional reactions. Becoming ontologically literate demands learning to become comfortable with being uncomfortable *on an existential level*. As such, I take care to generate an environment of *guided existential discomfort* that provides the necessary support as students learn to move through that discomfort.

In this spirit, each course starts with a forewarning:

> —Throughout this semester, be prepared to feel uncomfortable, uncomfortable with me, uncomfortable with you, with society, with the way you were raised, with how you understand existence, with the way you have been learning about IR until now... My goal is to help you become comfortable with being uncomfortable. It will pretty much take the whole semester to get to the point where you understand why you are going through this. All the while I will be intentionally triggering your fundamental belief systems that have been shaped by cultural, historical, socioeconomic, and academic factors.

I lend the discomfort a purpose:

> — When you feel uncomfortable in reaction to whatever comes up in class, it indicates that we have struck a chord with an idea or belief constitutive of your particular fishbowl. This is actually a good thing, because it flags for us where to pause and what to examine more carefully.[5]

As a multidimensional educator, it is also pertinent to review the possible range of emotional responses that can surge forth on the basis of this

---

[5]   At times when the triggering becomes too intense or when I point to something specific about Ecuadorian culture that might hit too close to home, I am quick to simultaneously acknowledge my own inherited *chuchakis* with which I personally struggle, like "the Protestant work ethic."

ontological training, such as resistance, shutting out, instability, sensations of betrayal or of having been misled, and the potential exacerbation of psychological instability. Due to the multiple referrals I make every semester, I add:

> — Many of you may not be in a place to face this challenge, so I will be reminding you regularly that I have connections with the staff in psychological services and can get you an appointment very quickly in the event that the ideas presented here are "too much" for where you find yourself on your own life path.

I also provide coping strategies. For instance, because I strive to have students recognize existential possibilities occluded through their current (predominant) ontological filter, they have to confront admitting "I don't know" to themselves or to me much more often than usual. When using the naturalized register of separation, having to say "I don't know" repeatedly only seems to reaffirm the existential supposition of uncertainty that derives from embracing separation in the first place and to justify the forms of existential anxiety that accompany it. To mitigate, we explicitly discuss their response and propose alternatives:

> — How does it make you feel to say "I don't know"?

Answers usually signal some form of frustration or discomfort.

> — Does the feeling last forever?

> — No.

> — Would it be possible for you to learn to take a deep breath the moment that you can feel yourself slipping into existential angst and focus on becoming comfortable with sitting in a space of "not knowing?" Once we can sit in tension with the momentary condition of not knowing, is it possible to call on another mode of engagement instead of fear?

The idea is to provide an alternative to drowning in an emotional response. They can become an observer of their response and examine how it derives from a particular constellation of existential assumptions.

— If hitting the emotional wall of "I don't know" can be reinterpreted as a trigger, what could it teach us about ourselves, about our fishbowl? Can we recognize that our response is based on existential assumptions that have been so naturalized that we hardly recognize them or imagine that we have a choice in the matter? Is it possible to see our emotional response as a learned reaction? If so, can we re-qualify uncertainty as an existential assumption itself, a hypothetical possibility as opposed to cosmic law? Can we assume otherwise? This maneuver will allow us to change it, just like that (or hold onto it again, just like that). It is important to get to the point of allowing yourself to recognize that you do not know right this very second without the emotional trigger, because this will enable you to pay attention to the new information that comes to you as part of the process of formulating an answer.

Not everyone will be excited about this kind of training or about the prospect of questioning their foundational assumptions. In fact, many will not be. When they start to feel discomfort, they will seek to avoid both it and the source of pain, a.k.a., the professor. Uncomfortable silences will also arise. These can all be turned into key teaching moments. Pedagogically, the task becomes one of knowing how to hold tension in a classroom and manage it so as to generate an environment of contrast that encourages growth. Over time, it is possible to recognize which silences require patience, which call for a re-stating, which might be best to have someone else explain in their own words, and which ones require emotional processing with questions like, "Does anyone want to talk about how this discussion makes them feel?" Overall, though, the activity of intentionally discomforting your students is not for the faint of heart. Nor is it a technique to use if you are seeking to be the most popular professor. Nevertheless, the significant shifts in perspective that I have witnessed among students, whereby they do not feel obligated to react out of fear or anger in the face of difference, are sufficient motivation for me to keep coaching them through existential calisthenics.

The pedagogical tools reviewed above provide a very small window into the kind of work that we need to undertake as a discipline to establish ontological literacy, which extends from recognizing that there are multiple ways for being, operating, and worlding to being able to read distinct forms of worlding and identify the fundamental existential assumptions that afford them. Once students realize that they have a choice about the assumptions they embrace and that the criteria behind their judgments regarding others obey particular ontological logics that are *not* universal, they will be ready to take "existential calisthenics" to the next level. This, however, does not take place until after their first semester with me. At that point, I encourage them to try applying one assumption now and another at another time in similar circumstances to see how they resonate differently. By comparing and contrasting the consequences of using one primordial assumption and the other, they can recognize the very direct impact that their embraced assumptions have on how we co-create. They may come to the realization that *we all* answer certain existential questions so consistently that *we* have become unaware that there are prior questions that *we* are constantly answering and that we all, actively or inactively, constantly make assumptions that shape the kinds of worlds that become possible. This exercise in learning about the various ways of assuming and participating in the world prepares them to eventually take responsibility for the existential commitments they choose to embrace and for the corresponding implications incurred.

In a field constituted through various forms of worlding that contribute to sites of contention, it is critical to have students undergo an existential calisthenics program while they are being taught about the theories that populate the discipline. This chapter asserts that it is our pedagogical duty to teach future graduates of IR programs how to be ontologically plural and endow them with the crucial life skill of ontological resilience and versatility, which will assist them to engage multiplicity and complexity more effectively. Hopefully, readers will be inspired to reflect on how their own teaching and learning praxis might reinforce the disciplinary ontological myopia that drives students to see the world from a reductionist ontological standpoint and to contemplate how we, as active co-creators, want to contribute to the worlds of IR in our teaching.

References

Acharya, Amitav and Barry Buzan, eds. 2010. *Non-Western International Relations Theory*, London, Routledge.

Agathangelou, Anna M. and L.H.M. Ling. 2004. 'The House of IR: From Family Power Politics to the Poisies of Worldism', *International Studies Review* 6, no.4: 21–49.

Arian, Anahita. 2021. "An Ethics of Understanding." *International Studies Perspectives* 22 no.1: 45–49. https://doi.org/10.1093/isp/ekaa008.

Behera, Navnita Chadha. 2021. "Teaching a More 'Rooted' IR!" *International Studies Perspectives* 22 no.1: 49–52. https://doi.org/10.1093/isp/ekaa008.

Bull, Hedley. 2002. *The Anarchical Society: A Study of Order in World Politics*. New York: Columbia University Press.

Capan, Zeynep. 2016. "Decolonizing International Relations: an essay in method." *Third World Quarterly* 38, no.1: 1–15.

Chakrabarty, Dipesh. 2000. *Provincializing Europe: Postcolonial Thought and Historical Difference*. Princeton: Princeton University Press.

Chandler, David, Franziska Müller, and Delf Rothe, eds. 2021. *International Relations in the Anthropocene: New Agendas, New Agencies and New Approaches*. London: Palgrave Macmillan.

Cox, Robert W. 1996. "Gramsci, hegemony, and international relations: an essay in method." In *Approaches to World Order*, edited by Robert Cox, and Timothy Sinclair, 124–143. Cambridge: Cambridge University Press.

Hagmann, Jonas. 2015. "Beyond Babylon? Teaching International Politics in the 21st Century." E-International Relations, May 7, 2015. https://www.e-ir. info/2015/05/07/beyond-babylon-teaching-international-politics-in-the-21st-century/

Hobbes, Thomas. 1996. *Leviathan (Norton Critical Edition)*. Edited by Richard Flathman, and David Johnston. New York: W.W. Norton & Co.

Hoffmann, Stanley.1977. "An American Social Science: International Relations." *Daedalus,* 106, no. 3: 41–60. http://www.jstor.org/stable/20024493.

Jackson, Patrick T. 2011. *The Conduct of Inquiry in International Relations: Philosophy of science and its implications for the study of world politics*. London: Routledge.

Lajo, Javier. 2004. *Qhapaq Ñan: La ruta Inka de la sabiduría*. Quito: Abya-Yala.

Linklater, Andrew. 1996. "Marxism." In *Theories of International Relations*, edited by Scott Burchill, and Andrew Linklater, 119–144. New York: St. Martin's Press.

Lüdert, Jan. 2016. "Signature Pedagogies in International Relations." E-International Relations, June 18, 2016. https://www.e-ir.info/2016/06/18/ signature-pedagogies-in-international-relations/

Nayak, Meghana, and Eric Selbin. 2010. *Decentering International Relations.* New York: Zed Books.

Patomäki, Heikki, and Colin Wight. 2000. "After postpositivism? The promises of critical realism." *International Studies Quarterly* 44, no. 2: 213–37.

Picq, Manuela. 2013. "Critics at the Edge? Decolonizing Methodologies in International Relations." *International Political Science Review* 34, no.4: 444–455.

Sen, Somdeep. 2020. "Race, Racism and Academia: A view from Denmark." The Disorder of Things, September 30, 2020. https://thedisorderofthings. com/2020/09/29/race-racism-and-academia-a-view-from-denmark/

Shani, Giorgio. 2008. "Toward a Post-Western IR: The 'Umma,' 'Khalsa Panth,' and Critical International Relations Theory." *International Studies Review* 10. no.4: 722–734.

Shilliam, Robbie. 2015. *The Black Pacific: Anti-Colonial Struggles and Oceanic Connections.* New York: Bloomsbury.

Shulman, Lee. 2005. "Signature pedagogies in the professions." *Daedalus* 134, no. 3: 52–59.

Tickner, Arlene B. and Ole Wæver, eds. 2009. *International Relations Scholarship Around the World,* London, Routledge.

Trownsell, Tamara. 2013. "Robust Relationality: Lessons from the Ontology of Complete Interconnectedness for the Field of International Relations." Unpublished Ph.D. diss., American University.

Walker, R.B.J. 1992. *Inside/Outside: International Relations as Political Theory.* Cambridge: Cambridge University Press.

Weber, Cynthia. 2014. "From Queer to Queer IR." *International Studies Review* 16: 596–601.

Wemheuer-Vogelaar, Wiebke, Ingo Peters, Laura Kemmer, Alina Kleinn, Luisa Linke Behrens, and Sabine Mokry. 2020. "The global IR debate in the classroom." In *International Relations from the Global South (Worlding Beyond the West)*, edited by Arlene B. Tickner, and Karen Smith, 17–37. New York: Routledge.

6

Marks That Matter: Slow Letters to Authors and Selves

ERZSÉBET STRAUSZ

Whenever I ask students at both Bachelor of Arts (BA) and Master of Arts (MA) levels what brings them to the study of world politics, most of the time there is some indication, even if hesitant, of wanting to make a difference to the world studied. While BA students, especially at the very beginning of their studies, may be quick to picture themselves as future UN diplomats or international lawyers, it all becomes more ambiguous and ambivalent at the MA level. "What is the purest intention, the strongest motivation that drove you here?" I start off the first seminars every year with this question. As I listen to the diversity of responses, I tend to hear the desire of wanting something "other" or "more" in an affirmative sense: more knowledge, more expertise, better job prospects, alternative opportunities to do something, searching for ways and means to be recognized, seen, heard and, as such, to be able to speak, act, and make a difference of some kind. I translate these responses for myself as an educator and my constantly evolving pedagogical philosophy as aiming for more agency, more *power* to do something and a wider horizon of sociological imagination to facilitate change at some level— be that personal, collective, local, global, or whatever form "change" may take beyond established categories of recognizability. When I ask my students, however, where they saw their place in International Relations (IR) as an academic discipline, if they felt that IR theory spoke to their lived experiences in any direct or meaningful way, most of them choose to remain silent. As the number of years of IR socialization increases, the silence, more often than not, deepens. Maybe, at first, the question doesn't even make sense to some – after all, getting to know the "discipline of the discipline" takes some time (Doty 2004, 380), but what may be the reasons for the disconnect to grow, rather than lessen as their knowledge base expands? Where and how have dreams, curiosity, ambition, passion, forward-lookingness slipped away, disappearing out of sight and thinking processes?

The affective and cognitive states of journeying in and through the discipline not only shape the kind of "knowing subject" that emerges after several years of active learning and socialization but also the future professional who—knowingly or unknowingly—will contribute to the making of the "world" in an even more intimate fashion through the intellectual, social, and ethical capital acquired. I engage Lee S. Shulman's notion of "signature pedagogy" for re-thinking pedagogical practice in IR primarily through one of the key questions asked by this volume: "What values and beliefs about professional attitudes and dispositions do we foster and in preparing students for a wide range of possible careers?"

Shulman describes "signature pedagogy" in terms of those formational practices through which "future practitioners are educated for their new professions" (2005, 52). My point of departure lies with the distance between "knowledge" and "life" that can be established, named, and felt early on in the journey and the corresponding "subjectivity"—a professional subjectivity in the making—that continues to carry this disconnect as an imprint within itself. The cultivation of "habits of mind," those internalized, routine-like modes of acting and behaving that we no longer think about since we learn to think with and also *through* them, takes place in teaching practice that imparts a sense of how "to think, to perform, and to act with integrity" in a given field, albeit with unequal emphasis on these three distinct elements (Shulman 2005, 52). Beyond the operational acts that are instrumental in delivering the subject matter ("surface structure"), there is also a pedagogical know-how ("deep structure") and a moral dimension ("implicit structure") that transmits "a set of beliefs about professional attitudes, values, and dispositions" (Shulman 2005, 54–55) about the epistemic community of scholars and the possible "worlds" that may emerge through an "IR" lens. The relationship to the discipline and the world that is simultaneously studied and inhabited by its students, teachers, and practitioners is crafted particularly through the latter two aspects. That is, to paraphrase Robert Cox's (1981, 129) original statement, who may IR (theory) be for and what can be done with this knowledge? It is through the below-the-surface planes of the architecture of classes, course design, the economy of small tasks and gestures, the often invisible staging of readings, debates and bodies of literature—who, what, and how is made visible, accessible, and rendered as legitimate sources of knowledge—that students (and teachers) make sense of both "the profession" and themselves as possible actors, stakeholders, participants, or passive recipients, objects, bystanders in it. Despite their strong discursive and communicative features, signature pedagogies "prefigure the cultures of professional work" (Shulman 2005, 59) in a fundamentally material, hands-on manner. "The way we teach" what we teach has a direct impact on what will be affirmed, validated, perpetuated as professional ethos and expertise for everyone involved.

While there may not be a single distinctive "signature pedagogy" in IR, the lived experiences of "early socialization" and exposure to particular texts, as well as ways of speaking, thinking, and writing uncover a cultivated sense of separation and disconnection where knowledge offered via disciplinary practice may not be immediately accessible, relatable, or translatable, let alone empowering. Shulman (2005) notes that already existing routines of imparting and receiving knowledge may be hard but not impossible to change, especially when external circumstances prompt a shift in the organization of professional life. The move to online teaching may act as such a trigger, making us reflect more, for instance, on knowledge, authority, learning, and responsibility in the virtual classroom and beyond. However, by directly engaging the "implicit structure" of IR pedagogy—for instance, by asking holistic questions about what kind of "mark" is made on future professionals as both knowing subjects and ethical beings—options become available from within. Turning these considerations into actual teaching practice may facilitate transformation from within the structures and habits of academic socialization as well as initiate a continuing mechanism of reflection that can guard against the shortcomings of a "compromised pedagogy," where the balance between "the intellectual, the technical, and the moral" legs of teaching is hierarchically distorted (Shulman 2005, 58). As Shulman (2005) stresses, signature pedagogies are important not least because contemporary societies' reliance on experts, the quality of their knowledge, and behavior is unlikely to lessen. What might the hologram, the blueprint of the future IR professional look like, who is able to hold on to their ambition to make a difference, is equipped with the appropriate thinking tools and ethical resources, and feels connected and empowered enough to act?

Writing, Telling, Slowing Down

I prefer to keep this question permanently open as a guiding principle that guards against closure in both what I could do as a teacher and how students may inhabit the frames and spaces of instruction. To facilitate a diversity of professional futures that are critically and ethically engaged, aware, and resourceful, I actively work with the affective landscapes of disconnection and alienation in learning experiences and academic study more broadly.

The literature on IR pedagogy documents two main sources of classroom failure. First, there is a lack of personal connection to the subject matter where a range of abstract concepts, data points, and distant considerations mark out the proper place of "International Relations" within the realm of "high politics." IR taught and represented as the terrain of rational statesmen, soldiers, and diplomats (Drainville 2003) seems far from the contingencies of everyday life and the actual circumstances of students who, despite what their training might suggest, experience, embody, and enact International Relations from one moment to the next. Second, the lack of alternatives in facilitating social change leaves students feel disempowered: while critical analysis throws light on what may be wrong with social and political structures, it often stops at projecting an even worse scenario without any indication of where more promising horizons and vistas of action may be found (Inayatullah 2013, 150–1).

I seek to transform such experiences by locating IR as already part of everyday life—showing how knowledge about International Relations and International Relations as lived experience are unfolding right in front of us—and affirming the possibility of other ways of sensing and sense-making, which may move us and our thinking forward, beyond the proverbial "boxes" of both the discipline and social structures. I design simple, accessible exercises emerging from everyday routine, which have the potential to open up and reveal surprising connections and new planes of solidarity across cultural, textual, and epistemic divisions. Taking inspiration from a growing interdisciplinary literature on slow scholarship (Mountz et al. 2015; Berg and Seeber 2016) as an alternative "signature pedagogy," I curate learning journeys where a range of encounters enabling ethical reflection on selfhood, Otherness, and lived experience are staged throughout the curriculum. While slow movements primarily aim to subvert the consumerism and labor politics of late-capitalist production, an important aspect of slow philosophy is to find ways of becoming present to ourselves and our circumstances. Cultivating such awareness makes possible more accommodating, more caring, embodied modes of being and being-together, and the recognition and appreciation of value, which may otherwise not be readily perceptible and recognizable. Slowing down is not only about "finding a slower way of doing scholarship," but rather, as Jasmine B. Ulmer writes, dwells in the open-ended question and quest for "how we can find a slower way of scholarly being" (Ulmer 2017, 202).

In my pedagogical practice, I draw on the transformational potential of narrative writing and the everyday politics of storytelling as sites of intervention. Slow scholarship inspired practices that refocus on the small, mundane aspects of "habit" and open them up for introspection, connection, and co-creation. Slowing down taught me to look for sources of inspiration and provocation in what is already here, turning the familiar into a site of surprise and learning by changing my relationship to it. I use the intellectual resources of IR's "narrative turn" both as texts that I systematically integrate into my syllabi in order to make visible the personal, political, lived, and living nature of knowledge production and as examples of non-mainstream, creative scholarly practice in the discipline. Stories, anecdotes, fragments, accounts of cultural encounters—of how people experienced and made sense of events, circumstances, that is, the everyday fabric of International Relations—invite closeness, intimacy, and emotional learning. They bring complexity to stripped-down notions of statehood, power, and the political, foregrounding the "how" of "know-how," which simultaneously emerges as IR knowledge and personal, perhaps accidental wisdom of how to live or, at least, strive towards a reflected, rounded life. In the process of telling, seemingly disparate worlds meet, dualities collapse, the usual divisions and distinctions—such as here and elsewhere, then and now, researcher and researched, student and teacher, us and them—no longer hold (Edkins 2013, 292). As we re-enter the discipline as vulnerable living beings who are already experts in their own lives and embrace the "other" in their same capacity (Nagar 2019, 31–33) world, self, and community lose their abstract qualities and take on a living, felt, hands-on dimension. When concepts are opened up to multi-dimensional engagement—intellectual, sensory, affective—new possibilities arise for both creativity and problem-based thinking and ethics. Learning how to engage with the "context" of what is habitually presented as "content" and its politics—that is, where representations, concepts, thoughts, images, ideas, practices may come from and with what significance—has the potential to fundamentally rewire sense perception and meaning-making. Equally, how to take the courage to think, feel, and explore beyond them are important transferable skills that nurture resourcefulness, sensitivity, and a reflexive self-presence when it comes to cultivating professional attitudes in and beyond academia.

"Letters to the Author"

In turning the habitual practices of reading and writing into a form of narrative exploration, I have developed a series of writing exercises within a Teaching and Learning Development Grant at Central European University titled, *Mindful Writing* and subsequently applied them in two MA-level IR theory courses, *Knowing, Narrating, (re)Writing International Relations* and *(Mis) Performing World Politics.* These exercises—developed in line with some of the philosophical underpinnings of slow scholarship—aim to craft alternative relationships to text, self, and the "lives of others" about which IR scholarship often writes uncritically.

One creative writing practice that I would like to share is an iterated, interactive, and adaptable exercise called "letters to the author," where students are asked to write letters to the authors of the assigned texts. I have used this practice with some surprising and mostly heart-warming results for teaching non-mainstream IR theory, which included in-class and asynchronous letter writing exercises, as well as responses in the form of video messages, emails, and Skype-ins by academics, artists, and professionals as "authors" whose work we have read. Expanding the range of interactions in this way not only brought "theory" to life in a democratic fashion where students' reflections drove the conversations but also enabled a more collaborative academic and professional spirit among students, teaching faculty, and guests when the context, ambitions, motivations, ethics, and politics of their own writing were shared.

Letters unsent

"Letters to the author" unfolded as an exercise that now has two iterations: letters unsent and letters sent. In its most basic format, letters remain unsent and their primary aim is to encourage a different kind of relationship to texts and knowledge by subverting the passivity of reading and re-staging it as part of an exchange or imaginary dialogue with another human being. The prompt is simple: "start with an address, as 'Dear...' and sign off by writing your name." In-between the frames of the letter form, the relationship can be established and molded in any way, with, of course, respect and appreciation. "You can ask questions, share your reading experience, you can tell the author anything that may come to you. Before you finish, please don't forget to thank them though—your reflections and whatever you may find out in the process were inspired by their efforts, research, and writing." The letters, written offline or on-site, are not shared in class, unless someone volunteers. Students discuss their experiences with each other and I only inquire about what it was like to write a letter to the author, maybe for the first time.

Letter writing is particularly fitting for the first three weeks of the course *Knowing, Narrating, (re)Writing International Relations,* titled "Situatedness: Where Are We, Who Are We in International Relations?" This section problematizes subject positions and what it may mean to "know" in and through the discipline, specifically engaging "the making of the knowing subject" and showcasing a range of intellectual resources for thinking about the lived experiences of research, teaching, and thinking. Through the personal accounts of established and junior scholars presented as auto-ethnography, autobiography, or in any other narrative or creative form, we discuss what may prompt curiosity, what life events and negotiations inform the production of "knowledge," when and how learning and discovery may take place, and what we bring with ourselves to these conversations as experience, wisdom, or "raw material" for intellectual, emotional, and creative processing.

I stage these encounters at the intersections of the "personal" and "the academic." We read, for instance, Carol Cohn's "Sex and Death," Roxanne Lynn Doty's "Maladies of our Souls," Ken Booth's "Reflections of a Fallen

Realist," Richa Nagar's *Hungry Translations*, Jenny Edkins's "Object among Objects," Oded Löwenheim's "The 'I' in IR," and Himadeep Muppidi's book chapter "Shame and Rage". I frame the invitation to write a letter to the author with the aid of a quote by bell hooks. In *Teaching to Transgress*, she writes that "theory is not inherently healing, liberatory, or revolutionary. It fulfills this function *only when we ask that it do so* and direct our theorizing towards this end" (hooks 1994, 61, my emphasis). In writing a letter to the author, the theorist, the scholar, the living being, we may experience a way of asking "theory" to do these for us.

Modes of address

"So how did you address the professor that you wrote a letter to? What followed after 'Dear?'" My first question already brings some interesting responses:

> dear bell (I stylized in all low caps like she does)
> Dear Professor Muppidi
> Dear Professor
> Dear Carol
> Dear scholar Edkins
> I started with "dear Oded," but switched to more formal "dear prof"

About half of the letters started formally. For one student, it was impossible even to think of addressing anyone, especially a professor by a first name, as culturally it was not permitted. Others, who chose to address the author by their first name, mentioned that they did so because they were talking to an author, *not* the professor. "Somehow I felt my letter was emotional, so there was no need to address them as 'dear professor' as I was not critical of their work, I was not suggesting different theories or nothing super professional, it was more like my personal feeling, how I felt reading her text." Someone else added, "I didn't even reflect much when I addressed the professor as dear Professor Muppidi. But then, when I looked at my letter and realized that it was extremely emotional, I could see that there was a disconnect maybe in some way of the address and the content of the letter." Going deeper into the process of writing and how students navigated the intersecting terrains of personal experience and academic reflection, I could see smiles on the screen, even if not everybody chose to speak. To engage in an unscripted manner brought a palpable sense of freedom. "In my previous university, I was encouraged to express my opinion but even if I liked the professor, I would refrain from expressing my reflection," recounts someone else, and "this letter encouraged me to give feedback more, of what we do, how it affects me," to share and show appreciation. This exercise helped to break through institutionally conditioned passivity and humanize relationships in other ways, too. "We should send more letters!"—someone interjects passionately. "We have been getting these very long letters from professors. You sent us a 15-paragraph email at the beginning of the course—you put a lot of thought into that. And then I don't respond. I feel bad! Maybe this is a sign that I should respond more."

The letter writing exercise will return later in the course. These responses made me appreciate and nourish even more the courage to express without judgement, the ability to put into words how something may *feel* in the first place, before intellectual processing and disciplinary ordering kicks in. In thinking about what it offered to students who had already done it multiple times, I asked Olga and Vladimir[1], who took the course last year and the year before, to look back on their experience. They recorded the following conversation:

OLGA: This was the first exercise of this kind that I have ever done in my life. The biggest impact it had on me was the realization that I actually have something to say, even though I am an MA student with no publications, no work experience. Our education is built in such a manner that there is always some kind of hierarchical relationship. Of course, I always feel the distance between me and the author. Whenever a professor assigns an article, even if I don't know anything about the author, I always approach it with respect and admiration. "Oh my God, I'm just a student, I haven't published anything, while this person has already written so many articles!" So my first feeling was not... aversion, but pure surprise. In the beginning I thought: "Does this person really want to hear my voice?" But then, after the professor's affirmations, "yes, you write for yourself, write no matter what," it was easier to begin. Suddenly, I realized that I had something to say. It is comfortable that no one is going to read it but even if someone does, it is not a big deal. You realize there are some things that you think about differently. This was really valuable for me.

VLADIMIR: Imagining a person behind the text, a *"you"* standing in front of my simplified writing. You do not have to know much about the author during reading/writing; the point is to understand that there is a living being behind the words which may seem like plain, academic prose. Understand, apprehend, and appreciate that person and their efforts. The exercise made me reflect on myself, the way I learn. When I was doing it, I paused to think: "What is actually happening here? Who, what am I in that situation?" And

---

[1]   Students have given explicit written consent for their answers and names to be used in this chapter.

then: "How *can* I write, what *can* I say in relation to another human being?" When you reflect on what you are actually doing here, right now, on the space, process, people, and objects involved, there is more room for ethical engagement with the text, for probing your own ethical approach towards theory, towards the case—in writing. There has been a lot of talk about intersubjectivity in IR but intersubjectivity never happens when you write *about* it (intersubjectivity objectified)—it takes place when you write *to* somebody. This exercise has never been purely subjective for me. It has been an opportunity for proper reflection about the "relations"—that part often forgotten in IR—interpersonal, intercultural, interdisciplinary—whatever.

OLGA: I agree, it is important to notice these things—intersubjective conversations between seemingly different levels in IR academia. What I realized is that, unfortunately, one read is not enough to comprehend the text. Whenever I re-read the text for the second time, it was always a revelation for me. And it is crucial that you not only understand that there is someone behind it but you put both yourself and that other person on the same level. You can address this person equally. And it is important to keep this thought with you along your studies and along your life. Only recently did I realize the importance of writing. I write to the professor because I have a deadline, I write to a bureaucratic institution because I need to get some papers. I always write for something, to someone. But this exercise is about writing for yourself. So, it is important to keep returning to that practice, that experience of writing to an author, or even writing to yourself. Even when you write a letter to an author you still write to yourself, and for yourself.

VLADIMIR: Yes. I used that exercise later on to begin writing whenever I experienced a "writing block." Writing in a dialogical form simplified even the most complex conceptual reflection, so crucial for my current PhD work. I find my "voice" through it.

Letters sent

Letters written to the author got actually sent to the addressee in the course *(Mis)Performing World Politics,* an experimental course that explicitly works with the scripts, dramaturgy, and performativity of knowledge practices, including pedagogical relationships and the design of class interactions as they unfold in real time. For a week on creative practice and performativity in IR, we watched two performance pieces by Catherine Chiniara Charrett: "Politics in Drag: Sipping Toffee with Hamas in Brussels" (2014) and her latest one, "The Vein, the Fingerprint Machine, and the Automatic Speed Detector" (2019). Catherine is a dear friend and co-traveler in the creative re-thinking, subverting, and re-invigorating of disciplinary practice and its politics. I asked

Catherine if she was willing to read letters from my students about her performances. She enthusiastically agreed and, upon the receipt of fifteen letters, sent us two video responses, addressing each letter writer and their questions. The power of the exercise was manifest when the author, the artist, the person writing and creating came alive, generously offering even more insight, more food for thought. The exercise, however, worked on multiple planes. As teaching faculty, I felt both liberated from the weight of "authority" of classroom design and fulfilled as a curator of learning journeys when viewers and artist entered a conversation on their own terms. I asked Catherine what it was like for her to receive "student letters" that directly engage her work, inviting her for an equal exchange. Taking forward the energy, the spirit of these serendipitous connections Catherine took genre-bending to the next level. This time she responded with a piece where "letters to the author" are further animated as objects, media, and vehicles of dialogue, extending beyond the question-response format and the initial queries of actual participants.

The original written collage composed by Catherine for the purposes of this book chapter explores and reimagines what a "letter" may do for our practices of sense-making when we embrace the profoundly relational quality of what it might mean to be human. In the space where habitual academic scripts no longer hold, ultimately, we arrive at the dimension of being and being-together:

"Receiving a letter.

Thank you for being you. The circulation of an object that allows me to show you me. And you saw; and you thanked me for it.

'I would like to express my gratitude to you for your impressing activities to support Palestinian people and to condemn aggressive Zionism.'

'Thank you for changing the safety of the writing desk for the exposition of the stage.'

'Thank you for the love, for the rupture.'

'Your research on Hamas and the EU is a result of your intense work, but it is a presentation.'

'Throughout the performance, I could not stop thinking about the type of person you are.'

'Through the openness of your performance to let the viewer make its own thoughts.'

We are always creating things. Writing things. Editing things. Sharing things. But what are those things that we share. And what do they do to us. What have they done to us?

Sara Ahmed (2006, 2-5) describes how bodies circulate around and through different objects. Bodies sit at desks. Bodies reach out to pens. And through this reaching out different objects are already in place. We are imprinted by the objects. As we use these objects in turn shape us.

I sit at the desk. I type. I worry. I read. I type. I try to cover my voice. I try to give you want I think you want from me. I seep out the edges. I fall out of the margins. You receive a completed blank sheet.

Our bodies circulate around and through these objects.

What if we didn't write? What if wrote differently? What if we inhabited objects differently? What if we inhabited different objects? What are the objects? And do they allow me to show you me?

I think about intention. What object turns me into a resource, and how does using a different object allow me to flourish?

I wanted you to see me. I wanted you to know what I felt about Palestine. I wanted you to know what I saw in Palestine. I wanted to account of the horror.

I made something that was a reflection of me and what I saw and felt.

You asked them to write me a letter. A letter circulates. It moves. It expresses. It carries. In the letter they put their thoughts. They put their gratitude. In the letter you asked them to say what they wanted to say.

Thanks.

Making objects. Always making objects. And, in those objects, we are lost and we are found. In those objects, we find and lose others. In these objects, we lose and find ourselves.

I receive a letter. I receive an expression of gratitude.

'I would like to thank you. For your courage, creativity, enthusiasm, and unhinged sarcasm.'

Thank you for being human and showing us what kind of human that is."

Making marks matter

"Letters to the author" as one particular feature of an alternative "signature pedagogy" transforms student experiences of disconnection into dialogue and (self-)discovery, facilitating embodied modes of learning that find value and creative opportunity in the already familiar. Slowing down, re-directing attention to the here and now, expanding our awareness of academic habit, and staging new relationships with how we read, write, or express reveal that neither IR, nor new social imaginations or windows for change may be that remote.

Through writing letters to the author, the scripts and subject positions of "student" and "teacher," novice and expert open up, enabling students to realize a form of agency that may not have been noticeable or accessible before—although it has been there all along. They turn from passive recipient of both "knowledge" and institutional support into active participants who may come to experience that communication, and with that, connection is already present. All of a sudden, it may be revealed to them that they already have something to say and have the power, the talent, the resources to express what they may carry in themselves. There may be room for dialogue in unexpected places. Beyond the default mode of disembodied critique, writing to the author and simultaneously, writing for oneself anchors the writer in their body, their own process of reflection. In this way, concepts lose their abstraction, exposing that disconnection is only one possible experience that has conventionally turned into a "habit of mind" and that it can be turned around by the creative labor of making, assuming connection, by acknowledging the text as "living." Actual responses from the author reinforced this message about communication and connectedness even more firmly. Catherine's collage shows how texts, letters, and video messages are "objects" only: objects of knowledge that we engage and produce, which also constantly point towards and circle back to life that provides context for anything that may appear as "content." There is always a bigger picture with more complexity, yet also resources for thinking, writing, and knowing otherwise. For me, a "signature pedagogy" for IR serves as a vehicle, a gateway for dwelling deeper into experiences and questions of living, being, becoming, and being-together. Our sensing, feeling, affective bodies and the practices that can activate emotional learning are the bridge—and the crux of pedagogical know-how as "deep structure." Whatever may be taught as the subject matter ("surface structure"), it can be made relatable, actual, or urgent, while always fluid and emergent, subject to negotiation in limitless ways. Students can be invited to probe into their call, what brought them to the study of IR and develop ownership over their formation as "knowing subjects" in a meaningful way for their purposes via small, everyday gestures. At its core, and as its "implicit structure," the teaching of IR (theory) should be life-affirming for everyone involved, where the hologram, the blueprint of the future IR professional would be designed, crafted in a fashion that its silhouettes merge with the singularity of other living beings, eluding narrative or disciplinary closure.

I thank Catherine, Olga, Vladimir, and all letter writers and receivers for their courage and ingenuity. Let us make marks matter—the ones that have been left on us via encounters with the social, the disciplinary, the human, and the ones that we choose to make from here.

References

Ahmed, Sara. 2006. *Queer Phenomenology: Orientations, Objects, Others.* Durham, NC: Duke University Press.

Berg, Maggie and Barbara Seeber. 2016. *The Slow Professor: Challenging the Culture of Speed in the Academy*, Toronto: University of Toronto Press.

Booth, Ken. 1994. "Security and Self: Reflections of a Fallen Realist." YCISS Occasional Paper, No. 26.

Chiniara Charrett, Catherine. 2019. "The Vein, the Fingerprint Machine and the Automatic Speed Detector." Performance.

Chiniara Charrett, Catherine. 2014. "Politics in Drag: Sipping Toffee with Hamas in Brussels." Performance.

Cohn, Carol. 1987. "Sex and Death in the Rational World of Defence Intellectuals." *Signs: Journal of Women in Culture and Society* 12, (4): 687–718.

Cox, R. W. 1981. "Social Forces, States and World Orders: Beyond International Relations Theory". *Millennium* 10, (2): 126–155.

Dauphinee, Elizabeth. 2010. "The Ethics of Autoethnography." *Review of International Studies* 36, (3): 799–818.

Doty, Roxanne Lynn. 2004. "Maladies of Our Souls: Identity and Voice in the Writing of Academic International Relations". *Cambridge Review of International Studies* 17, (2): 377–392.

Drainville, André C. 2003. "Critical Pedagogy for the Present Moment: Learning from the Avant-Garde to Teach Globalization from Experiences." *International Studies Perspectives* 4, (3): 231–249.

Edkins, Jenny. 2013. "Novel writing in international relations: Openings for a creative practice." *Security Dialogue* 44, (4): 281–297.

Edkins, Jenny. 2011. "Objects among objects." In *Autobiographic International Relations: I, IR*, edited by Naeem Inayatullah, 19–30. London: Routledge.

hooks, bell. 1994. *Teaching to Transgress: Education as the Practice of Freedom.* New York: Routledge.

Inayatullah, Naeem. 2013. "Impossibilities: Generative Misperformance and the Movements of the Teaching Body." In *International Politics and Performance: Critical Aesthetics and Creative Practice*, edited by Jenny Edkins and Adrian Kear, 150–168. London, Routledge.

Inayatullah, Naeem. 2011. "Falling and Flying: An Introduction." In *Autobiographic International Relations: I, IR*, edited by Naeem Inayatullah, 1–12. London, Routledge.

Löwenheim, Oded. 2010. "The 'I' in IR: An Autoethnographic Account." *Review of International Studies* 36, (4): 1023–1045.

Mountz, Alison, Anne Bonds, Becky Mansfield, Jenna Loyd, Jennifer Hyndman, Margaret Walton-Roberts, Ranu Basu, Risa Withson, Roberta Hawkins, Trina Hamilton, and Winifred Curran. 2015. "For Slow Scholarship: A Feminist Politics of Resistance through Collective Action in the Neoliberal University." *ACME: An International e-Journal for Critical Geographies* 14, (4): 1235–59.

Muppidi, Himadeep. 2012. *The Colonial Signs of International Relations.* London: C Hurst & Co Publishers.

Nagar, Richa. 2019. *Hungry Translations: Relearning the World through Radical Vulnerability*. Chicago: University of Illinois Press.

Shulman, Lee S. 2005. "Signature pedagogies in the professions." *Daedalus* 134, (3): 52–59.

Ulmer, Jasmine B. 2017. "Writing Slow Ontology." *Qualitative Inquiry* 23, (3): 201–211.

7

Travel Learning Clusters as Signature Pedagogies

SHANE JOSHUA BARTER

This chapter analyzes travel "Learning Cluster" (LC) courses as signature pedagogies. Taught at a small liberal arts university in southern California, LCs are intense winter block courses that typically focus on unique topics, with some involving travel. After locating LCs in various pedagogical concepts and explaining how these courses work, this chapter analyzes some challenges and successes in teaching travel LCs. Challenges include selecting students, addressing racial and gender identities, health and safety, etiquette, assessing firsthand experiences, and returning to campus. These challenges are offset by some incredible benefits of field-based education, including achieving primary and secondary learning objectives through experiential education, meeting people with diverse perspectives, making enduring local connections, elevating less privileged students, and future learning opportunities. All told, field-based LCs have represented some of the most exhausting, rewarding moments of my teaching career, representing a signature pedagogy in international studies.

In 2018, I was contacted by a recent alumnus asking for advice. It was not for him, but instead for an Indonesian student he had met during our 2015 course. Our "Learning Cluster" took place in the province of Aceh, where we studied the local politics of coffee. We stayed at Almuslim University, with my students making meaningful connections with Acehnese students amidst this exhausting course. Two of my students would later volunteer at our host university, some would go on to study related topics at graduate school, and most kept in touch with their Acehnese friends. Years later, my former student was helping his Acehnese friend apply to a program in Singapore, an unexpected but welcomed outcome of a field-based seminar.

This chapter analyzes field-based seminars as signature pedagogies. It examines my experiences with LCs, intensive winter block classes at Soka University of America (SUA). First, this chapter defines some key terms and situates LCs as signature pedagogies. Second, it provides some context, introducing SUA, LC classes, and LCs I have led. Third, it discusses challenges in teaching such courses: selecting students, racial and gender identities, health and safety, etiquette, representing firsthand experiences, and more. Fourth, it discusses some of the many strengths and unexpected opportunities that have come from travel LCs. One key insight is that field-based courses seem to privilege students from poorer and working-class backgrounds, with their ability to cook, communicate, and wayfind providing advantages compared to their classmates. In this sense, travel LCs feature important implicit learning structures, engaging life skills beyond standard classroom learning. All told, LCs represent signature pedagogies at my university, with travel LCs standing as a signature form of experiential education.

Concepts: Study Abroad, Experiential Learning, and Signature Pedagogies

First, it is important to discuss some related terms in order to situate travel LC classes. Study abroad refers to courses taken in foreign countries, typically under the supervision of local teachers and institutions. Study abroad is often related to language acquisition over at least one semester. At SUA, Study Abroad refers to mandatory semester-long experiences at foreign universities geared mostly towards language acquisition. In contrast, most LCs remain on campus or else travel regionally, with only a handful leaving the United States. Once abroad, LCs are overseen entirely by the SUA professor, not by host institutions. LCs last only a few weeks, lacking the duration necessary for developing cultural or linguistic competencies (Anderson et al. 2006). Travel LCs might usefully be understood as field seminars, a specific form of study abroad with focused learning goals, but do not necessarily involve international travel (Furco 1996).

A related term that might describe LCs is experiential education. Experiential education can be understood as learning through doing, allowing reflection of raw experiences beyond traditional classrooms (Dewey 1938; Katula and Threnhauser 1999). Again, LCs fit imperfectly. On one hand, they typically take place outside of traditional classrooms and involve firsthand experience. On the other hand, LCs are not necessarily learning by doing. LCs are not like apprenticeships or volunteering, as they still involve conducting research, even if it is *in situ*. As I suggest below, the primary learning goals of LCs may not involve experiential education, but various secondary learning provides experiential education along the way.

Another related term is service learning. Although service learning is often mentioned in the same breath as experiential education, they are hardly synonyms. Service learning is education through actions that help others, a specific form of experiential education (Lim 2015). Service learning is typically optimal in a domestic context, as students are more likely to understand the needs of local communities, and service learning abroad invites criticisms of voluntourism. LCs mostly do not involve service learning, as they are about studying a topic, not directly promoting welfare or humanitarian aims.

To illustrate, suppose I planned a travel LC on armed conflict in Southeast Asia. We might arrive at safe adjacent areas to interview key stakeholders, such as NGOs or officials, and perhaps victims' organizations. We might visit key sites such as monuments or museums, or collect resources and information, all the while experiencing local culture. This course would involve studying abroad and experiential education. But the experience would not teach students directly about war—they would only "experience" war through research (unless I armed the students). And it would not involve service learning unless I encouraged them to distribute aid to conflict victims. I would encourage neither without proper training.

LCs are thus scholarly seminar courses that involve experiential education and some elements of study abroad, but not necessarily service learning. As this chapter argues, these courses embody a signature pedagogy of our institution and of international studies as an interdisciplinary field.

As articulated by Shulman (2005, 52), signature pedagogies are "types of teaching that organize the fundamental ways in which future practitioners are educated for their new professions." The idea of signature pedagogies is primarily intended to speak to professional education, areas such as legal education, design, clergy, engineering, and the like, professions into which instructors socialize students. This framework applies imperfectly to liberal arts education, which in some ways eschews training in place of creating well-rounded, adaptable citizens. For Gaposchkin (2015), liberal arts students are able to adapt and create because they are "not pigeon-holed into a single vocation and thus a single career path." Shulman (2005, 58) believes that liberal arts education can learn from "the pedagogies of the professions." There is little sense here that learning might be reciprocal, nor is there a clear sense of signature pedagogies in the liberal arts (see Chick, Haynie, and Gurung 2012).

What are some signature pedagogies of liberal arts education, specifically international studies? Schrand and Eliason (2012, 52) echo Shulman, stating that the signature pedagogy of the liberal arts is the large lecture. Many liberal arts instructors might recoil at this, as our classes are often small and our students rebel against lectures. Certainly, Williams' Tutorial and other applications of the Socratic Method look very different than this. Although liberal arts education is not geared towards professional training, it is commonly said that the goal is to create informed, democratic persons. For Nussbaum (2010), liberal arts cultivate "informed, independent, and sympathetic democratic citizens." Thus, a signature pedagogy in the liberal arts would likely involve pervasive teaching methods that seek to develop democratic citizens, and for international studies, global citizens.

Soka University of America's Learning Clusters

Established in 2001, SUA is a private liberal arts university in southern California. Informed by Buddhist humanism, SUA seeks to shed some of the Eurocentricity sometimes associated with liberal arts. SUA features a diverse student body, with about 40 percent of students being international. Students are required to study a new language and complete a semester of study abroad. SUA's oft-repeated mission statement is to foster "a steady stream of global citizens committed to living a contributive life." Sometimes criticized as a slogan instead of a framework for confronting injustice (Andreotti 2014), global citizenship refers to the cultivation of a sense of awareness and fluency in the wider world regardless of national borders, often with a commitment to contributing to the well-being of others. If SUA were to have a "profession" that a signature pedagogy might seek to cultivate, it would likely be global citizens, in whatever profession(s) our graduates find themselves.

LCs thus embody a signature pedagogy for a liberal arts university seeking to cultivate global citizens. Taught in a winter block of just under four weeks to classes of 10–12 students, SUA's LCs vary immensely in scope and content. These courses are mandatory for first- and second-year students, with many students opting to take an additional LC in their third year. Some are taught like more traditional classes, while others tackle topics well beyond the instructor's expertise. Many LCs are led and designed, partly or entirely, by students, allowing for a sense of shared ownership. This challenges a core part of signature pedagogies, the idea of instructors as professionals socializing students into specific fields, with many LCs instead favoring models of mutual learning. LCs are intensive and exhausting courses, meeting daily, and for instructors, almost always representing new "preps." The block concludes with an "Learning Cluster Fair" in which we share our activities with wider audiences.

The block format has students taking only one course. This enables LC classes to move beyond classroom hours and places, disrupting traditional course "surface structures" such as lectures and seminars. Most LCs travel off-campus for field excursions and to meet various figures. Due to generous, committed donors (we forbid students from paying for LC expenses), SUA is able to award a handful of travel grants through a competitive proposal process. These grants can be used for extended regional or international travel, with about 3–4 classes per year going abroad. Travel LCs can be taxing for faculty members. Unlike other universities, faculty are responsible for writing proposals, designing and teaching the course, arranging travel logistics, managing the budget, and supervising students in the field. We must consider visas, health, transportation, communication, and perhaps trans-lation—a daunting set of tasks, but a system I prefer, as it would be difficult for staff to arrange logistics in remote corners of Southeast Asia.

Travel LCs typically begin with 3-5 extended classroom sessions on campus before embarking for just under two weeks in the field, returning to campus for a handful of concluding classes. These courses involve several instit-utional challenges. There are concerns that they represent a form of tourism (they are!). SUA often publicizes travel LCs in admission materials, creating a false sense that this is the norm and exoticizing serious academic courses. My approach is to confront the issue, being clear that these brief courses are forms of educational tourism; we should own this, but work hard to make the most of our privilege. Next, it has been true that younger male professors have been more likely to take classes abroad, demanding that we reflect on age and gender dimensions for LC faculty. More reasonably, they also tend to favor faculty with language skills and networks abroad.

Table 1: Overview of Author's LC Courses (2011–19)

2012	Growing up in Sumatra: Child Rights in Indonesia	Travel (North Sumatra, Indonesia)
2013	Power in Movement: Mass Transit in Comparative Context	Travel (Vancouver to Los Angeles)
2014	Intimate Economies: Tourism and Sex in Southeast Asia	Local Travel
2015	From Field to Cup: The Politics of Sumatran Coffee	Travel (Aceh, Indonesia)
2016	Liberal Arts in Action	Local Travel
2017	Multiculturalism in Asia	Travel (Singapore and Malaysia)
2018	Southeast Asian America	Local Travel
2019	Indigenous Development in Asia	Travel (Sabah, Malaysia)

My travel LCs are informed by my field of study and personal experiences. I teach in the International Studies concentration, studying politics and conflict in Southeast Asia. I worked in Southeast Asia for many years with domestic and international organizations before conducting extensive dissertation fieldwork. I thus came to SUA familiar with politics and society in Southeast Asia, and with an itch to leave the classroom. Over nearly a decade, I have taught eight LCs, all involving some travel and four involving international travel (see Table 1). These courses have been some of the most exhausting, rewarding parts of my teaching career.

Challenges

I was advised not to take students abroad for my first LC in 2012, as I was still learning the ropes and was unfamiliar with our students. But I was 30 years old, so I ignored good advice and organized an LC to Sumatra. I entered the class with a skewed view of student tastes and capacities. I became frustrated when they wanted to eat Kentucky Fried Chicken and when some complained that we were eating too much rice (!). On our lone afternoon off, I took students to a national park to visit orangutans. I learned that the students were not accustomed to hiking, heat, leeches, or fire ants. Even though we saw an orangutan family, the students felt I downplayed the difficulty of the hike. I had to develop empathy to stave off a mutiny. For this first travel LC, I did not know the students and they did not know me, with some divergent expectations creating hiccups, but only some, in an otherwise successful course. This experience enabled me to adjust as well as clarify my expectations for future classes. Over the next few years, I was able to reflect further on various challenges associated with travel LCs, including student selection, issues related to identity, health and safety, local etiquette, assessing firsthand experiences, and returning home.

One of the more complex challenges has involved selecting students. Typically, students select classes and instructors, but for ever-popular travel LCs, professors select students. Reviewing applications, I learned that some students shine on paper, having traveled around the world, but are unaccustomed to even moderately rough conditions. It can be difficult to parse out which students are genuinely interested in the topic, and which just want to travel. I have questioned whether I should favor students with whom I am familiar, namely those who have taken my courses. It would be unwise not to select students that I know and trust (and they me), as effective communication is integral to a productive and safe course. My response has typically been to save a couple of spots for first-year students and those who have not taken my classes. Another concern is the potential of ableism, as travel LCs demand considerable physical endurance, especially when planned with a limited budget in developing countries.

Related challenges involve managing religious, racial, and gender identities. On campus, a student's personal identity may be none of the professor's business unless the student wishes otherwise. For travel LCs, I tend to initiate such conversations with students; although this can be awkward, it may be more problematic *not* to discuss identity before going abroad. Before traveling to conservative Islamic regions, my Jewish, African American, and LGBTQ students have not relished sitting down with me to discuss identity. But it is important to prepare them for some of the questions and comments they might expect, and how to interpret local responses. For example, Acehnese students may hold negative stereotypes surrounding Israel, but have never met a Jewish person; explaining this to one of my students before departure helped to prepare her for awkward comments. Another example is explaining to an African American student that Indonesians might call her Papuan, referring to darker-skinned people from Papua, then discussing how she might feel and respond. Throughout our classes, it is important to encourage respect for local cultural values, but also to emphasize that I am an ally and would never expect them to closet any part of their identity. I have been so proud to see LGBTQ students ask about gender and sexuality in interviews, challenging local figures, but in ways that encourage mutual respect.

Another set of challenges relate to health, diet, and safety. Thus far, my classes have yet to encounter major problems. Happily, Southeast Asia has a variety of food items that are vegan, vegetarian, halal, and the like. Safety is always a concern, whether it is crossing the street with jetlagged students, eating local foods, or managing nightlife. It helps for students to have data on their phones, allowing us to create WhatsApp groups for instant communication. Things can be difficult at night, as it is unclear if instructors should be on duty at all hours of all days. Enforcing curfews can be difficult. Much depends on the instructor staying with students in group accommodation, sacrificing some much-needed distance for the ability to monitor. I have always tried to allow some room to maneuver, as university students are adults. This said, I also emphasize a responsibility to our institution and donors—using privilege to encourage short nights so as to prepare us for long days. This speaks to a core aspect of signature pedagogies, of encouraging visibility and accountability (Shulman 2005, 57).

A fourth challenge relates to etiquette, both in local society as well as within our class. I have been surprised at how few students know local etiquette in North America, including sharing your seat on the bus, doing dishes, recycling, or sharing space at crowded coffee shops. In all countries, students sometimes struggle with appropriate dress. In Indonesia, the issue has often been more with male students, who perhaps believe that conservative societies only pressure women. It can be hard to explain that proper dress is not just an Indonesian thing, but is consistent with professionalism in any country. Within our group, it has sometimes been difficult to communicate what may, for some, be obvious social norms. This can include cleaning the house, cooking, laundry, and the like. I recall one time when a student flooded a toilet and left it; as the professor had to fix the problem, it was unclear how to describe this particular form of pedagogy.

A fifth challenge relates to interpreting firsthand experiences. One strength of field-based courses is their intense learning experiences. However, their brief nature and limited contextual knowledge often leads students to misunderstand events, with misinterpretations potentially being cemented as facts because they register as raw, firsthand knowledge. This is especially important since, at least in my courses in Southeast Asia, students typically lack training in local languages. For example, we might meet with progressive Islamic leaders or gravitate towards English-speaking NGOs, leading students to develop partial yet powerful understandings of local society. I have had respondents mistranslate important terms, likely to please my students, so I later explained what was missed and why. It can be difficult to encourage students to question their firsthand experiences, since this cuts against the very purpose of such courses. However, doing so remains an important responsibility for travel LC faculty. It can also be challenging to explain why students should not quote people we met in their papers or on social media, as we lack institutional review clearance and informed consent, and their rough notes are not reliable transcripts.

A final challenge relates to returning home. It can be difficult to influence how students share their images and experiences. I have had to dissuade students from posting images of local children, as they did not have parental consent; I will never understand the desire of people from developed countries to photograph anonymous children from poorer countries. Students typically return to campus to complain to their friends about our insane workload and brag about amazing adventures, accounts which are true, but can take on a life of their own. Sometimes, the photos students opt to share can make the course look like a vacation more than a scholarly seminar. As we return with souvenirs, I have also had to deal with concerns about cultural appropriation. On one occasion, our entire class purchased sarongs, a staple form of clothing from South Asia through Polynesia. One student felt that wearing a sarong represented cultural appropriation, even though this is not likely to be a common view among Malay communities. The appropriation critique has, however, been a useful reminder for students wishing to obtain souvenirs and dress with deeper religious or cultural significance.

Successes and Strengths

In addition to the obvious hard work involved, travel LCs clearly involve many major challenges. With some reflection and communication, these challenges can be managed, and there are some exceptional rewards in these classes.

It is useful to separate primary, scholarly learning objectives from secondary, indirect ones. Regarding the former, I have always been impressed with how much students learn about course themes and scholarly theories in LC courses. Be the topics Southeast Asian American communities, indigeneity in Asia, coffee politics, or rapid transit, students finish with a surprising amount of knowledge and sustained interest. This may be due to the intense nature of the classes and the process of learning alongside instructors. It is also likely due to the excitement of travel, and perhaps the feeling that the student must work hard given the opportunity. Whatever the reason, I have seen many students go on to further explore LC themes in their coursework, thesis, graduate studies, and careers. For example, the students from my Southeast Asian America LC later joined students in demanding more courses on Asian American communities, and one would work at an Asian American museum. One student from my course on coffee politics in Sumatra went on to graduate studies in philosophy, focusing on ethics in Fair Trade regimes.

The gains are at least as great in terms of secondary learning objectives. This echoes what Shulman (2005, 55) refers to as "implicit structures," the moral dimension of professional attitudes and actions in the field. Learning about travel, local cultures, and housework is not exactly unexpected, but involve indirect learning objectives; it is here where LCs embody experiential education. Students learn about planning travel, public transport, reading maps, new foods, cultures, gender relations, and more. According to one student evaluation from 2013, they learned about scholarly themes, "but we also gained some much needed 'real life' skills. Cliché as it might sound, it truly was life-changing." Or, from 2015, "I thought this class would be more like experience than academic training, but I feel I hugely improved in both ways." Some of my favorite moments have involved seeing students practice local languages, something not necessarily expected in these brief courses. In 2019, I had two students rush back to the house, excited to tell their peers that they ordered food in Malay! The experiential learning from travel LCs is deeply rewarding.

A related benefit is that LCs enable students to meet persons with very different views than their own, leaving the campus echo chambers of similar worldviews. From kind old Islamic leaders who shelter refugees but find varied gender identities to be "unfortunate," to a Filipino American businessman's stringent anti-liberalism, a Sumatran leader's brazen sexism, or a Chinese owner of a tour company joking about lazy indigenous workers, I have always appreciated seeing my students navigate genuine disagreements. As guests, we must be polite, and would hate to sustain neocolonial relations by telling them the right way to think. However, we should also challenge the views of our hosts when they say things we truly disagree with, making them aware of our perspectives.

As suggested in this chapter's introduction, travel LCs encourage students to develop enduring relationships with local people and organizations, conn-ections that outlast our course. Early on, I realized the value of organizing activities with local universities. In planning joint workshops, I try to introduce core course themes, then allow all of the students to discuss in small groups, allowing my students to learn what local students think about our topic. The students quickly become close, exchanging social media contacts. During precious moments of free time, my students tend to meet up with their new friends, who introduce them to sites and provide further insights on course themes. For example, in my 2019 class to Sabah, we began by visiting Universiti Teknologi MARA (UiTM). Despite just finishing exams, UiTM students were excited to return to campus for a workshop with my students. I enjoyed connecting with local professors, including a future collaborator. Days later, my students were taken by their new friends to visit local mosques, markets, and beaches. I have seen my students go on to volunteer at travel LC sites and maintain social media connections for years, including later helping their friends, embodying a sense of global citizenship.

Another strength of travel LCs is that they can subvert usual class-based dynamics in university classrooms. It is well understood that students from higher class and educational backgrounds enjoy several advantages compar-ed to less privileged students (Ostrove and Long 2007). This can be amplified at SUA, as some of our students are from less privileged communities in developing countries, benefitting from generous financial support to study in the United States. One thing I have noticed repeatedly during travel LCs is that students from poorer families sometimes really shine. They are often more capable of wayfinding, connecting with local communities, adapting to difficult circumstances, and doing chores. For example, one Nepali student from a very poor background proved highly capable of navigating towns, recognizing cultural norms, and teaching other students about housework. This student emerged from the course with new confidence, accelerating his development as an exceptional young scholar.

Finally, I would like to emphasize some long-term benefits of LCs. I have enjoyed seeing students become excited to take related courses and continue to develop their knowledge. Selfishly, I often gain highly motivated, knowledgeable students in my classes. I am also pleased to see students pursue interests in LC themes about which I am not an expert, including, for instance, several taking environmental studies after my transit LC or Asian American studies after my Southeast Asian America LC. Travel LC experiences have enabled me to write in-depth reference letters for my students, as I have gotten to know them very well, having observed their adaptability and ability to work as part of a team in new contexts.

Analysis and Conclusions

Travel LCs are exhausting. For instructors, they involve far more work than already intense on-campus LCs. Not only are there no additional monetary rewards, teachers of travel LCs invariably lose money to various minor expenses or missing receipts. Travel LCs demand that I leave my family for two weeks. My youngest child's birthday is during the LC period, meaning that I miss his birthday every time I take students abroad. I return exhausted, but with concluding classes to teach and obligations to make up for lost time at home. Travel LCs entail serious costs for the instructor, but also for students, whose endurance is tested as I demand book reports over the holiday break and research papers when we return. Despite some real challenges, these field seminar classes also provide considerable rewards.

This chapter has examined how travel LCs move beyond classroom lectures and seminars, disrupting surface structures in our teaching. This enables LCs to cultivate a deeper learning structure, imparting local know-how, and implicitly teaching normative dimensions that will be useful for a variety of professions, central to a sense of global citizenship. Travel LCs foster learning related to course themes, but also skills related to travel, cultural competencies, social norms, wayfinding, networking, and teamwork.

Learning Clusters can be considered as a signature pedagogy at Soka University of America, and for me as an international studies professor, travel LCs are my signature pedagogy. More than any other courses, they enable me to cultivate the knowledge and values I want to see in my students, producing more informed and reflective global citizens.

The author would like to thank Jan Lüdert, Ian Read, Tomas Crowder-Taraborrelli, Jay Heffron, Bryan Penprase, and Kelsey Castanho for their feedback.

References

Anderson, Philip H., Leigh Lawton, Richard J. Rexeisen, and Ann C. Hubbard. 2016. "Short-Term Study Abroad and Intercultural Sensitivity: A Pilot Study." *International Journal of Intercultural Relations* 30:4; pp. 457–469.

Andreotti, Vanessa. 2014. "Soft versus Critical Global Citizenship Education." In *Development Education in Policy and Practice*, edited by Stephen McCloskey. London: Springer, 21–31.

Chick, Nancy L., Aeron Haynie, and Regan A.R. Gurung (eds.). 2012. *Exploring More Signature Pedagogies: Approaches to Teaching Disciplinary Habits of Mind*. Sterling, VA: Stylus.

Dewey, John. 1938. *Education and Experience*. New York: Simon and Schuster.

Furco, Andrew. 1996. "Service-Learning: A Balanced Approach to Experiential Education." *Building Connections*; pp. 2–6.

Gaposchkin, Cecilia. 2015. "Just What Are the Liberal Arts Anyway?" *Huffington Post,* July 20, 2015. https://www.huffpost.com/entry/just-what-are-the-liberal_b_7829118

Katula, Richard A. and Elizabeth Threnhauser. 1999. "Experiential Education in the Undergraduate Curriculum." *Communication Education* 48:3; pp. 238–255.

Lim, Sook. 2015. "Distinguishing Service Learning from Other Types of Experiential Learning." *Education for Information* 31:4; pp. 195–207.

Nussbaum, Martha C. 2010. "The Liberal Arts are not Elitist," *The Chronicle of Higher Education*, February 28, 2010. https://www.chronicle.com/article/the-liberal-arts-are-not-elitist/

Ostrove, Joan M. and Susan M. Long. 2007. "Social Class and Belonging: Implications for College Adjustment." *The Review of Higher Education* 30:4; pp. 363–389.

Schrand, Tom and John Eliason. 2012. "Feedback Practices and Signature Pedagogies: What Can the Liberal Arts Learn from the Design Critique?" *Teaching in Higher Education* 17:1; pp. 51–62.

Shulman, Lee S. 2005. "Signature Pedagogies in the Professions." *Dædalus* 134(30); pp. 52–59.

8

Student Led Advocacy and the "Scholars in Prison" Project: Experiential Learning and Critical Knowledge(s) in International Relations

WILLIAM J. SHELLING II AND JENNY H. PETERSON

This chapter explores the interplay between didactic and experiential learning in the context of International Relations (IR) teaching. Using the case study of a course designed around a community partnership with the Scholars at Risk Network (SAR), it examines impacts on student learning as well as instructor delivery. Confirming the benefits of experiential learning in providing experience in a range of professional skills to students, the study also points to the realities of the emotional labor involved in experiential learning. It also reveals how such pedagogical approaches alter the understanding of "expertise" and how this can impact students' understanding of their role within the discipline. These findings provide important insight into the utility of blending didactic and experiential modes of learning, the learning opportunities and ethics of exposing students to the emotional labor of academic work as well as important reflections on reciprocity when experiential learning takes the form of partnership with external actors.

Although IR is not normally seen as a vocational training program, many of our students go on to have careers in related fields and we hope that much of what they learn in our courses will prepare them for their future professions. With this, experiential learning (EL), which provides students with hands-on experience, or the opportunity to "learn by doing," is increasingly seen as integral to IR education. Not only do these types of experiences provide students with much desired transferable skills that will help them profess-ionally, but they are also assumed to encourage deeper and/or different forms of learning of disciplinary knowledge(s) that more traditional forms of didactic learning often do not easily facilitate.

Following a brief exploration of the history and use of EL, this chapter will present an example of EL, which was integral to the running of an undergrad-uate IR seminar at the University of British Columbia. Run in partnership with SAR, this human rights course saw students produce various deliverables on four cases from SAR's Scholars in Prison Project, which aims to free wrong-fully imprisoned scholars around the world. After presenting an overview of how the course ran, including essential inputs from the community partner (SAR), this chapter will explore how a combination of both didactic and experiential learning created unique learning outcomes.

Using survey data[1] and author reflections (comprised of both the faculty member who ran the course and a student who took the course), we demonstrate how the types of learning that stem from experiential pedagogies not only provide students with professional development opportunities, but also challenge students to think more critically about core conceptual and theoretical content, the realities of political praxis outside of the discipline, and, finally, what learning looks and feels like in International Relations. The findings from this analysis point to several key conclusions regarding the use of experiential pedagogies that instructors should consider in their course design and that are worthy of further research. These include the impact EL has on teaching faculty (not only on students) in terms of emotional labor, ethical issues regarding the reciprocity in some EL opportunities and the importance of exploring the emergent outcomes when didactic and EL are used in tandem. All of these impacts, explored in detail later in the chapter, can be considered as examples of what Shulman (2005) describes as either "implicit" or "deep structures" in IR as they illustrate both the moral elements of teaching and how students come to attain such forms of knowledge(s). In other words, emotions, ethics, and being open to emergent outcomes are not simply results of learning, but are central to underlying (and sometimes changing) ethical assumptions about IR and about the realities of how we learn or "come to know" the discipline.

Experiential Learning: A Complement to Traditional Didactic Learning

The goal of experiential-based learning is to integrate and synthesize learning

---

[1]   Behavioural research ethics approval for survey obtained: Certificate UBC BREB H20-02341

through the application of client-focused or project-based learning (Riefen-berg and Long 2017, 580). The majority of such pedagogies are geared towards facilitating student opportunities to make important connections between their academic skills and prior didactic learning to real-world practice (Hauhart and Garage, 2014). These learning opportunities require the ability to succinctly communicate project issues and develop relationships between students and their colleagues (Nordin et al. 2015, 127). Scholars such as Barr and Tagg have noted that collaborative models of teaching where students work with teachers to construct knowledge create strong and meaningful learning environments (Barr and Tagg 1995 as cited in Lantis 1998, 41). This often emulates real-world models of collaboration, meaning that EL often seeks to prepare students for professional life after they graduate.

EL can be contrasted with didactic learning, which focuses on the modes of instruction with which scholars are most familiar in a university classroom—namely instructor-led lectures alongside student discussions of course material and coursework related to the content set by the instructor. This didactic content is generally seen as setting out core concepts and debates related to the discipline. Assignments are largely set for students to showcase a mastery of this canon—generally in the form of research essays or exams (for a discussion of didactic learning and alternatives, see Walks 2015). As an interesting aside, academic disciplines such as nursing, which are often founded on much more experience-based modes of learning, are paradox-ically interested in increasing didactic knowledge in their curriculum (Westin, Sundler and Bergland 2015).

With regard to IR, EL has existed alongside didactic learning for several decades. One of the most obvious forms of EL can be seen in the use of simulations, which has roots in Cold War-era classrooms. In these cases, EL has been used as a means of interacting with real-world issues in a controlled classroom setting (Lantis 1998, 39). Simulations of peace negotiations, trade talks, and other global gatherings, such as those related to climate change are also common features within IR classrooms. Experiential pedagogy in IR has also evolved to include internships, field courses, and involvement in faculty research, leading to an increased understanding of political science through application (Kenyon 2017, 98).

As an example, Kenyon describes a work opportunity where students investigated ethical dilemmas and worked in dialogue with development practitioners. These experiences came with unique teaching needs both in terms of pacing and resourcing. They found that, due to the structure of the course and the need for swift communication, smaller classes and teaching assistants were necessary for detailed feedback and assessment of students

(Kenyon 2017, 98). Another example from Gammonley et al. (2013) describes a study abroad trip that involved cases concerning human rights violations ranging from gender-based violence to human trafficking. Students were directly involved in policy practice, working to create "global community building and social change" and "exposing them to values about human rights and providing them opportunities to develop practice skills" (619). This experience had ongoing impacts on students' understanding of their role within international politics, with the authors noting that participants found that they were more compelled to "intervene" in the human rights situations following the study abroad trip (631). Policy advocacy education based on EL, therefore, took on a greater depth and led to more work upon their return to the classroom (621).

In another study, the pedagogical approach of combining in-class learning with collaborative projects regarding leadership and policy demonstrated that students came to understand the subject matter better, and that, alongside this, there was evidence of increasing competencies in policy analysis and other tools used in students' placements. Students noted that their professional competencies such as written communications, teamwork, and leadership capacity increased following their placement (Sandfort and Gerdes 2017). Indeed, what the above studies observe is that EL is uniquely positioned to teach students far more than content or traditional academic skills, such as critical thinking, research, and writing. It left students feeling more compelled to dig deeper into the subject matter and left them, in some cases, with a sense of responsibility to act on what they had learned. Further, it equipped them with several transferable skills that would serve them in a broad range of future professions. At the same time, these opportunities created logistical dilemmas that instructors may not have to consider if delivering courses more traditionally, as EL often requires a more responsive, hands-on approach from instructors. These findings guided the initial questions asked and explored the case study at hand and are explored in greater detail in the remainder of the chapter.

The SAR Student Advocacy Seminars: Background and UBC Experience

SAR Student Advocacy Seminars offer a template for experiential human rights learning. Support for running a seminar, or integrating elements of the seminar into already existing courses is provided by SAR staff to professors whose universities are SAR members. The seminars have multiple aims, one of which is having students produce deliverables that support SAR's wider mandates of furthering academic freedom and the human rights work this entails. SAR describes the seminars as an "experiential program [that] is tailored to each institution and group of students and is designed to give students a foundation in Human rights research, standards, and mechanisms; Organizing and advocacy; Persuasive writing; Leadership and teamwork skills" (Scholars at Risk Student Advocacy Seminars n.d.). In this sense, the seminars are based on the important principle of reciprocity, in which both the community partner (SAR) and the student participants gain from collaboration.

At the authors' institution, the University of British Columbia (UBC), the seminar took the form of a for-credit 13-week Political Science course, which met once a week in a three-hour block. It is important to also note that SAR experiences can be integrated as illustrative cases into other already existing courses including but not limited to those on on human rights, international politics, legal studies, sociology, or EL programs. Such integration of components of SARs work into other courses and programs is taking root across UBC via a wider teaching and learning initiative that seeks to embed SAR's work within a range of undergraduate courses and programs (UBC, n.d.).

Before engaging in further analysis, it is useful to note the "surface structure" (Shulman 2005), the mechanics of how the course was delivered—this will vary from seminar to seminar, depending on the preferences of individual instructors. At UBC, 22 Political Science and IR students participated in the course. They were split into four groups, with each group being assigned cases from SAR's Scholars in Prison Project. These cases had been selected in consultation with SAR staff based on a range of issues including, but not limited to, cases that SAR deemed as most needing further advocacy work or cases in which the UBC student body may have had a particular interest or expertise. For example, one of the scholars in prison had been imprisoned alongside a UBC Alumni, so there was already a strong circle of advocacy and awareness surrounding this case.

Each week was split into three one-hour blocks. The first hour consisted of a lecture and discussion of academic research related to the topic of transnational human rights. Topics included concepts central to the study of human rights, such as bearing witness, transnational-advocacy networks, human rights treaties and legal mechanisms, and a range of critical perspectives, such as the role of celebrity in the field of human rights. In the second hour, students would often hear from a guest speaker. Staff from SAR would occasionally video-conference with students to provide advice related to the cases. This was supplemented by video-calls from a faculty member that assists SAR in the running of these seminars globally. Additionally, several other individuals also acted as virtual guest speakers throughout the term. These included a "scholar at risk" who had needed to leave their own country and had been provided with a placement at a North American university (as part of SAR's protection work), a close family member of a scholar who had been freed, as well as a close family member of one of the scholars-in-prison who remained detained and whose case students were actively working on. SAR staff assisted in identifying and connecting these latter guests with the instructor. An optional component of the partnership with SAR, these speakers provided incredible insight for students, as they were meeting scholars at risk and those immediately impacted by the human rights abuses they were studying. These were no longer textbook cases, and access to the personal side of international politics had a profound impact on students, both personally and in terms of their scholarship.

The third hour was generally allotted to the experiential component of the course. This is where students worked towards completing deliverables for the community partner, SAR. These deliverables are ultimately set by the instructor with guidance from SAR and vary depending on the topic of the course and the aims of individual instructors. In the case of the UBC seminar, this primarily took the form of a human rights report (comprised of a biography of the scholar, analysis of domestic and international laws relevant to the case, media monitoring reports, and reports on completed and future advocacy). Students also produced a research poster on their case, which was later presented to the other groups and, in some cases, at a national academic conference. Alongside these deliverables, students also completed more traditional academic assignments utilizing the wider literature on human rights advocacy and non-SAR cases.

From Skills Development to Emotional Labor: Impacts of Experiential Learning on Students and Instructors

To explore the impact on learning that occurs through experiential opportunities, the authors surveyed participants of SAR advocacy seminars globally and included their own auto-ethnographic reflections alongside this. The survey focused on two groups: students and instructors of SAR advocacy seminars. With regard to the student side of the survey, we aimed to explore what they gained and/or learned (broadly speaking) from participating in SAR advocacy seminars. Questions included asking students why they decided to enroll in a SAR student advocacy seminar and what skills they developed as a result of participating. For the instructor arm of the survey, questions focused primarily on why they chose to run SAR advocacy seminars—what learning did they envision would happen within their classrooms and what evidence existed for if and/or how this occurred? Further questions were asked regarding course delivery and their experiences of implementing this form of EL. Some key insights from the data are explored below.

Deepening Disciplinary Knowledge(s) and Understandings of Knowledge Production

Although the survey was not designed to assess the quality of the seminars, findings did confirm an overall benefit in regard to student learning in SAR seminars from both the student and instructor experiences. What was striking were the noted benefits from both didactic and experiential learning activities within the seminar. Here, it is important to note that a majority of instructors adopted a blended model of didactic and EL. The responses to the survey were overwhelmingly in favor of the benefits of SAR advocacy seminars as a form of didactic and experiential learning—offering students a solid understanding of disciplinary canons whilst also providing students with work experience to complement their theoretical learning.

The most striking statistics lie in comparing the student perspective before and after their participation in the SAR seminars. Respondents wrote that before they participated in the seminar, a majority of them lacked a sound knowledge of the link between academic freedom, human rights, and global politics. Following their participation, an overwhelming majority (90 percent of 43 students) cited that they gained a clearer understanding of these links. What is particularly exciting about this finding in the context of this case and its contribution to signature pedagogies is the foregrounding of academic freedom in this EL opportunity. As instructors, we generally understand the importance of academic freedom insofar as it allows us (in most circumstances) to engage in our teaching and research without fear of repercussions. It is central to our understanding of our role and rights in the academy generally and our disciplines specifically. This is often not the case for students, who are rarely if ever challenged to think about their academic freedom and how it impacts their learning in IR. As signature pedagogies often have as their goal, helping students understand how knowledge is produced and their role within it, an experience that asks them to explore the academic freedoms they have (or in some case do not) and how, in so many cases, academic freedom is under threat, gives students a new appreciation for their studies and how these are undertaken.

Strengthening Student Skills and Employability

Survey data confirmed that students enrolled in these seminars for a wide variety of reasons. And whilst course design should never rest solely on student preferences, as instructors, it is invaluable to understand the types of learning students are hoping to gain in classes. As junior scholars, they too have a role to play in the shaping of the discipline. Here, the findings are again insightful. Over 46 percent of respondents enrolled because it would expose them to the topic of human rights. This suggests that many students are signing up for such experiences not primarily due to an interest in the topic but for other reasons. The survey found that approximately one-third of respondents felt that it would provide them with work or professional experience, alluding to the fact that EL is often seen by students as providing a new means for graining work experience. As the student-author of this chapter notes in their reflections:

> My academic interests before this class focused on human rights as a general topic, rather than specific instances of advocacy. This class was the first experience I had of doing human rights advocacy with an NGO and provided me with a wealth of opportunities to be involved, make mistakes, and execute deliverables. I took this course for the specificity of the coursework, and the interesting course title. It was only after the first class that I found out it was a work experiential-based course that I felt sold on my decision, because of the distinct lack of academic-related professional experiences on my resume. One of the follies of social science degrees is that outside of co-op education or internships, there is a severe deficit when it comes to allowing for work experience in a collaborative setting... I felt that the SAR advocacy seminar allowed me for an opportunity to delve a bit into what NGO work would be like so that I could make more informed decisions on what to do potentially following completion of my undergrad.

Our survey confirmed what the student-author and other studies on EL have found in terms of the valuable transferable/professional skills gained through EL. This is actually somewhat of a challenge to implicit structures in IR pedagogies (Shulman 2005), as the valuing of professional skills leads to a renegotiation of established norms and values within the IR classroom. It challenges scholars to rethink the general reliance on primarily didactic forms of learning, as there is increasing value being placed on experience and political praxis *within academic settings*. Within the survey, data initially suggest students primarily value concrete professional skills (such as advocacy skills, communication, and research skills) insofar as these offer development opportunities that might further their own job prospects. However, what is actually occurring is more profound. Students are coming to value and center skills development and political advocacy within IR education itself.

Worth noting, only a small percentage of students enrolled specifically because they knew about the work of SAR, hinting that the appeal was not based on working specifically with SAR, but rather seeing it as a general work experience opportunity. This finding is also significant in that the top reason for faculty offering SAR student seminars was to increase their university's commitment to SAR's mandate. In one regard, data confirms that these seminars help faculty and universities in this aim, but that so few students knew of SAR's work coming into the seminar suggests that universities and their faculty can be doing more to educate the study body and highlight the aims of SAR on their campus. This finding also raises questions about the ethics of reciprocity in such partnerships that will be explored later.

Bringing to the Fore the Emotional Labor of Academic Work

Over 85 per cent of survey respondents agreed that their experience in the SAR advocacy seminars resulted in an increase of empathy within themselves for human rights issues. This aligns with the personal experience of the student-author, who reflects more deeply on this issue:

> As a student, I knew very little about the subject matter outside of the typical conversations surrounding "freedom of speech" vs. academic freedom, but thankfully, I gained a stronger understanding of exactly the nuances of this topic. I was extremely curious when it came to understanding the differences between the two, and once I learned that individuals were imprisoned for similar reasons that I gained a stronger empathy for these scholars. The method of learning that we took was not just conceptual, but it was learning more about these individual scholars that we were advocating on behalf of, and gaining something that I didn't expect to learn when it came to NGO work, that you would begin to take this work extremely personally and internalize the struggle that these individuals would face. A significant moment for my group was when we discovered that our Scholar was facing a diagnosis of cancer while in prison, which was a major blow to our morale.

Speaking from the instructor-author point of view on empathy and emotion in the classroom, by the time the course had ended it was clear how (unintended) pedagogies of discomfort (Zembylas and Papamichael 2017) emerged as central to student learning. This discomfort in the learning process should not be seen as a negative—often, learning is necessarily uncomfortable. These moments of discomfort appeared as the instructor watched students struggle with what they knew to be true or important through their traditional, didactic learning (exploring academic debates through readings, lectures, and their academic writing) and how this did not always align with what they were experiencing through coursework and their work on their case for SAR specifically. For example, some students were well versed in some of the critiques of human rights work. These accepted academic critiques, however, did not always sit easily in terms of some students' profound personal commitments to the cases on which they were working, where there were unquestionable human rights abuses that needed the care and attention of human rights organizations such as SAR. Students who were skeptical of states' and politicians' commitments to human rights work from their readings and previous learning were at the same time fully committed to raising their cases with state actors and government representatives.

As another example, many students were very much drawn to and appreciated an article the instructor-author assigned on the importance of bearing witness (Kurasawa 2009). Several found the argument convincing and central to both the study and practice of human rights. Multiple students wrote incredibly strong assignments drawing on the importance of bearing witness and the impact it had on several (non-SAR) cases. At the same time, many of these same students expressed to the instructor that, in reference to the scholars on whose cases they were working, bearing witness, was simply "not enough." Frustration and feelings of being ineffectual were common. Watching students sit with and internalize these two competing forms of learning—engaging with valid critiques *of* the human rights industry alongside working vigilantly *for* a human rights organization was a striking phenomenon to watch play out as a professor. Their traditional (didactic) learning revealed many truths to them that did not align with the experiential arm of the course.

Why is this important and why highlight student frustration and grappling with uncomfortable paradoxes? Simply put, it is where deep learning occurred. Their didactic learning had taught them one truth, their EL presented them with an alternative truth. These findings clearly illustrate Shulman's (2005) concepts of both implicit and deep structures. These learning experiences forced students to explore deeply held values (both personal and academic), demonstrating and impact on implicit structures within this IR pedagogy. At the same time, there are important findings here in terms of deep structure—how to impart knowledge. Our findings also clearly indicate a difference in traditional (didactic) deep structures of pedagogical learning for IR, as changing the learning outcomes from traditional lecture-based methods resulted in different learning outcomes. Observing these discussions, as a professor, the instructor-author witnessed numerous, unexpected learning outcomes as students unpacked and analyzed these uncomfortable paradoxes in learning. In doing so, it was clear that students were learning lessons about human rights work that neither didactic nor EL could have taught them on their own.

Indeed, it was in students dealing with the confrontations of the didactic and the experiential that, from the authors' observations, led to the most meaningful lessons both in terms of content and knowledge production in the discipline. It offered a very concrete experience of the reality that knowledge is deeply contested in the discipline, and there are rarely simple answers to the questions we pose as IR scholars.

Challenging Notions of Expertise and Instructor Professional Development

Whilst the authors of this article began this study primarily interested in these seminars from an IR perspective, our survey instead illustrated the breadth of disciplines integrating SAR seminars into their programming; instructors from the arts, social sciences, and hard sciences have participated in this program. This emphasizes the need for us to also un-silo ourselves and be open to more interdisciplinarity and to expose our students to the realities of how such topics as human rights and academic freedom transcend traditional disciplines. Indeed, an acceptance and integration of interdisciplinarity, with academic freedom as a unifying theme, challenges us to (re)consider disciplinary pedagogical practices (whether they be structural, implicit or deep-seated features of IR).

Beyond highlighting the need for and benefits of interdisciplinarity, other key findings regarding faculty learning emerged from the study. From the survey, instructor experiences seemed overwhelmingly positive, despite some notable challenges to be overcome through their own learning and development. As one respondent noted, "It's been such a privilege and enriching experience, both for me and my students, working with SAR. Advocacy seminars are a unique opportunity for students to practice human rights advocacy. SAR offers excellent support and guidance to faculty and students." With this, another instructor noted in the survey, "We do struggle a bit to get the right balance between theory and practice and I still feel less confident in the advocacy work side, but with each iteration of the course (I've now taught it 4 times) it gets better." This highlights the important role that SAR as a community partner provides. Indeed, as previous studies on experiential learning note—these types of learning experiences often require more timely responses, as well as increased human resources, to succeed. The SAR seminar is no exception, and the faculty support and training provided by SAR in these cases cannot be underplayed.

Indeed, the reflections of the instructor-author of this article illustrate the centrality of SAR in the success of this experience (for both instructors and students) and also highlights how experiential learning not only changes classroom dynamics in important ways but often results in profound learning outcomes for the instructor.

As an instructor, I planned and launched the case with much trepidation. Although I had worked with NGOs on experiential learning opportunities for my students on many occasions, working on the theme of "Academic Freedom" and the Scholars in Prison project was an entirely new exercise for me and far outside of my own expertise (peacebuilding policies). Further, recent debates around Academic Freedom related to so-called "Controversial Speakers" on campus have been very divisive and I was worried about managing these conversations with students. My fears were largely unfounded in that the course was oversubscribed and the students were more than willing to engage in debates around academic freedom in ways that were always scholarly, if not difficult and controversial. I was open and honest with my students about where my lack of knowledge and experience existed. We worked through struggles regarding the cases and the advocacy plans together. In many instances, students taught me about potential paths for advocacy and important details of the case. The way that this "flipped" or challenged the "sage on the stage" model of teaching, felt like an important step in helping students recognize their own role in knowledge production and thus their place in the discipline. Experiential learning often means our students are engaged in research experiences that are not documented in the literature.

What the above highlights is how EL often and necessarily destabilizes preconceptions that stem from the prevalence of traditional didactic learning in IR: that instructors will come to the course with all the answers, that they are the experts who have produced and mastered the knowledge that will be imparted to students. EL instead requires instructors to arrive in their classrooms prepared to learn alongside their students. Indeed, our survey found that close to half of these instructors do not consider themselves experts in academic freedom, but confidently took on the running of a seminar on academic freedom, showing a commitment to learn and become experts along the way, alongside students and with the guidance of a community partner. In this sense, EL democratizes and widens notions of who creates knowledge in IR and how it is learned.

From "Either/Or" To "Both/And": The Value of Didactic and Experiential Learning

Although some seminars focused almost entirely on the experiential element of the SAR program with many positive outcomes, our analysis points to results that stem from a merging of didactic and experiential pedagogies. Importantly, it is argued here that the combination of experiential and didactic learning reveals emergent learning outcomes that were often unexpected, unplanned, and, in some cases, transformative. This leaves instructors hoping to integrate EL with a range of options in terms of what Shulman (2005) refers as "surface" structures—the mechanics of teaching. Each pedagogical tool (didactic or experiential) contributes to different and, at times, complementary learning outcomes. In many instances, lessons learned by both students and faculty members would not have been achieved without the interplay between different modes of learning. This wider finding suggests that future research could explore if or how specific forms of didactic learning are perhaps best suited for the specific forms experiential opportunities that are increasingly part of IR signature pedagogies.

Our findings also suggest the need for further investigation and frank discussions of the emotional labor that stems from EL. In the analysis above, we have largely presented EL as "transformative" and broadly positive—but this is not universally true. The emotional labor of mentoring students through these opportunities as well as the emotional labor of academic work as experienced by students needs more careful consideration. Additionally, the change in deep structures within IR education, how we teach and learn, from traditionally non-advocacy based to being heavily advocacy based align with the following questions: How do faculty prepare for this? How do we manage cases when emotional labor becomes overwhelming for students? How do we balance this non-traditional form of learning within IR whilst maintaining traditional standards of academic rigor and what is generally considered the "canon"?

Finally, our findings re-affirm but also problematize the issue of reciprocity when EL takes the form of working with organizations and real-life stakeholders. The discussions above raise the issue of how to ensure ethical engagement in EL opportunities. What discussion do we have with students in relation to this? How do we handle cases where students see such opportunities primarily from a personal gain point of view—an opportunity for career advancement rather than supporting the partner? How do we handle students who, over the term, become disengaged or even disenchanted by the experience, perhaps starting to question the programming of the community partner? How do we handle these situations as instructors who have a responsibility both to student learning and students' academic freedom, but also to the community partner to whom the class has committed to working alongside? These are all questions that are normally not explored when instructors are preparing traditional lecture materials, when instructors are considering how to effectively communicate content. The dilemmas raised above pose further questions as opposed to concrete answers about what is or *should be* the deep structures (how to impart knowledge) within IR. And this is intentional. EL as a signature pedagogy forces us to continually disrupt and (re)imagine the contours of the discipline. Such disruptions are necessary to ensure IR teaching remains dynamic and responsive to the changing state of global affairs.

In conclusion, our analysis, whilst confirming the already cited benefits of EL, has also expanded on these, noting how, in the case of SAR seminars, EL, when combined with didactic learning can very much help challenge and (re) form both the instructor and student understanding of what counts as knowledge and expertise in IR. At the same time, there is more work to be done to explore how exactly didactic and experiential learning can be synergistic. In ending our analysis, for the benefits of EL to be even more fully realized, the authors urge both ourselves as actors, as well as others implementing any form of EL, to pay close attention in addressing both the emotional labor and ethical dilemmas surrounding reciprocity that are also key features of such forms of learning.

References

Barr, Robert B., and John Tagg (1995). "From Teaching to Learning A New Paradigm for Undergraduate Education." *Change* 6: 13–25.

Gammonley, Denise, Karen Smith Rotabi, Janett Forte, and Amanda Martin. 2013. "Beyond Study Abroad: A Human Rights Delegation to Teach Policy Advocacy." *Journal of Social Work Education* 49: 619–634.

Keng, Shao-Hsun, Chun-Hung Lin, and Peter F. Orazem. 2017. "Expanding College Access in Taiwan, 1978–2014: Effects on Graduate Quality and Income Inequality." *Journal of Human Capital* 11, no. 1 (Spring): 1–34. https://doi.org/10.1086/690235.

Kenyon, Kristi Heather. 2017. "Bringing the field into the classroom: Methods and experiential learning in the 'Politics of Development'." *Learning and Teaching in Politics and International Studies* 37, no. 1: 97–112.

Kurasawa, Fuyuki. 2009. "A Message in a Bottle: Bearing Witness as a Mode of Transnational Practice." *Theory, Culture & Society*, 26(1).

Lantis, Jeffrey. 1998. "Simulations and Experiential Learning in the International Relations Classroom." *International Negotiation* 3, no. 1:39–58.

Nordin, Rohaida, Muhamad Sayuti bin Hassan, Rohimi Shapie, Faridah Jalil, Matthew Albert Witbrodt. 2015. "Experiential Learning via Intervention Programme in Teaching and Learning Human Rights Subject." *Mediterranean Journal of Social Sciences.* 6, no. 6 (November): 120–128.

Riefenberg, Steve, and Sean Long. 2017. "Negotiating the Client-Based Capstone Experience." *International Journal of Teaching and Learning in Higher Education* 29, no. 3: 580–588.

Sandfort, Jodi, and Kevin Gerdes. 2017. "The design, pedagogy and practice of an integrated public affairs leadership course." *Teaching Public Administration* 35. no.1: 50–65

Shulman, Lee S. 2005 "Signature Pedagogies in the Professions" *Daedelus* 134(3): 42–59.

Scholars At Risk. n.d. "Student Advocacy Seminars." Accessed September 30th, 2020. https://www.scholarsatrisk.org/actions/student-advocacy-seminars/

UBC. n.d. "Scholars at Risk." Accessed February 28, 2021. https://scholarsatrisk.ubc.ca/

Walks, 2015. *Listening to Teach: Beyond Didactic Pedagogy.* New York: State University of New York Press.

Westin, Sundeler and Berglund, 2015. 'Students' experiences of learning in relation to didactic strategies during the first year of a nursing programme: a qualitative study' *BMC Medical Education* 15(49)

Zembylas, Michalinos & Elena Papamichael. 2017. 'Pedagogies of discomfort and empathy in multicultural teacher education' *Intercultural Education*, 28(3), 1–19.

9

Killing Your Students: Signature Pedagogies and the Use of Violence in In-Class Simulations

DAVID ANDERSEN-RODGERS

The field of political science, but particularly the field of International Relations, is one of the few academic disciplines in which professors can openly discuss, in the classroom, the mass slaughter of human beings in what may come across as amoral terms. Much of this, of course, derives from the questions that drive our research. When studying why wars start or escalate, the researcher may be driven to the subject for normative purposes, but the requirements of supposedly impartial research have in many ways sanitized our variables—deaths become data, not bodies. While this may be necessary for research purposes, when translated back into the policy world, it may have the unintended consequence of minimizing, in a policymaker's mind, the full range of consequences that accompany decisions to use violence. This creates critical ethical problems if one of our purposes as teachers is to, in fact, train the next generation of foreign policy decision-makers. In short, how do we teach and train students who may be entering a profession in which they could ultimately be called on to make critical choices on the use of violence? This chapter engages this question by questioning how we use in-class simulations—which often have a violent component—as a method for developing a signature pedagogy for the discipline.

A signature pedagogy encompasses the ways that we train the next generation of professionals in our field to think, perform, and act with integrity (Shulman 2005). One important difference between the field of International Relations and many of the fields highlighted by Shulman (i.e., law, medicine, engineering, etc.) is that the total number of people who are ever put into positions of leadership with the authority to make foreign policy decisions for a state is very small. Therefore, it becomes very unlikely that someone sitting in our classroom will one day be personally making those decisions— although there may be a higher likelihood that they would be responsible for crafting the analysis and justifications that could assist in making those decisions. This assumed distance of the learner from the possible future act may mean that, at times, instructors do not feel the burden of developing a signature pedagogy around questions of initiating war and violence—these are decisions made by others, we just study them.[1]

This distance is amplified due to the fact that the field of conflict studies has largely relied on the collection of secondary event data to construct datasets that then are used to statistically test different hypotheses.[2] This reliance on event data and large-n studies to understand war, along with the, thankfully, speculative underpinnings of nuclear deterrence theory, meant that how we have tended to talk about war in our classrooms has either been reduced to an easily observable variable (e.g., 1,000 battle-deaths) or presented in highly abstract terms (e.g., the consequences of deterrence built on mutually assured destruction failing). Ironically, these approaches to the study of war also meant that an area of research specifically concerned with the harm and death of human beings could largely avoid falling under the human subject requirements of Institutional Review Boards (IRB). This distancing of the human-made choice to use violence in international politics from the human bodies that absorb that violence raises serious questions about how we teach these topics, particularly when choosing to construct in-class simulations designed to mimic decision-making processes.

Games and in-class simulations are one mechanism to meet the goals of a signature pedagogy within our teaching. A well-designed simulation can expose students to the complex decision-making processes that foreign policy actors may face in their jobs. Games and in-class simulations have shown themselves to be effective ways for teaching and reinforcing course content (Asal and Blake 2006; Giovanello, Kirk, and Kromer 2013). These activities engage students in ways that traditional forms of teaching are frequently unable to and can help highlight each of the core elements of a signature pedagogy—how to think, perform, and act with integrity. However, what may

---

[1]   Of course, this is not universally true, as many courses and textbooks on ethics in International Relations exist. However, these courses often exist *outside* what may be deemed as more traditional courses in International Relations and security studies.

[2]   Thankfully, this is changing as we are beginning to see more methodological diversity within the field, as well as more forthright discussions about how to ethically conduct both desk and field research (see Hoover, Green, and Cohen 2020; Cronin-Furman and Lake 2018).

be overlooked when designing and implementing in-class simulations is the way in which violent assumptions are often embedded within them and how these might undermine training our students in how to act with integrity. This issue emerges in two ways: first, through the effects that violent decision-making has on those participating in the simulations; and, second, through the built-in assumptions of classroom simulations that can make the use of violence seem like a forced choice.

All in-class simulations are designed to be played by humans. Consequently, they typically mirror the type of research that would require IRB approval, but because they do not fit under the federal definition of research (46.102.l), they would not be required to go through an IRB process. Just as with human subject lab experiments, most simulations introduce a scenario, a treatment, and then a set of choices that the students have to make based on their evaluation of the situation. These decisions are often interdependent with other students' decision-making within the class—students who, not inconsequentially, may have to interact with each other in other contexts throughout their day. Research has shown that participating in these simulations create emotional affect for these students, and that these affects effect how students both play the game and view the world (Zappile, Beers, and Raymond 2016; McDermott et al. 2007). A simulation that forces students to make choices around the use of violence may have unintended emotional consequences from feeling uneasy about instigating said violence against another student or feeling unfairly targeted by students who are instigating violence against them. A study by McDermott, Johnson, Cowden and Rosen (2007) showed that men were much more likely to use aggressive actions than women. A game that rewards aggression may have unintended consequences for what already are difficult classroom gender dynamics. As educators, we should think deeply about the long-term implications that our pedagogical approaches have on our students' thinking about the world and to consciously work to design simulations that teach the basic principles of the class while avoiding unnecessary harm to our students and the potential of harm to others.

Games, it should be recognized, are a central component of most students' lives and many games—both video and board—have the players engage in a continuous stream of violent decision-making. That said, these games are almost universally understood to be for entertainment and do not reflect the player's daily reality. Classroom simulations, on the other hand, are not designed to entertain, but to provide students with the opportunity to engage and learn about actual decision-making processes. The ultimate goal of these simulations is that the experience or the lessons learned from that experience can then be used in real world scenarios. As teachers of international politics, we should, despite its low probability, always assume that the students in our classroom may, one day in the future, be in a position to make the very types of decisions that are being role played in our simulations. This obligates us to take the design of these simulations seriously and consider carefully what the possible real-world consequences of the game, if drawn out to its obvious conclusions, could be.

As with data collection on war, sanitization—by which I mean the presentation of concepts that have been stripped from the trauma one experiences when said concept is being performed on you—can be a useful, but consequential aspect of simulation design. One common type of simulation follows the parameters found in rational choice models in which players are asked to coerce or accommodate an opponent who also has an identical or similar set of choices. These simulations will typically give the option for one of the players to opt out of the game and declare war. Who "wins" the war will sometimes be determined by a coin-flip or some other method of randomiz-ation (see for example Kraus et al. 2008). These are very straightforward simulations and they do a good job helping the student work through some of the game theoretic logic of rational choice models. Because the choice environment is simple, the simulation is easy to explain and play. However, just as with rational choice models they run the risk of minimizing the layered and complex costs of war.

First, wars are rarely "won," at least not in the definitive way captured by a coin toss. A coin toss is predictable in that one can calculate the outcome and compare it to the other available options. A player versed with very basic knowledge of expected utility theory can easily do the math to determine whether they should risk initiating a war. For those participants who are math-averse, they can still rely on a wide range of social-psychological heuristics to make somewhat predictable choices. In the real world, however, these choices to use force are riddled with both known and unknown risks as well as costs, and will often have long-term consequences far beyond the immediate coin-toss outcome. Underspecifying costs and risks within a simulation may have the unintended consequence of training students to under-determine the risks of war within real-world scenarios—a basic win the war, but lose the peace outcome. Of course, there is also the possibility of over-specifying costs and risks, but the very nature of the simplified odds found in most simulation designs make under-specification more likely.

The mechanics of any game are going to affect how the game is played, when and how the choice to use violence is made, and the range of possible outcomes. The field of International Relations is highly contested over the likelihood of conflict or cooperation. Many simulations can be used to demonstrate how certain sets of assumptions can lead to certain outcomes. A "state of nature" game, for example, is based on a very narrow premise about the condition of the world. This premise, of course, is highly contested, but without appropriate context a participant can leave the simulation believing that that is, in fact, how the world works. If the real world is not actually a "state of nature" game, but behavior is driven by the assumption that it is, there is a high likelihood for inefficient outcomes. The same can be said of Prisoner's Dilemma or Stag Hunt or any of the other simplistic scenarios we have concocted over time to make sense of a complex world.

Of course, a more realistic capturing of the dynamics of violent conflict means that we are asking participants to make choices for which they may not be adequately prepared, either on an emotional or maturity level. This problem is reflected in how roles are assigned and how participants respond to those roles. Psychological experiments have consistently shown how immediately participants take on the roles that are assigned to them. Often this role adaption will reflect the extremes of what the participant believes the role is. In the Stanford Prison Experiment, in which undergraduates were put in a basement and assigned the roles of prisoners and guards, participants reflected on how they took on the characteristics that they *thought* that role would have. Of course, it is highly unlikely that undergraduates had much real-world experience as either guards or prisoners, thus their performance in the simulation was more akin to familiar tropes than the actual day to day behavior of guards or prisoners (Carnahan and McFarland 2007; Texier 2019; Zimbardo 1973). The Milgram experiments, in which participants were asked to administer electric shocks to an actor who they believed to be a co-participant, also demonstrate the impact of forcing participants to behave in ways that they understand to be immoral (Milgram and Gudehus 1978). Films of the experiment as it was being conducted show high levels of stress on the participants as they comply with the administrator's orders. A simulation like the Wave at Cubberley High School in Palo Alto, California, in which a teacher created an in-group and out-group to demonstrate how easily they could be pulled into and adopt the behaviors of a pseudo-fascist organization, may also have had unintended psychological effects as participants were unwittingly forced to self-reflect about their conduct in the grossest of possible ways (Saari 2020). Even when guarding against these high-profile excesses, some of the same dynamics may play out in subtler, albeit similar ways.

Knowing the strong effect that situational determinants can have on part-icipants, simulation designers should consider how role assignment shapes the simulation and the lessons that participants take away from it. One assumption that should underlie our thinking is that participants will gain sympathy for the roles that they are assigned—or at least will not fully question any underlying moral problems that the role might require. These issues may manifest themselves differently depending on whether the simulation is based on fictitious or real-life scenarios, but they are present in both types of designs. A second assumption is that a simulation that is specifically designed to garner hostility and competitive play between students could break those boundaries outside the classroom. This can be particularly amplified when gender or racial dynamics start driving how the game plays out.

When designing a simulation with a real-life scenario it is possible that some of the roles will be actors that have committed atrocities. How are the parameters around atrocity crimes handled? Do the game mechanics allow for atrocities and, if so, how are payouts weighed for these types of actions? If participants can choose to engage in atrocities, what is our moral obligation regarding consequences for these choices? If atrocities are not included within the choice set, meaning the role has been sanitized, how is this addressed? Similar questions can be raised for simulations that are based on a fictitious scenario modeled around real-world events. While such scenarios do provide for both more flexibility as well as constraints in what can be addressed, fictitious countries or groups cannot be studied and therefore cannot be understood outside the parameters of the simulation itself. Consequently, participants may be more inclined to adapt tropes in their role-playing approaches. If "Trope-playing" only reinforces preexisting stereotypes it is less likely to help the student develop a deeper understanding of the complex set of preferences and interests that underlie political decision-making.

These are complex questions that go to the roots or our moral obligations as instructors. Frankly, the vast majority of atrocities that have been committed throughout world history have gone unpunished. Many times, these atrocities have advanced the strategic objectives of those who have carried them out, meaning they cannot simply be made exogenous to these simulated worlds. Thus, we need to engage the deeper question of what pedagogical purpose the simulation has and what ultimate lessons may come out of playing the game. If the simulation does not go beyond "crime pays" or similar types of lessons, then should we be engaging students in these scenarios? Without this reflection the question of whether a simulation can serve as a tool for presenting a meaningful signature pedagogy comes into question.

The questions raised here serve as a starting point for a broader discussion on how we use games and simulations in the classroom. Its main call is to be more reflective about how we approach these activities and to more closely consider the short- and long-term impacts they may have on our students. This final section engages some steps we can take now to improve the environment in which we conduct these simulations that would more closely align with the development of a signature pedagogy for International Relations.

Think about how violence is used, who gets to use it, and against whom: Violence is a key component of International Relations, therefore, it is unrealistic to develop scenarios that eliminate the option for violence altogether. However, it may not be necessary for the students to take on that role or to be the ones who are targeted with violence itself. This role can be taken on by the instructor or it could be embedded within the scenario. For example, in a simulation that occurs over multiple rounds, violent acts can provide the background for the negotiations that are taking place between players. The players themselves are not choosing violence or even having violence used against them directly, but are instead responding to "spoilers" who use violence to disrupt the negotiations. Importantly, one should ask what the violent options of the scenario ultimately teach us. If they are not a core part of the pedagogical purpose of the exercise, they should be de-emphasized.

Engage students in the process of simulation design: A simulation that is simply presented as a given requires little critical evaluation on the participant's part. When students design their own simulations, they begin to challenge the assumptions underlying the basic gameplay. A say in the game's design might also decrease the emotive effect that role-playing will often elicit. When they think about the roles and the interests of the actors, they may be more inclined to challenge stereotyped assumptions. At the very least, as instructors, we can challenge them to question those assumptions. This activity may not result in the actual playing of the simulation, but the exercise can help them engage with many of the theoretical assumptions that were engaged during the course of the semester.

Leave time for reflection and discussion: Simulations can be intense experiences, particularly simulations that involve violence. A simulation that includes any level of ruthlessness in which participants take advantage of each other should not be ended without closure. As an instructor, it is important to engage with the participants on the emotionally intense moments that participants experienced. Highlighting how easy it was to develop these emotions, though, can provide insight into how real-life conflicts can escalate and persist.

Be willing to stop the simulation if emotions get too high: Sometimes, things do not go as planned and, as an instructor, it is important to recognize when a simulation needs to be stopped. If such an event happens, discuss what happened and how they escalated. After the conversations, the students may be in a better place to re-engage with the simulation. If not, it is ok to move on. A simulation is only as good as the core ideas it is teaching. If those core ideas cannot be engaged, there is little need to move forward.

Conclusion

This chapter engages some key questions associated with simulations that incorporate violence into their gameplay and links it to the question of whether such simulations are an appropriate vehicle for a signature pedagogy in our classroom. While simulations are useful pedagogical tools, as instructors, we need to be cognizant of the potential impact that these exercises have, particularly as they relate to training future foreign policy decision-makers. Thinking of our students as future decision-makers puts the onus on us to design scenarios that adequately prepare them to engage in matters of life and death from both a strategic and moral position. However, we should also be aware of the intense emotional effects that these games may have on students participating in them. Being aware of these effects and being adequately prepared to address them can make the simulation environment a much more useful experience for all participants.

*I would like to thank Amy Eckert for her comments on the initial draft of this piece and dedicate it to her memory.

References

Asal, Victor, and Elizabeth L. Blake. 2006. "Creating Simulations for Political Science Education." *Journal of Political Science Education* 2 (1): 1–18. https://doi.org/10.1080/15512160500484119.

Carnahan, Thomas, and Sam McFarland. 2007. "Revisiting the Stanford Prison Experiment: Could Participant Self-Selection Have Led to the Cruelty?" *Personality and Social Psychology Bulletin* 33 (5): 603–14. https://doi.org/10.1177/0146167206292689.

Cronin-Furman, Kate, and Milli Lake. 2018. "Ethics Abroad: Fieldwork in Fragile and Violent Contexts." *PS: Political Science & Politics* 51 (03): 607–14. https://doi.org/10.1017/S1049096518000379.

Giovanello, Sean P., Jason A. Kirk, and Mileah K. Kromer. 2013. "Student Perceptions of a Role-Playing Simulation in an Introductory International Relations Course." *Journal of Political Science Education* 9 (2): 197–208. https://doi.org/10.1080/15512169.2013.770989.

Hoover Green, Amelia, and Dara Kay Cohen. 2020. "Centering Human Subjects: The Ethics of 'Desk Research' on Political Violence." *Journal of Global Security Studies*, July, ogaa029. https://doi.org/10.1093/jogss/ogaa029.

Kraus, Sarit, Penina Hoz-Weiss, Jonathan Wilkenfeld, David R. Andersen, and Amy Pate. 2008. "Resolving Crises through Automated Bilateral Negotiations." *Artificial Intelligence* 172 (1): 1–18. https://doi.org/10.1016/j.artint.2007.05.007.

McDermott, Rose, Dominic Johnson, Jonathan Cowden, and Stephen Rosen. 2007. "Testosterone and Aggression in a Simulated Crisis Game." *The ANNALS of the American Academy of Political and Social Science* 614 (1): 15–33. https://doi.org/10.1177/0002716207305268.

Milgram, Stanley, and Christian Gudehus. 1978. "Obedience to Authority."

Saari, Antti. 2020. "Transference, Desire, and the Logic of Emancipation." In *Handbook of Theory and Research in Cultural Studies and Education*, edited by Peter Pericles Trifonas, 179–92. Cham: Springer International Publishing. https://doi.org/10.1007/978-3-319-56988-8_1.

Shulman, Lee S. 2005. "Signature Pedagogies in the Professions." *Daedalus* 134 (3): 52–59. https://doi.org/10.1162/0011526054622015.

Texier, Thibault Le. 2019. "Debunking the Stanford Prison Experiment," *American Psychologist*, 74 (7): 823–839. https://doi.org/10.1037/amp0000401.

Zappile, Tina M., Daniel J. Beers, and Chad Raymond. 2016. "Promoting Global Empathy and Engagement through Real-Time Problem-Based Simulations." *International Studies Perspectives*, February, ekv024. https://doi.org/10.1093/isp/ekv024.

Zimbardo, Philip G. 1973. "On the Ethics of Intervention in Human Psychological Research: With Special Reference to the Stanford Prison Experiment." *Cognition* 2 (2): 243–56. https://doi.org/10.1016/0010-0277(72)90014-5.

10

Supervising IR Dissertations: Using Personal Anecdotes to Reflect a Strategy for Supervision

ARCHIE W. SIMPSON

It can be said that the dissertation (or honors thesis) reflects the culmination of undergraduate studies. It is an opportunity for the student to pursue an independent piece of research into a topic of their own choosing. It can also be a daunting prospect for students, as often they have not been involved in such a research project before. For the supervisor, it is a chance to foster new research and to pass on some of their own experiences and knowledge to students. As part of the signature pedagogy of International Relations (IR), the dissertation presents an intellectual challenge for students, in which they have the opportunity to create new knowledge. As a dissertation supervisor at a number of British universities since 2006, the author has accumulated great experiences of the dissertation process. In this chapter, anecdotal evidence will be used to set out good practice in the supervision of dissertations in IR. Anecdotes are stories with a purpose, and they often reflect real-life incidents or examples. Aronson (2003, 1346) writes, "Anecdotal reports... should be published... a fact that is not emphasized by the evidence hierarchy." Anecdotes can elucidate good practice, they can demonstrate teaching techniques, and they can provide testimony of pedagogical experiences. A novel strategy based upon establishing a two-way interactive dialogue with the student will be presented. The signature pedagogy of International Relations involves, mass lectures, small tutorials, and private study. Mass lectures, due to their sheer size, tend to limit student participation and interaction and can therefore lead to passive learning" (Harris 2012, 176). The dissertation therefore presents an opportunity for the student to become research-active, to engage in critical thinking, and it is, "preparation for 'good work'" (Shulman 2005, 53). This chapter will set out what a dissertation involves, offer a strategy for supervision, suggest ways to encourage originality, and offer some conclusions. According to Todd et al. (2006, 163), "Most literature relating to dissertation supervision is aimed at masters and doctoral level students," and this chapter aims to fill the gap in relation to undergraduate dissertations involving IR.

There are several differences between undergraduate and postgraduate dissertations in terms of length/word count, depth of analysis, length of literature review, methods of data collection, and purpose of study. Usually, undergraduate dissertations are shorter in length and tend to be more general or broader in scope, while postgraduate dissertations are more focused, more advanced, and more detailed on a given topic. The undergraduate dissertation introduces the student to the idea of research projects and promotes the signature pedagogy of IR, whereas postgraduate dissertations demonstrate some advancement in scholarship that can fill a gap in the knowledge of IR. *Ergo,* a postgraduate dissertation can contribute to ongoing research and identify openings for future research. This chapter aims to offer some insights into the supervision of undergraduate dissertations and thus focuses on how to introduce the idea of a dissertation to students rather than on experimental issues that involve postgraduate studies.

What the Dissertation Involves

The undergraduate dissertation usually happens in the final year of studies in the third or fourth year. In Scotland, this means in the fourth year of undergraduate studies and, in the rest of the UK, it typically means in third year – though there are some exceptions. It is part of the signature pedagogy of IR in which students "engage critically with a body of knowledge. This engagement facilitates understanding of key concepts and theories, and also provides students with the methodologies to analyze material" (Harris 2012, 176) and to apply this in practical terms. This involves the student picking a research topic and then carrying out research under the supervision of a lecturer or tutor. The dissertation is regarded as a course module, though there are no lectures[1] or tutorials throughout the term(s), unlike other modules. Each university department has its own regulations regarding the dissertation, and this usually involves the length of the dissertation (usually involving between 10,000 and 12,000 words with a 10 percent upper or lower threshold), the time period involved, an ethics procedure, formatting of the

---

[1]   There is usually one introductory lecture to review and explain the dissertation process and to encourage students to begin thinking about the dissertation topic at the start of the process.

dissertation, deadline details, general regulations about the dissertation, and means of assessment. Some universities prescribe a formal process in which various elements of the dissertation study are set out with deadlines (e.g., submission of a literature review).

The dissertation is an independent research project carried out by the student under supervision. The purpose of the dissertation is to encourage the student to pursue research into a subject of their own choosing, in which they can demonstrate a range of research skills, show their analytical skills, interpret relevant information, and present their knowledge of the subject by writing up results in a logical and coherent manner. It also develops a range of practical skills and abilities, including time management skills, writing and editing abilities, negotiations (with supervisors and possibly interviewees), organizational skills, and to put into practice what they have learned during their degree studies. The dissertation is also a part of the peroration of the signature pedagogy of IR at undergraduate level. The dissertation becomes an opportunity for students to study a topic in more depth than they may have encountered previously in their studies. Importantly, the dissertation fosters critical thinking by the student themselves. Greenbank and Penketh (2009, 463) write that the dissertation "provides the vehicle for students to engage with their own thinking". Moreover, the dissertation allows the student to take responsibility for their own learning; students have to think, plan, act, and reflect upon their work in order to learn and earn a good grade (Gibbs and Habeshaw 2011, 34-35). Producing a good dissertation can be satisfying for the student (and the supervisor), but it could also be cited in job applications or in postgraduate applications following graduation.

The dissertation is an assessed piece of work that contributes towards the final degree classification. In British universities, the norm is that the supervisor is the first marker, and there is a second marker, whose identity is usually unknown to the student. Sometimes a third marker might be called in or the external examiner gets involved where there are significant disputes by the markers. As the supervisor is also (usually) the first marker, this means that they cannot see the entire dissertation before its submission. Normal regulations are that the supervisor can read 1–3 draft chapters (or 30 percent) before submission, and this normally includes the introduction; in practice, the supervisor will have a good idea about what the dissertation is likely to look like. The assessment follows the usual departmental assessment scale, whatever that is. However, two key points about the assessment of dissertations should be made here. Firstly, the unique nature of the dissertation means that markers take assessment particularly seriously as they agree what the grade should be. Secondly, in final exam board meetings at the end of the academic year, the dissertation grade is (often) given added weight especially when a student is on the borderline between degree classifications. The author has attended many exam boards where the question has been raised, "what did they get for their dissertation?" A good dissertation grade can therefore help the student improve their final degree classification.

A Strategy for Supervision

There is no right way to supervise a dissertation student, as each supervisor has their own different experiences of being supervised themselves. The convenor of the dissertation module has overall responsibility for dissertations, and they try to match supervisors with students as best as possible or allow students to find their own supervisors within their department. Once the student has a supervisor, the dissertation process begins. The strategy for supervision involves establishing a two-way dialogue with the student beginning at the first meeting. The first meeting should set the tone for the supervision process and establish a collegial working relationship between student and supervisor.

In my experience, the first meeting with the student is important as several outcomes should be achieved. For the student, they should have a better idea as to what the dissertation involves, they should have some initial work to do, and they should feel reassured that their supervisor is going to be helpful in their efforts. For the supervisor, they should know what the student wants to look at and why, they should pass on relevant information to the student, and they should establish a working relationship with the student. The first meeting should be as friendly as possible and the student should discuss the dissertation idea as much as possible. Supervisors should take notes throughout each meeting with students. As part of the signature pedagogy of dissertations, students, "are expected to participate actively in the discuss-ions, rounds, or constructions; they are also expected to make relevant contributions that respond directly to previous exchanges" (Shulman 2005, 57). As preparation for this meeting, the author has developed a simple hand-out (or checklist) to show based on experience to explain to the student. This involves five points:

1. What is the topic?
2. What is the most appropriate theory?
3. Structure of the dissertation
4. Research issues
5. Presentation of the dissertation

Each point is explained to the student beginning with "what is the topic?" Todd et al. (2006, 167) write, "The first major task, which the dissertation supervisor undertakes is to provide support for students in identifying and defining the research question". It is important that the student explains what it is they want to study and why they want to study the topic. Sometimes the student does not have a topic and, in such cases, a discussion about the subjects in which they are interested should elicit a potential topic. Roselle and Spray (2012, 6) write, "Choosing a topic is often the most difficult component of writing a research project". Where students are involved in a joint degree, the other discipline should be incorporated into the dissertation, where possible. In IR, the topic could be contemporary, historical, theoretical, policy-related, or thematic; this also applies to other social sciences and, perhaps especially, politics. The student does not necessarily need an actual question at this stage, but they should be asked to develop a hypothesis (or several related hypotheses) to help generate a question or proposition; this will also help develop the eventual title of the dissertation. The hypothesis will also encourage the student to *think more coherently and critically* about the topic.

Anecdote 1: The author usually asks students to pick a topic in which they are interested as this helps their motivation OR choose a subject about which they know little/nothing, and this becomes a motivation for the study. As students are researching in an autonomous manner with no set timetable, self-motivation becomes an important factor.

The second point is to ensure that the student incorporates an appropriate theory or concept(s) into the study. Matching a theory to a topic is *a central part of achieving a good grade* for the dissertation in IR. This is a point that the supervisor should convey to the student as early as possible. Sutch and Elias (2007, 4) write, "IR theory is basic to the study of world politics... IR theory attempts to elaborate general principles that can help orientate us in our encounter with the complexities of world politics". By the time students are considering their dissertations, they should already have completed a module(s) on IR theory; this is an important part of the signature pedagogy of IR. By incorporating IR theory into the dissertation, the student can demonstrate their theoretical knowledge in a practical manner. It is incumbent on the supervisor to ensure that the student recognizes the need to incorporate a theoretical or conceptual dimension into the study. As signature pedagogies involve, "defin[ing] how knowledge is analyzed, criticized, accepted, or discarded" (Shulman 2005, 54), the inclusion of IR theory into the dissertation becomes important as part of this process. The dissertation should include *a golden thread* of theory, meaning that *each chapter* should have some theoretical component. The integration of theory into the dissertation is part of the vocabulary of IR, and it "also provides possibilities for students' emancipation" (Marsden and Savigny 2012, 128). The theoretical element also contributes towards the originality of the dissertation and demonstrates the *implicit structure* (Shulman, 2005, 55) of IR as an academic discipline. The inclusion of theory in the dissertation also symbolizes that the student is actively learning and is being socialized into having the mind-set of an IR thinker.

The third point concerns the structure of the dissertation. This relates to the number of chapters, the order of chapters, and the word count for each chapter. Usually, departmental regulations will stipulate that dissertations have a title page, an abstract, contents page, chapters, bibliography, and appendices. Appendices[2] are not usually included as part of the word count. If the dissertation is 10,000 words long, then there are, broadly, two structural models to recommend to students. The first is a simple five-chapter dissertation with approximately 2,000 words assigned to each chapter. This should include an introduction, three substantial chapters, and a conclusion. This provides scope for a methods/theoretical/historical background chapter and two case studies. The second involves a six-chapter dissertation involving an introduction of 1,500 words, four chapters of 1,750 words each and a conclusion of 1,500 words. A 12,000-word dissertation would follow a similar format.

The contents of each chapter differ from dissertation to dissertation, but the student should follow some structure as this will help form a clearer focus for each chapter and help them to keep to the word count as much as possible.

Table 1: Structure and word count

Model 1: 10,000 words	Model 2: 10,000 words	Model 3: 12,000 words
Introduction 2,000	Introduction 1,500	Introduction 2,000
Chapter 2,000	Chapter 1,750	Chapter 2,000
Chapter 2,000	Chapter 1,750	Chapter 2,000
Chapter 2,000	Chapter 1,750	Chapter 2,000
Conclusion 2,000	Chapter 1,750	Chapter 2,000
	Conclusion 1,500	Conclusion 2,000

The fourth part of the discussion is about research issues. Many students will have taken a research methods module in their studies by the time they begin their dissertation. The supervisor should explain (or remind students) to carry out a literature review, and to consider carefully what research method(s) to consider. Roselle and Spray (2012, 5) write, "Political scientists must build on

---

[2]   Appendices are useful ways to add information, such as interview transcripts, maps and diagrams, evidence of ethics, and other additional information.

the research of others". Todd et al. (2006, 167) write, "The supervisor's role is also to ensure that what the student intends to do is feasible in scope and sensible in terms of ethics". Methods could be qualitative, quantitative, or a mixture of methods. A range of methods or approaches should be discussed at this point with the student. In some ways, this reflects the *surface structure* (Shulman 2005, 54–55) of the signature pedagogy of supervising IR dissertations. Sources of information, such as the university library, online sources, journals, broadcast media, print media, and official documentation, should be identified to the student to consider utilizing. Depending on the dissertation topic, other sources of information could be discussed, such as films, departmental research seminars, and sitting in on lectures (from their department or other university departments where appropriate). If the student considers interviews, then the supervisor should set out some of the practical aspects of this (e.g., setting up meetings, recording, etc.) (Todd et al. 2006, 168). In addition, all universities now have an "ethics policy," and this should be explained to the student. At some point during this initial meeting, the author usually tells the student that they should consider themselves as being "a researcher" and not "a student"; for some students, this becomes a gateway into thinking about postgraduate education. This should help establish a working relationship which, in turn, should facilitate a two-way dialogue. It is important that the views of the student are aired during this meeting and at subsequent meetings, as they are the one working on the study; the student should be *active* and *not passive* throughout the dissertation process. Time management should also be discussed; 5–8 hours per week minimum should be scheduled into the student's timetable for dissertation work.

The final point relates to the presentation of the dissertation. This includes some discussion about technical issues, such as font size, the use of maps or diagrams, what the title page should look like (sometimes it can include the title, author, and year, but sometimes it can include a picture/image), using margins,[3] and including page numbers. It is useful for the supervisor to show old dissertations to the student as examples; good and bad. Showing the student "the final product" is helpful so that the student has a better idea of what they should aim towards; many students have said to the author that this was helpful. The referencing system should also be discussed; whether using footnotes or the Harvard system.[4] The regulations for the dissertation might dictate which referencing system is used. The author has suggested to students that each chapter could begin with a short quote as a means to

---

[3]   As a supervisor, I usually ask students to "justify" the text instead of "left align," as the end product looks better, but this is subject to university regulations.

[4]   The author *always* advises student to begin a running bibliography for the dissertation partly as good practice, partly to ensure they adopt a systematic approach to the dissertation, but largely to avoid problems when finishing writing up the study.

introduce each chapter. Some students like this, while others do not, but it is an interesting thing to mention.

Anecdote 2: The author prints out this five-point checklist for students at the first meeting. At the end of term, one student told me that he carried the note with him throughout the term and used it to add notes and comments, and to remind him to work on the dissertation.

When this first meeting is ending, the supervisor should ask the students if they have questions. The supervisor should also agree some schedule for future meetings, exchange e-mail details, and ensure that both parties know what is happening. It is advised that students should try to have *at least* one face-to-face meeting once a month throughout the term(s) and maintain e-mail contact; the use of social media such as Facebook or Twitter is also useful to maintain contact. Woolhouse (2010, 137) writes, "Much of what happens between tutors and students is 'semi-public'." By engaging with the student throughout, a two-way dialogue should identify any problems, facilitate good research by the student, and be pedagogically rewarding for student and supervisor. In subsequent meetings, the student should report what they have done and what they are going to do. Supervisors should ask questions, provide feedback, and offer appropriate advice at each meeting in a collegial manner.

Encouraging Originality

To an extent, all dissertations are original as students write in their own way, include their own analysis, and present their own findings. Gill and Dolan (2015, 11) write, "The concept of originality is commonly associated with something truly novel or unique." However, in IR, over the past decade or so, there have been a number of popular topics relating to 9/11, EU politics, US foreign policy, the rise of China, and the financial crisis of 2008. Originality is important (and better grades usually follow), and it evinces the student as a knowledge creator. The supervisor should encourage as much originality as possible in terms of subject matter, use of theory, research, and reading. Originality can be discerned in a number of ways: if the topic is new, if a new theory is being used, if the research involves the gathering of new information, if new interpretations are offered on an old topic, or if a new concept or idea emerges from the study (Gill and Dolan 2015, 12). There are various ways in which a supervisor can encourage originality, and this is done in conjunction with the student. By incorporating different layers or components into the dissertation, originality can be developed. For example, one student wanted to explore the intelligence capabilities of small states. A discussion was held in which possible case studies were mentioned, theories were suggested, and some practical issues were raised. It was agreed that a comparison between Israeli and Cuban intelligence would be feasible partly because of the amount of literature on each case. It was suggested that game theory might be an interesting approach as the student had not looked at this before, and the student was able to interview another member of staff whose main research involved Cuba. During the research, the student also identified "prospect theory" (a theory of economic behavior), and this was incorporated into the analysis. In addition, small state perspectives added another dimension to the study. These various components (theories, comparative case studies, qualitative research, and literature review) cumulatively created an original piece of dissertation research. Throughout the term, the student consulted the supervisor, and an ongoing exchange of ideas were expressed.

Anecdote 3: At one university I was asked to supervise a dissertation on "reform of the UN Security Council" (an important and interesting topic). The following year, I was asked to do this again. On the second occasion, the student involved was from Ireland, and I suggested a slight variation: what is the Irish position about UN Security Council reform? This would have been a (slightly) more original topic at a British university.

A second example involves a student who wanted to study the problem of Somali piracy off the East coast of Africa. The subject was both topical and important. The Copenhagen School approach, and especially the "five types of security" (Buzan 1991) was suggested as a theoretical lens for the study; this also helped the structure of the dissertation. The student identified a law lecturer in another university, who was an expert in maritime law, and a group of Somalis living in the area. The student was able to carry out interviews with the expert and a Somali person, which focused on the piracy issue. The combination of original interviews, literature, theory, and a focus on the piracy issue resulted in an original piece of research. Again, these different elements combined to create an interesting and original dissertation.

A third example in which originality was found came through an initial discussion about the dissertation. The student wanted to explore the concept of "soft power" as expressed by Joseph Nye (2004) in IR. The student had carried out a brief literature search and, in this discussion, mentioned the Jimmy Carter Library. As supervisor, the author asked if this was possibly a source of US soft power. The student used this idea in the subsequent research, which included two interviews using Skype. In an extended literature review, the student found that no one had ever written about US Presidential foundations as a source of US soft power before; this constituted an original piece of research. The two-way dialogue between supervisor and student can encourage original thinking and original research outcomes.[5]

Anecdote 4: One student was studying the accountability of British intelligence agencies and he wanted to carry out an interview(s). The nature of the topic meant this was problematic, but the author suggested that a possible interviewee could be the local MP. An interview was carried out and this was both informative and original. While an MP might not be an "expert," they will have opinions that can be of interest.

Conclusions

Researching and writing a dissertation is a form of active learning that transforms the student from a consumer of knowledge to a creator of knowledge. It also demonstrates that the student follows a signature pedagogy of IR. The supervisor, in this context, becomes a conduit to this learning process. Supervising involves imparting knowledge and instilling the student into the culture of IR as an academic discipline. In crude terms, supervision is somewhat akin to an indoctrination process. By creating a two-way dialogue and acting in a collegial way, the supervisor can encourage good research by the student. The supervision process involves a *surface structure* in which the supervisor sets out many aspects of the dissertation, a *deep structure* in which thinking like an IR scholar is encouraged, and an *implicit structure* in which the attitudes and dispositions of IR are imparted to the student (Shulman 2005). The student should be active and enthusiastic about the research, and should be as professional as possible.

Using anecdotes, based on personal experiences throughout this chapter, highlights good practices and how a dialogue with the student can foster originality in undergraduate dissertations involving IR. The efficacy of good supervision following the signature pedagogy of IR becomes a rite of passage for the undergraduate. Moreover, the inclusion of appropriate IR theories coupled with original research, such as interviews, can foster better (and more interesting) dissertations. Supervising undergraduate dissertations can also be pedagogically and intellectually rewarding for the supervisor, especially when the students get good grades as a result.

References

Aronson, Jeffrey K. 2003. "Editorials: Anecdotes as Evidence" *British Medical Journal (BMJ)* 326, 1346.

---

[5]   In each of these three examples, the dissertations each got a first in their grade.

Buzan, Barry. 1991 (First edition). *People, States and Fears.* Hemel Hempstead: Harvester Wheatsheaf.

Gibbs, Graham and Habeshaw, Trevor. 2011. "Preparing to Teach." Creative Commons. Accessed July 2020. https://www.scribd.com/document/245250244/Preparing-to-Teach

Gill, P. and Dolan G. 2015. "Originality and the PhD: What Is It and How Can it be Demonstrated?" *Nurse Researcher,* 22:6, 11–15.

Greenbank, Paul and Penketh, Claire. 2009. "Student Autonomy and Reflections and Writing the Undergraduate Dissertation." *Journal of Further and Higher Education,* 33:4, 463–472.

Harris, Clodagh. 2012. "Expanding Political Science's Signature Pedagogy: The Case for Service Learning." *European Political Science,* 11, 175–185.

Jimmy Carter Library 2020. Accessed July 2020. https://www.jimmycarterlibrary.gov/.

Marsden, Lee and Savigny, Heather. 2012. "The Importance of Being Theoretical: Analyzing Contemporary Politics" in *Teaching Politics and International Relations*, edited by Cathy Gormley-Heenan and Simon Lightfoot, 123–131. Basingstoke: Palgrave.

Nye, Joseph. 2004. *Soft Power: The Means to Success In World Politics.* New York: Public Affairs.

Shulman, Lee S. 2005. "Signature Pedagogies in the Professions." *Dædalus* 134 (Summer), 52–59.

Sutch, Peter and Elias, Juanita. 2007. *International Relations: The Basics.* London and New York: Routledge.

Todd, Malcolm J., Smith, Karen and Bannister, Phil. 2006. "Supervising a Social Science Undergraduate Dissertation: Staff Experiences and Perceptions." *Teaching in Higher Education,* 11:2, 161–173.

Roulston, Carmel. 2012. "Supervising a Doctoral Student" in *Teaching Politics and International Relations*, edited by Cathy Gormley-Heenan and Simon Lightfoot. 210–225. Basingstoke: Palgrave.

Woolhouse, Marian. 2010. "Supervising Dissertation Projects: Expectations of Supervisors and Students." *Innovations in Education and Teaching International,* 39:2, 137–144.

11

Teaching and Learning International Relations Professional Skills Through Simulations

PATRICIA CAPELINI BORELLI, PATRÍCIA NOGUEIRA RINALDI, ROBERTA SILVA MACHADO AND TALITA DE MELLO PINOTTI

The field of International Relations (IR) attracts students who are interested in understanding global problems and are willing to make a difference in the world. However, newcomers to the field have many doubts regarding their careers and what exactly they can do with an IR degree. These doubts are understandable because IR is not a discipline "in the occupational-career sense" (Jackson 2018, 334), which means it is not directly associated with a specific professional path. IR experts can exercise different jobs in a broad range of segments, such as public and private sectors, international organizations (IOs), academia, and non-profit organizations. This is why an education in IR must entail not only a theoretical but also a practical dimension. There is a consensus in the literature on IR pedagogies about the importance of incorporating professional training in the curriculum so students can turn into practitioners equipped with the most important skills required to perform any job: analytical and critical thinking, active learning, creative problem-solving, leadership, and emotional intelligence (World Economic Forum 2018, 12).

This chapter explores the use of simulations as an effective tool to develop such professional skills and considers them a fundamental part of IR signature pedagogies. There are examples in the literature attesting that simulations positively contribute to the formation of IR students and, in this chapter, we advance this debate by arguing that simulations themselves can be professional experiences. If planned and structured with this objective in mind, simulations can develop professional skills as a desired outcome, not as a mere side-effect. Drawing from our knowledge in implementing FACAMP Model United Nations (FAMUN)—a simulation project composed by a discipline and a conference organized by *Faculdades de Campinas* (FACAMP), a private Brazilian university—we demonstrate how simulations can build students' capacity in essential dimensions of IR career performance. In this chapter, we incorporate the views and perceptions of the students who attended the discipline in 2019 and 2020. Twenty-six students responded to an online survey (from 1 to 4 December 2020), which comprised six questions that evaluated the skills developed during the project. The form was anonymous, and students could add extra comments or suggestions in the last question.

The first section of this chapter analyzes the use of simulations to teach and learn professional skills, as part of our signature pedagogy in the IR field. Section two addresses a specific format of simulations, namely Model United Nations (MUNs), and their potential to develop professional abilities. The third section focuses on how our signature pedagogy is embedded in FAMUN, which makes the simulation not only an experiential learning activity but intentionally also a professional experience. In the conclusion, we underscore the importance of adopting simulations as part of a signature pedagogy in the field of IR more broadly.

IR Signature Pedagogy and Simulations

The debate on signature pedagogies offers a fruitful perspective on how to incorporate the teaching and learning of professional skills in IR education through simulations. Shulman (2005, 59) argues that a signature pedagogy is responsible for educating future practitioners into the "three fundamental dimensions of professional work—to think, to perform, and to act with integrity." The importance of a signature pedagogy is that it entails the deliberative effort to provide students with a broad set of abilities to be good professionals in a determined area (Ciccone 2009, xv).

Shulman (2005, 54–55) defines three structures of a signature pedagogy: the surface, the deep, and the implicit structures. In the IR field, the surface structure involves the way IR teaching and learning are operationalized, and the literature emphasizes the use of approaches that go beyond the lecture-seminar style. Student-centered active learning lies at the core of our signature pedagogy in IR because professionals in the field are asked to connect different perspectives and propose concrete solutions to specific global problems. The deep structure addresses the way knowledge is approached in IR education. Bartell and Vespia (2009, 139, 141), when discussing signature pedagogies in human development, affirm that such pedagogies are more challenging—and exciting—for interdisciplinary areas because there is not a unified perspective on how knowledge is transmitted. This is also the case for our IR signature pedagogy because interdisciplinarity characterizes the way IR professionals impart their knowledge, regardless of their job or occupation. The implicit structure relates to the principles, values, and moral dimension of the teaching and learning processes. From our perspective, the IR field encompasses building a professional character based on global citizenship, collaboration, responsibility, and empathy for others.

Considering these structures, the literature highlights the importance of experiential learning tools for the development of professional skills in IR. Lewis and Williams (1994, 15) show that when students engage in learning by doing, they acquire "a repertoire of attitudes, skills, and understandings that allow them to become more effective, flexible, and self-organized learners in a variety of contexts," which is crucial to the formation of an IR expert. Simulations are experiential activities based on active learning and have become increasingly popular in the IR courses. They replicate the reality of a given institutional setting, which is translated into specific rules of procedure and decision-making processes. The most common simulations reproduce the structure of international organizations, such as the United Nations, the African Union, the European Union, etc. But there are also simulations of governmental organizations, such as Congresses, Parliaments, Ministerial Cabinets, and Councils.

Drawing from Shulman's (2005, 59) three dimensions of professional work, the literature is consensual about the positive effects of simulations for IR students. Firstly, simulations address the intellectual dimension of IR professional work through problem-based learning. Students mobilize concepts and theories to comprehend the nature of cases of the international agenda. Asal and Blake (2006, 2) argue that simulations allow students to understand "the subtleties of theories and concepts" in a more engaging way, improving content retention in comparison to traditional class discussions. Besides, simulations are research-engaged activities, so students have to ground their performance in factual content (Obendorf and Randerson 2012, 4). Students prepare statements and position papers that express the perspective of their specific roles, which improves both their research abilities and critical thinking.

Regarding the technical dimension of IR professional work, students practice their professional behavior during simulations (Simpson and Kaussler 2009,

423). Participants can assume the role of Heads of State and Government, Ministers, diplomats, or other representatives from countries or organizations. They keep their own personalities and have autonomy over their decisions, but they do so while performing the functional role of decision-makers "with the power and authority of professionals who are trying to cope with a developing situation" (Jones 1995, 12–13). As in a professional setting, they learn how to address international issues as experts, under a predefined time frame.

In simulations, participants are required to act based on ethical and responsible behavior, fostering the moral dimension of IR professional work. Obendorf and Randerson (2012, 9) emphasize that simulations are a platform to encourage students' voice, educating them to address different points of view and listen to others with empathy. Students learn through simulations that integrative solutions are the best option, dealing with problems as a common challenge instead of a competition (Simpson and Kaussler 2009, 421). Given that simulations are grounded in the real world, "it is the environment that is simulated... but the behavior is real" (Jones 1995, 7). Students progressively incorporate the attitudes of an IR professional because simulations raise their awareness of what they already know about IR, what they want to know about the field, and what they have learned during this experiential activity.

MUNs as Pedagogical Tools

One of the most popular formats of simulations is a MUN, in which participants (delegates) play the role of diplomats in a UN organ or venue, and they debate current international topics and follow specific rules of procedure (McIntosh 2001, 270–271). The origin of MUNs precedes the creation of the very UN (1945). There are records of MUN simulations since 1943, when non-governmental organizations (NGOs) and universities in the United States simulated the negotiations among 26 countries that signed the "Declaration of the United Nations," a document that sealed the commitment to fight the Axis in World War II (National Model United Nations 2020).

MUNs can provide various benefits as an IR practice. First, there is an agreement in the literature on the advantages of using a student-centered approach that combines the academic demands with professional practices (Obendorf and Randerson 2012, 3). Shaw and Switky (2018, 5–6) explain that, in this case, faculties need to set out their learning objectives when preparing a MUN simulation. For instance, they can focus the activity on content—to understand a specific international topic—or on the process—to understand possible scenarios and outcomes during a negotiation. Second, students actively engage in research: the research process for a MUN involves not only the collection of information about different international topics, but also about a country's foreign policy. In this sense, students expand their sources of research; besides textbooks and academic papers, they research UN documents and reports, official databases, and diplomatic documents (Crossley-Frolick 2010, 189). As a result, they acquire refined research skills and become familiar with research sources that will be part of their professional routine. Third, Obendorf and Randerson (2013, 351) explain that students are involved in drafting supporting materials, such as study handbooks and rules of procedure. These have specific formats and language, helping them to improve writing skills and vocabulary required in IO careers. Also, since they need to understand the procedure of organizations in order to write the rules' manual, students also develop a keen understanding of the dynamics of multilateral negotiations. Fourth, the organization of a MUN conference involves practical and logistical aspects, meaning that students will develop abilities on how to plan and implement projects, which otherwise may not be acquired during their undergraduate path since many IR courses are so focused on teaching content that they fail to notice the importance of learning such practical skills (Lüdert and Stewart 2017).

Still, MUNs have also been subjected to some strong criticism towards their relevance in teaching IR content. The first simulations, organized by NGOs and universities in the United States and Europe, created the rules of procedure for MUNs based on the decision-making processes of American and European national legislative bodies, which are basically voting systems. However, this use of parliamentary rules fails in portraying the real UN and does not achieve the goal of imparting IR content because, in the UN, voting is used as a means of last resort. In the UN General Assembly (UNGA), for instance, in the last decades, states have made an effort to adopt resolutions by consensus (approximately 80% of the time) instead of by vote (United Nations 2020a). Considering the variety of agenda items within the UNGA, consensus entails complex negotiations, not only among states, but also among different political groups, which makes the decision-making process more inclusive and collaborative, a reality that is not captured by MUNs based on parliamentary rules. Another issue of voting systems used in parliamentary rules is that they create a competitive environment among students aiming to prove *who is the strongest/most dominant*. In fact, many students complain that MUNs are more centered on competition than cooperation and fail to portray real UN procedures (Parrin 2013). These are some of the issues discouraging professors to consider simulations as an effective pedagogical tool.

The UN addressed this shortcoming only at the end of the 2000s by becoming more supportive and seeking to translate actual UN rules and procedures into MUNs. First developed within the UN Department of Global Communications, as the project UN4MUN (United Nations 2020b), the initiative was further advanced by NGOs, such as the World Federation of the United Nations Associations (WFUNA). WFUNA annually hosts WFUNA International Model United Nations (WIMUN), a flagship conference that offers participants an approach that draws from the project UN4MUN and is more accurate in terms of replicating the decision-making process of the UN (World Federation of United Nations Associations 2020). With an emphasis on consensus, students learn how to negotiate, aiming at collaborative decisions instead of pushing for majorities, minimizing simplistic zero-sum mentalities. Consequently, negotiations take longer, but once decisions are reached, they are more legitimate and express more robust compromise positions by stakeholders.

Interestingly, by bringing the rules of procedure of MUNs closer to the real dynamics of the UN, it is possible to enhance the potential that such simulations have in teaching IR students how to think, perform and act with responsibility as professionals. In order to achieve this goal, we suggest that educators need to combine approaches developed by the UN and WFUNA with activities and exercises that build students' fundamental characteristics as IR experts. While most MUNs are developed to teach IR content and negotiation, gaining additional professional skills, we argue that it becomes possible to conceive of MUNs as a pedagogical approach within an applied IR signature pedagogy.

Designing MUNs for an IR Signature Pedagogy

FAMUN is a distinctive MUN project designed to teach diplomacy, negotiation, global governance, and especially the role and relevance of the UN system, while developing a range of professional IR skills. Since 2013, FAMUN has been one of the core activities of the Bachelor's degree in IR offered by FACAMP. It consists of an eight months-long course in which 25 pre-selected IR students are trained to host an annual conference in September. While the discipline only enrolls FACAMP IR students, the conference is open to university and high school students, who simulate eight to ten UN organs and entities, totaling around 400–500 participants.[1] In partnership with WFUNA, FAMUN adopts the WIMUN approach, which is fundamental for guaranteeing the accuracy of the simulation.

The project is based on team teaching with the presence of four professors that—although all IR graduates—share different research backgrounds. While planning the project, we as professors design interdisciplinary activities targ-

---

[1]   For more information, please check the official website: www.famun.com.br

eted at fostering professional abilities, which can be seen as corresponding to the three structures of a signature pedagogy. As characteristic of the surface structure, we apply different teaching methods, namely student-centered active learning, problem-based learning by scaffolding, and application method. The very first task is to select the team of IR students, enrolled in different semesters, that will organize and conduct the conference, assuming a professional commitment. The Secretariat is entirely composed by students, who are encouraged to apply for different positions. The selection process is conducted by the instructors considering the students' profiles and interest areas. In this sense, undergraduates experiment with how to apply for a job position during their degree program. Some students, when asked to add extra comments to the survey given at the end of the discipline, even mentioned that they considered FAMUN to be their "first truly professional experience."

Following the UN structure, one student plays the role of Secretary-General, being responsible for monitoring the work of all areas and dealing with the politics of conference preparation. The interaction between more and less experienced students is paramount in this process. The latter usually assume the position of UN officials to work as mediators in the simulations, while the former occupy Secretariat positions that are directly related to the organization of the conference, separated in three main areas: academic, logistics, and communications.

Once the team is selected, they are assigned with research tasks to define the conference theme and the topics of the simulations, which draw from the real UN agenda and campaigns. We, as professors, are responsible for choosing the organs and entities that will be simulated, but the students are responsible for doing research and choosing the topics. For example, in 2019, the conference theme was "Living Together in Peace," and some of the topics discussed were "Harmony with Nature" and "Women, Peace, and Security." In 2020, the conference theme was "Be the Change: Shaping our Future Together" and among the topics selected were "The Situation in Burundi" and "Human Rights and Climate Change." In smaller groups, students write a paper and a report about the topics chosen. The material is then published as an e-book to be used as a study guide for the participants of the conference. In the survey, 25 out of 26 students affirmed that their research abilities greatly improved through these activities. This is an example of how to engage the students in an active learning process under the mentorship and facilitation of the professors.

Our role as professors is to assist and support the team during the preparation process. Through different activities, we offer the intellectual tools with which students can accomplish the tasks that will familiarize them with the theoretical approach to diplomacy, the UN system, and its rules of procedure. This scaffolding strategy is necessary to equalize the knowledge among students from different semesters. We also introduce an application method (Bartell and Vespia 2009, 148): practical activities to develop skills required both for simulations and students' professional careers. One example is public speaking exercises with a perspective-taking approach: first, students watch videos of statements from political leaders; then, they are asked to identify any fallacies in the speeches and point out what drew their attention or distracted them. This type of brainstorming fosters critical thinking and reflections on how to write and deliver an effective and persuasive speech. Students are later encouraged to put these considerations into practice, preparing short statements to address the class. Noteworthy is that due to the previous activity, they are able to correct themselves when realizing they made the same mistakes of the videos they watched before.

Considering that FAMUN students are not native English speakers, our approach emphasizes effective English pronunciation drills that focus on practicing words commonly used in simulations. These are prepared as collaborative games, so students can help each other, avoiding a competitive atmosphere among them. Practicing helps them to improve their fluency and confidence with a foreign language, something that will be expected from them as IR professionals. When responding the survey, 20 out of the 26 respondents affirmed that these activities highly contributed to improving their command of English.

FAMUN also aims to ensure that students internalize IR practices, which is paramount to the deep structure. To this end, it is important to instruct undergraduates in how to perform as real stakeholders in a decision-making process. During in-class simulations, the professors offer a two-week intensive training so that students can learn—in practice—the rules of procedure. Following the WFUNA's approach, consensus plays a central role because it avoids the "who is the strongest" mentality, since students are encouraged to find common ground to make decisions. Thus, they learn how to listen and negotiate their interests amongst each other. They are not only encouraged to look for win-win solutions, but also learn how to do it, how to think in a way that is conducive to building compromise positions or reaching consensus across differences. Interestingly, once they learn the process, they can apply consensus-building techniques while solving issues in other environments. When responding the survey, 23 out of 26 students affirmed that they developed the skill of applying consensus-building to daily problem-solving.

Consensus requires students to prepare their negotiation strategy in advance. First, they identify their country position and list their interests; second, they are tasked with prioritizing some points over others: to choose their red lines, which are non-negotiable, as well as their middle and low priorities. Hence, they understand which of their positions can be loosened during negotiations to achieve consensus. In our survey, 73 percent of the students considered that this activity highly contributed to their skill in identifying priorities in a negotiation.

The decision-making process also includes different political and regional groups that, in specific moments, are the main subjects of the negotiation. This mirrors the dynamics of the UN through which countries regularly rely on groups to advance negotiations on their behalf. Students need to interact simultaneously across multiple levels of negotiation: with their respective group and with the whole group. They are motivated to take their decisions considering that they should be accountable to their national interests and also to their peers. The lesson is to build collective strategies and routinely engage in exchanges with a great diversity of stakeholders.

Students playing the roles of Secretariat members and officials learn to identify common grounds amidst concurring interests. As mediators, officials play a significant role in building consensus by helping delegates prioritize issues in which less bargaining is needed and where the negotiation can advance easily. This creates a positive environment leading into more controversial items later on in the negotiation process. Mediators are taught to listen to the different positions and to look for overlapping ideas aiming at consensus. After routinely practicing active listening and appreciating various perspectives, students master key skills for IR professions.

IR experts are typically focused on how to adequately express their ideas, especially when confronted with multicultural environments. Hence, another central exercise is for students to understand the substance of the documents they are negotiating. Usually, the focal point of MUNs lies in the bargaining process rather than in the decision itself. But, in FAMUN, students also learn how to analyze and understand the language of the documents they are approving. Some classes are dedicated to present students with the verbs and expressions used in UN resolutions and the specific meanings of agreed language. Then, undergraduates are encouraged to reflect on them and question the reasons for choosing specific wordings. This is especially useful for understanding the particularities of IR negotiations, and the relevance of thinking about the specificity and importance of precise language used in official UN documents.

Considering that FAMUN deals with IR students, abiding by UN procedures creates a near-real experience that helps them to better understand how the institution works and provides professional training for those who want to follow a career in multilateral entities. That is why instructors should not assume leadership roles in the simulation. Especially in curricular MUNs, it is common that professors play the role of officials or the Secretariat in order to guarantee the rules of procedure or the equality of participation among students (Engel, Pallas and Lambert 2017, 5; Obendorf and Randerson 2013, 357). But in FAMUN, students have full autonomy to conduct the debates and rely on professors' support and guidance to solve doubts and master procedures. This is an aspect that characterizes our signature pedagogy when, as Shulman (2005, 57) noted "[s]tudents are accountable not only to teachers, but also to peers in their responses, arguments, commentaries, and presentation of new data."

Other than that, FAMUN presents insights into how this methodology comprehends the implicit structure. First, by putting students in the role of decision-makers and creating space for them to own their learning experience, simulations create an atmosphere of uncertainty that challenges the students to engage in active performance. When supported to embrace their choices and make their decisions based on their own strategy, students develop a greater sense of responsibility. Second, simulations enhance autonomy and self-confidence, and foster meaningful participation of students in political processes. Noteworthy is that consensus is key: challenged to find collective answers for common problems, students need to consider their counterparts' perspectives and dedicate themselves to understand the very logic sustaining the concurring position, while exercising critical thinking and reflexivity (Bartell and Vespia 2009, 144). Students are encouraged to put themselves in someone else's shoes, developing a sense of empathy and understanding, which is indispensable to cross-cultural communication.

Third, FAMUN fosters peer-to-peer teaching, teamwork, and the development of professional networks by bringing together students from different stages of the undergraduate course. When more advanced students interact with newcomers, an enriching experience-sharing takes place that motivates students to learn from their peers and strive for a career within FAMUN. It is different from Crossley-Frolick's (2010, 194) observation that a "simulation is best run in a class with predominantly advanced students." Although more advanced students tend to centralize the discussions, in FAMUN, we notice that mixing students from different levels does not constrain the learning process of younger students, as they usually consider older students as role-models. As highlighted by Lüdert and Steward (2017), a diverse team in terms of interests and levels of experience is crucial to the learning process, since students are encouraged to have different perspectives and to collaborate among themselves to reach a common goal. Fourth, FAMUN creates an environment of affective empathy (Lüdert and Stewart 2017), in which students dedicate not only their time and work to the project but are emotionally invested and feel passionate about it. When responding the feedback survey, one of our students mentioned the following: "FAMUN awakened my personal, academic, and professional development. If I could, I would be a part of it until my senior year at university and I am sure I would still have new content to learn." Finally, we also noticed that this process fosters political engagement: as students are dedicated to conduct a long-term research project about global issues, they develop critical thinking and a keen interest in politics, becoming more sensitive to the potential of their agency as youth. These are desirable outcomes of simulations and deep learning, and are extremely valuable for future IR professionals (Hammond and Albert 2019, 3). As a central part of our signature pedagogy, FAMUN develops "the habits of the mind" by teaching students to master IR thinking. It also fosters "the habits of the hand" by immersing students in a near-real UN decision-making environment. It works for the "habits of the heart," as students stand up for values and attitudes that are key to be a responsible professional, regardless of the career they choose.

Conclusion

IR is not directly associated with a specific professional orientation, and students must have a broader formation, based on skills that can be applied in different professional settings. Departing from this assumption, the chapter revisited some aspects of the literature on the use of simulations as experiential teaching and learning tools that can develop and improve IR professional skills. We advanced the debate, showing that simulations can offer a professional performance as a desired outcome, rather than a side-effect. To this end, professors need to consciously plan and structure activities aiming at the targeted abilities. This chapter demonstrated that simulations, as a practice of IR education, are more than pedagogical tools; they are a real part of a signature pedagogy in the field. We presented our experience with FAMUN, a bold academic project that involves a long period of preparation and requires students to have an active participation in all aspects of the process. Responsibilities towards the project are equally shared among students, and they learn how to deal with uncertainties and address issues with empathy in a collective effort. There is a real sense of ownership, as they are responsible for the outcomes. Furthermore, by applying accurate procedures and selecting a decision-making process based on the reality of multilateral environments, FAMUN fosters multiple abilities. Students learn how to prepare and prioritize their negotiation strategy, to interact with stakeholders, to identify consensual positions, and to better express their ideas using meaningful language, which grants them a truly professional experience while in university. In sum, when simulations are conceived as part of an IR signature pedagogy, they can build a professional character based on autonomy, collaboration, responsibility, and empathy, which are key values to IR experts.

References

Asal, Victor and Elizabeth L. Blake. 2006. "Creating Simulations for Political Science Education", *Journal of Political Science Education*, 2:1, 1–18.

Bartell, Denise S. and Kristin M. Vespia. 2009. "Teaching and learning in the 'interdisciplinary discipline' of human development". In: *Exploring signature pedagogies: Approaches to teaching disciplinary habits of mind.* edited by Reagan A. R. Gurung et al., 139–160. Sterning, Virginia: Stylus Publishing.

Ciccone, Anthony A. 2009. "Foreword". In: *Exploring signature pedagogies: Approaches to teaching disciplinary habits of mind.* edited by Reagan A. R. Gurung et al., xi-xvi. Sterning, Virginia: Stylus Publishing.

Crossley-Frolick, Katy A. 2010. "Beyond Model UN: Simulating Multi-Level, Multi-Actor Diplomacy Using the Millennium Development Goals", *International Studies Perspectives*, 11, 184–201.

Engel, Susan, Josh Pallas and Sarah Lambert. 2017. "Model United Nations and deep learning: theoretical and professional learning", *Journal of Political Science Education,* 13 (2), 1–14.

Hammond, Augustine and Craig Douglas Albert. 2019. "Learning by Experiencing: Improving Student Learning Through a Model United Nations Simulation", *Journal of Political Science Education,* 1–18.

Jackson, Patrick Thaddeus. 2018. "'Does It Matter if It's a Discipline?' Bawled the Child". In: *The SAGE Handbook of the History, Philosophy and Sociology of International Relations*, edited by Andreas Gofas et al., 326–339. London: Sage Publications.

Jones, Ken. 1995. *Simulations: A handbook for teachers and trainers*. 3rd edition. London: Kogan Page.

Lewis, Linda H. and Carol J. Williams. 1994. "Experiential learning: Past and present". *New Directions for Adult and Continuing Education*, 62 (Summer): 5–16.

Lüdert, Jan and Katriona Stewart. 2017. *Nurturing Cognitive and Affective Empathy: The Benefits of Perspective-Taking*. E-International Relations, 19 November. Accessed 03 December 2020. https://www.e-ir.info/2017/11/19/ nurturing-cognitive-and-affective-empathy-the-benefits-of-perspective-taking/

McIntosh, Daniel. 2001. "The Uses and Limits of the Model United Nations in an International Relations Classroom", *International Studies Perspectives*, 2, 269-280.

National Model United Nations. 2020. *Historical Timeline of the NMUN Conferences 1927-69*. Last modified May 2020. https://www.nmun.org/assets/ documents/about-nmun/mission-and-history/history-timeline- conference-1927-69.pdf

Obendorf, Simon and Claire Randerson. 2012. "The Model United Nations simulation and the student as a producer agenda", *Enhancing Learning in the Social Sciences*, 4:3, 1–15.

Obendorf, Simon and Claire Randerson. 2013. "Evaluating the Model United Nations: Diplomatic simulations as assessed undergraduate coursework", *European Political Science*, 12, 350–364.

Parrin, Anjli. 2013. "The Dog-Eat-Dog World of Model U.N". *New York Times*, August 02, 2013. https://www.nytimes.com/2013/08/04/education/ edlife/a-new-student-run-breed-crisis-oriented-and-fiercely-competitive. html?auth=login-google

Shulman, Lee S. 2005. "Signature pedagogies in the professions". *Daedalus*, 134(3) (Summer): 52–59.

Shaw, Carolyn M. and Bob Switky. 2018. "Designing and Using Simulations in the International Relations Classroom", *Journal of Political Science Education*, 1–12.

Simpson, Archie and Bernd Kaussler. 2009. "IR Teaching Reloaded: Using Films and Simulations in the Teaching of International Relations", *International Studies Perspectives*, 10, 413–427.

United Nations. 2020 a. "How Decisions are Made at the UN". Model United Nations. Accessed 2 December 2020. https://www.un.org/en/model-united- nations/how-decisions-are-made-un

United Nations. 2020 b. "Model UN Guide". Model United Nations. Accessed 28 September, 2020. https://www.un.org/en/mun/model-un-guide

World Federation of United Nations Associations. 2020. "The WIMUN Advantage". WFUNA International Model United Nations. Accessed 28 September, 2020 https://wfuna.org/wimun/advantage

World Economic Forum. 2018. *The Future of Jobs Report.* Cologny/Geneva: World Economic Forum, Centre for the New Economy and Society.

12

Teaching IR Through Short Iterated Simulations: A Sequenced Approach for IR Courses

XIAOYE SHE

International Relations (IR) as a field has long traditions of employing simulations for both practitioners and educational audiences (Starkey and Blake 2001). Simulations help students deepen their understanding of relevant IR concepts and theories (Ellington et al. 1998; Asal 2005). For introductory IR classes, the primary challenge is that time and resources are limited. As a result, instructors need to carefully balance between lecture content and active learning components. As Wakelee (2008) points out, it is sometimes not feasible to spend substantial course time conducting elaborately constructed, in-depth simulations, such as Model United Nations (MUN) simulations. Drawing on Asal and Blake (2006), and as part of my IR signature pedagogy, I suggest that students in an introductory IR class can benefit from a sequenced approach of short simulations that requires little prior knowledge. Rather than treating simulations as stand-alone exercises, it is possible to create short-duration United Nations (UN) simulations and integrate them as a semester-long active learning sequence.

Prior to the simulations, the instructor can lecture on the differences between the United Nations Security Council (UNSC) and the United Nations General Assembly (UNGA) in terms of their decision-making structure, processes, and the nature of resolutions. No matter which simulation structure the instructor chooses, this allows the instructor to review these differences during debriefing and discuss potential alternative scenarios. Once the simulation structure is determined, students begin the simulation sequence with a mock simulation based on the hypothesized scenario of a zombie pandemic (Michelsen 2010; Horn et al. 2016; Fischer 2019). The goal is to involve students in a low-stakes preparation activity to get familiar with the basic structure and flow of the simulation. This ungraded mock simulation therefore helps students build foundational literacy in UN simulations and greatly reduces their anxiety when the graded simulations based on real-world scenarios occur later in the semester.

The graded simulations focus on each main subfield in IR, namely international security, international political economy, as well as transnational issues and global governance. To ensure student engagement and preparedness, the instructor creates a list of potential simulation topics at the beginning of the semester and asks students to vote on their favorite topics. Students are also introduced to two mobile apps, UNdata and MUN, which allow them to do basic research on their country positions and learn how to draft preambulatory and operative clauses and resolutions.

The quality of each simulation session depends on a few key factors. First, in order to help students quickly immerse themselves into the simulation environment, the instructor can adapt the idea of "immerse theater" developed by Dacombe and Morrow (2017) and create a sense of formality through use of diplomatic and formal language, rearrangement of the classroom space, and adding a short opening ceremony to each simulation. The instructor can provide more structured guidance in earlier iterations, and gradually allow students to operate the simulation without too much intervention. During the debriefing stage, the instructor can consider using some combinations of written and oral debriefing, a follow-up theory exercise, and self-and peer-evaluations to help students to connect the simulation experience with content learning, personal growth, and simulation design feedback. While the decision-making structure of the UN is fixed in reality and can be cumbersome and frustrating, rules can be more flexible in the simulation setting. Once students get familiar with the formal rules in earlier iterations and are exposed to real-world UN reform proposals, they are encouraged to experiment with rule and procedural changes through a voting process and then examine the significant differences in simulation outcomes.

The rest of the chapter is divided as follows. Following a brief review on the simulation literature in IR, I will discuss the deep and implicit structures behind the integrated and sequenced approach for simulations. To demonstrate how simulations as a signature pedagogy work, I will discuss the surface structure of simulations by outlining challenges and strategies in each stage of preparation, simulation in action, as well as debriefing, reflection, and assessment. The chapter will conclude with critical reflections on certain limitations and future directions for improvements of this teaching approach.

Simulation as IR Signature Pedagogy

IR as a field increasingly emphasizes active, cooperative or collaborative, and problem-based learning (PBL) (Lamy 2007; Sharan 2010; Baker & Clark 2010; Burch 2000). As a popular pedagogy tool, simulations in IR take a variety of forms, ranging from formal, cross-institutional or semester-long Model United Nations (MUN), to computer-assisted simulations inside and outside of classroom, to embedded short simulations in introductory and upper-division IR courses (Engel et al. 2017; Hammond and Albert 2019; Horn et al. 2016; Leib and Ruppel 2020; McCarthy 2014; McIntosh 2001; Wheeler 2006; Boyer 2011).

Simulations have therefore become an integral part of signature pedagogies in IR. Lüdert (2020) argues that signature pedagogies share three key characteristics of surface structure, deep structure, and implicit structure. For simulations, the surface structure is often divided into distinctive stages of teaching and learning. The instructor takes a leading role in helping students prepare, observes and intervenes when students play in action, and finally helps students reflect on their simulation experience through oral and written debriefing (Asal and Blake 2006). Taylor (2013) identifies different styles of learning opportunities in simulations, including content learning, theoretical learning, and experiential learning. According to Taylor (2013, 148), there is "no one-size-fit-all prescription" and, when resources allow, the more diverse the simulation experience, the better.

Using simulations as a signature pedagogy involves prioritizing certain teaching and learning approaches. Simulations are often based on deep and implicit structures that highlight active, problem-based, and often student-centered learning to teach IR theories and subject matter. When incorporating simulations into their classes, instructors need to make hard choices between simulation content and lectures (McIntosh 2001). Asal and Kratoville (2013) underline the connections between two pedagogy theories, constructivist learning theory and PBL, and the use of simulations in IR classes. A few others have highlighted opportunities for student ownership, research-based learning, and deep learning through the usage of real-world scenarios, fictional stories, or both (Engel 2017; Obendorf and Randerson 2013; Fischer 2019). Applying this pedagogical tradition, the simulations I developed help create space for student-centered learning in an introductory IR class that used to be mainly lecture-based.

With proper design, simulations can help connect abstract theories with complex empirics on the ground. They also provide avenues for recursive processes that help students grasp threshold concepts, which are "conceptual gateways" or "portals" that must be negotiated to arrive at new, transformative knowledge (Meyer et al. 2008; Lüdert 2019). To convey the concepts of anarchy, cooperation, and conflict, Young (2006) and McCarthy (2014), for instance, created games and simulations based on Putnam's "Two-Level Games." Through a simulation in Middle Eastern politics, Sasley (2010, 67–68) demonstrates how simulations can teach students about "miscommun-ication, misunderstandings, misperceptions," as well as failure and complexity in global politics.

This chapter proposes a similar strategy to integrate simulations into introductory IR classes. Drawing on Asal and Blake (2006), I suggest that students of introductory IR can benefit from a sequence of short simulations that allows scaffolding of both content knowledge and transferrable skills over the course of the semester. To achieve these goals, I argue it is essential to have a constant yet flexible structure for the simulations, with iterations across subject matter and varying rules. The following sections provide an overview of this approach, as well as concrete strategies to implement short, simplified UN simulations in an introductory or survey IR class.

Integrating UN Simulations into Introductory or Survey IR Courses

An introductory or survey IR class is an important steppingstone for students to learn about how politics work on the global stage, no matter if the student is a political science major or not. Introductory or survey IR classes can serve multiple purposes, including, but not limited to, preparing political science majors for upper-division IR electives, attracting potential students who are interested in becoming political science majors, and improving information literacy and critical thinking about global politics among non-major students. The question then is how we can level the playing field for students, create a sense of community, and facilitate active learning among a diverse student population across majors and non-majors.

Following Lamy (2007), I argue that using simulations as an active learning strategy can teach students about competing world views or theories in IR, while allowing students to follow through the "describe, explain, predict, and prescribe" sequence in PBL. Simulations often require students to work in groups, focusing on a problem, case or scenario, and create a sense of ownership and responsibility, which are essential features of PBL (Burch 2000). In addition, simulations can facilitate cooperative or collaborative learning on topics outside of students' comfort zones, which in turn can help promote diversity, reciprocity, scaffolding, and friendships within the class-room (Sharan 2010; Baker and Clark 2010). Most importantly, integrating the simulations with regular lectures and discussions means no prior knowledge of students is required as long as the instructor provides students with opportunities to learn and prepare in class before the simulations start.

The simulations I used were based on the structure of MUN simulations, with several significant adaptations. First, the decision to implement a UNSC or UNGA structure of the simulation often depends on class size and students' knowledge level. A UNGA simulation is ideal for a large lecture class with easily 50–100 students or even more, while the UNSC decision-making structure is clearly more appropriate for small to medium class of no more than 50 students. The size of student teams can also vary whether it is a lower-division introductory or upper-division survey course. A general rule of thumb is that the size of the team can decrease as the knowledge level of student increases. Prior to the first simulation, I go through a lecture on intergovernmental organizations (IGOs) as well as a case study of the UN in class, during which students are exposed to key differences in UNSC and UNGA decision-making structure and processes, as well as the nature of amending texts towards a vote and final resolution.

Second, simulations are not stand-alone techniques, but are rather understood to be part of an integrated active learning sequence. During the first few weeks of the semester, I use a few simple games to help students warm up to the idea of role-playing. The games that I most frequently use are Asal's (2005) classical realist "Hobbes Game" and the Prisoners' Dilemma game. These games are primarily used to illustrate theories of realism and neoliberal institutionalism, though students can also use constructivism to explain the game dynamics. Asking students to stand up and walk around in the classroom almost always immediately changes the classroom dynamic as they engage students in active interactions. These types of shorter, simpler games therefore help students with no prior experience get comfortable within the class dynamic and interact with others, and then extract from their roles and discuss the results during debriefing. For the actual simulation sequence, I first begin with a hypothesized scenario of zombie pandemic (Michelsen 2010; Horn et al. 2016; Fischer 2019) and an ungraded mock simulation. This immediately follows a lecture on IGOs and a case study of the UN with the dual purposes of helping students reinforce their content learning and reducing their anxieties about the upcoming simulation sequence.

Third, students in the later part of the course have the opportunity to choose simulation topics other than the first mock simulation. This strategy encourages students to take more ownership of the simulations as they become more comfortable with the simulation structure. The graded simulations focus on subfields of international security, international political economy, and transnational issues. To ensure student interest and preparedness, I create a list of potential simulation topics early in the semester and ask students to rank their favorite topic in each subfield through an online survey. Each simulation topic suggestion presents a real-world problem or case, and I regularly update the list as new issues are discussed and considered in the UN system. The benefit of doing so is that students apply their learning to current "hot topics" in the UN while taking part in choosing topics of their own interest, a technique sometimes referred to as dotmocracy. In addition, using real-world problems allows students to conduct in-depth research on the topic using UN databases and news articles. Conducting research allows students to gain skills and improve their understanding of competing preferences and official stances of each member state, along with making informed choices when drafting their simulation documents and responding to other groups.

Furthermore, the rules of the game can be more flexible than the real-world UN meetings. The first graded simulation follows the exact decision-making structure in the real world. From then on, I allow students to review, propose, and vote on potential changes to the decision-making structure in subsequent iterations. This serves a few purposes. First, students are priorly exposed to the debates on various UN decision-making reform proposals. This provides them an opportunity to think in the shoes of the countries they represent and identify the country's preferred choices from a list of real-world UN reform proposals. They can also propose something new, although it is often more difficult to garner sufficient support from other teams. Once all proposals are on the table, all teams have a chance to vote based on simple majority rule, then potentially implement the reform proposal, which is not possible in a real-world scenario. In addition, this helps students critically reflect on failures and frustrations in earlier iterations, which can frequently occur in the case of UNSC simulations. Given that the simulations are short, often lasting only one or two class sessions, it is very likely that students may not be able to achieve consensus with fixed rules in such a short time frame. By changing the rules and seeing an immediate effect, students become more engaged in critical reflections of the current UN decision-making structure.

Simulation Preparation

Although no prior knowledge is assumed before the semester starts, the first few weeks of lectures, discussions, and case studies can provide students with a necessary knowledge base and skills for the simulations to succeed. Failures can happen without proper preparation of students. When I taught introductory IR for the first time, I rushed to run the simulations in the first few weeks. Not surprisingly, students were confused and stressed as they were not ready. Except for a few, most students did not know what to do in the simulation, and they were not engaged as a result. This also affected their ability to critically reflect on the simulation experience through theoretical lens. Reflecting on this failure, I redesigned the course structure in later semesters. The most significant changes I made were to begin with smaller, low-stakes warmup exercises, to add an ungraded mock simulation based on a hypothetical scenario, and to provide more preparation guidance and time for earlier simulations.

During the first week of class, I introduce to students the idea of active learning and the pedagogy tools that are used in this class. I also ask students to play the first iteration of the classical realist game or the Hobbes game adapted from Asal (2005). Then, in the week concerned with IR history, students read about the League of Nations and why it failed. Once this is complete, students participate in relevant in-class case study work and related discussion activities. In the following two weeks, I introduce main IR theories with a focus on various levels of analysis during lectures. During these two weeks, students are asked play another iteration of the classical realism game, as well as the large-N Prisoner's Dilemma game from Asal (2005). With these practice games, students become increasingly comfortable with role-playing in the classroom. As they leave or change their seats and interact with other students, the in-class dynamics change significantly as more students begin to talk, interact, and laugh with each other. Following each game, students are asked to collectively debrief on the game dynamics and then apply theories and levels of analysis to interpret the outcomes. This helps them prepare for the simulation debriefings later in the semester.

By now the class enrollment stabilizes and, as such, a good time to divide students into simulation teams. This is also when I ask students to sign up for states that they will represent in the first mock simulation. Students will have the opportunity to represent non-governmental organizations (NGO) later in the semester, but the first mock simulation includes only states. While it would be ideal to include all actors in the first mock simulation, adding NGOs as observers would significantly increase the complexity to the simulation structure. By now, students only have a vague idea about NGOs through lecture content, without understanding their concrete roles in specific issue arenas. Students can play the NGO roles more effectively as their comfort level with the simulations, their content knowledge on issue topics, and their understanding of NGOs' rules increase.

During the week prior to the simulation, the lectures focus on the role of states in the international system and various tools of statecraft. Students work together in their teams for the first time by working through a case study of foreign policy and diplomacy of the country they will represent in the first simulation. Although time does not allow for each team to present individually,

I pair the teams so that they can present their case studies to each other to encourage facilitated interactions and collaborative learning between teams. In the lecture right before the simulation, I officially introduce the UN decision-making structure along with the processes thereof.

With sufficient knowledge on the country they are going to represent, the student teams are ready to participate in the first simulation on the zombie pandemic. This mock simulation was adapted from Horn et al. (2016) and an online simulation developed by the United Nations Association (UNA). The simulation begins with a news report on zombie attacks in Los Angeles International Airport with the potential of the next outbreak taking place anywhere, anytime within a matter of hours. As their countries' delegates to the UN, the student teams are charged with the task of coming up with a resolution to manage and contain future outbreaks. Since it is a hypothetical scenario, little prior research on the topic is required other than some general knowledge from popular culture. Nonetheless, students do need to learn how to write an effective position statement to present at the beginning of the simulation, and how to draft preambulatory and operative clauses that accurately represent their country's positions.

Each simulation comes with a prompt that offers some background, the mission of the student teams, preparation steps and guidance for document drafts, sample position statement with resolutions from past classes on a different topic, and links to additional resources. In addition to lecture slides and handouts that provide examples, I also introduce students to two mobile apps: UNdata and MUN. These apps provide background information about their own and other member countries, a short summary of rules or procedures, and examples of preambulatory and operative clauses. Students are encouraged to use both mobile apps to prepare their statements, and they are able to refer back to the apps whenever they need during the simulations.

For all the subsequent graded simulations, I do some preliminary research on the issue topics students have selected, and prepare prompts following the same structures of the first prompt on the zombie pandemic. This iterated structure allows students to become familiar with the process before midterm point, and then continue to practice to improve as they are entering the second part of the semester. Student teams are asked to submit the written position statements and attach draft preambulatory and operative clauses as an appendix. They are also encouraged to predict other countries' reactions to their proposals in a second appendix. While initial predictions are often less accurate or even completely wrong, students can improve their prediction accuracy for future iterations based on interactions with other teams during the simulation. Written submissions, therefore, provide important foundations for both their opening statement during the simulation and further negotiations during the simulation itself.

Simulations in Action

With these preparatory steps of lecture and collaborative writing, students should ideally be ready to participate in the actual simulations. Still, it is important to recognize some unique challenges of an integrated approach to simulations. In a semester-long class that is dedicated to MUN, students can have more opportunities to practice and improve over time. In an introductory or survey IR class, however, the simulation iterations require no more than a few instances in the semester. Although I can help students get used to role-play exercises through smaller games, students may still be too distracted, nervous, or anxious to play their specific roles effectively. The key question, therefore, is how we can help students immerse themselves in the simulation environment, feel comfortable, and stay engaged throughout.

The first strategy I use is to reorganize the classroom and create a space that resemble the actual UN meetings as much as possible. When the classroom environment allows, I ask some student volunteers to arrive a little early and help reorganize the chairs. For the UNSC simulations, I reorganize the chairs to a roundtable, with the representatives sitting at the front, and the rest of the delegation sitting behind the representative. Each representative makes their statements or proposals at their seats, just as enacted in actual UNSC meetings. For the larger UNGA simulations which are often located in lecture halls, each country's delegation sits in a group and faces the podium. When called by the chairperson on the speakers' list, the member-states and NGOs send their representatives to the podium to make statements or proposals. In either case, some designated empty spaces remain on the periphery of the classroom that can be used as "lobbying area" where student teams negotiate informally when formal meetings are adjourned.

In addition, it is possible to create a sense of formality through language use and an opening ceremony. While I do not require students to dress up formally, they are asked to use formal and diplomatic language to the extent possible. Each student team should elect a representative before each simulation. For member-states, the person elected is called "Ambassador XX." For observer states and NGOs, the person is called "Representative XX." The rotating ambassadors and representatives need to stand up, come to the front of the class, and take a picture together shaking hands. Although this does not happen in actual UN simulations, I find this helpful for students to settle in their roles. These strategies were inspired by the "immersive theater approach" by Dacombe and Morrow (2017) and first implemented in my regional politics class where I ran simulations of the Association of Southeast Asian Nations. Although it may cost a few minutes of the actual simulation, it provides students an efficient way to immerse themselves in their assigned roles and stay focused during the simulation.

Following the opening ceremony, the simulation begins with a formal announcement by the chair and a series of opening statements by the ambassadors and representatives. As the instructor, I always chair the first mock simulation on the zombie pandemic to set an example for students. I also prepare a written provisional agenda, a speakers' list and a flow chart of the meeting that students can refer to when they need guidance. The simulations begin with the opening statements, followed by debates and possible motions. A motion can be made to adjourn the formal meeting to allow behind-the-door negotiations in "lobbying areas," to discuss draft resolutions, make amendments, or make roll call votes on the resolutions. Interestingly, students quickly figure out ways to sabotage a draft resolution they do not like by making unfriendly amendments to a resolution, such as proposing strict conditions on lifting sanctions or providing humanitarian aid. As a result, even though there are a plethora of motions, sometimes the simulations would end without a resolution being passed.

As students iterate the simulations and become more comfortable during the semester, the instructor can take a back seat to observe during the simulation and facilitate learning. Starting from the second simulation, I ask student teams to volunteer to serve the chair role. Once they see me playing the chair for the first time, they often realize that this role is not as intimidating as they thought, and that the chair may enjoy some perks, such as agenda-setting and increased visibility. The smaller, non-permanent member-states that tend to be ignored in negotiations often quickly find out that this is an effective strategy for them to get their voice heard. Once selected as the chair, the student team need to prepare the written provisional agenda and a speakers' list similar to the one I created for the mock simulation. I also provide written tips to the team to ensure the class as a whole follows the same rules and procedures. During the simulation, I minimize my direct intervention and only remind the chair team when rules are not followed.

Voting is an important part of the simulation as it determines the fate of proposed resolutions and therefore simulation outcomes. As the deadline or time limit approaches, student teams often rush to vote on one draft resolution after another, and usually the process become chaotic and disorderly. It is therefore important to specify the rules of voting before each simulation and make clear which rules can be changed and which cannot. First, I specify a set of rules that are fixed or constant for all simulation iterations. Specifically, I make a distinction between a procedural vote and a substantive vote. Only a substantive vote allows abstentions and excludes any observer states or NGOs represented. This is important when we begin to include observers and NGOs in later iterations. It helps us connect the rules to the concepts of sovereignty as well as state and non-state actors' involvement during the debrief and assessment.

Additionally, I encourage students to debate the majority voting rules and the use of veto in the UNSC. The latter is clearly highly controversial, as other student teams become frequently frustrated by permanent five members (P5) of the UNSC. By reviewing these frustrations in debriefings sessions, students can easily connect them to core concepts of IR, such as anarchy, rationality, self-interest, and relative gains. As mentioned before, I allow students to change rules in later simulations if they can get it to pass through a motion using the existing decision-making structure. Students often find out that they cannot persuade P5 teams that act like realists, and the only times that a change of voting rule can occur is when they have very liberal P5 teams. The differences in simulation outcomes depending on the dominant culture or norms also provide an ideal opportunity to examine the theory of constructivism. Whether passed or not, rule change attempts provide an ideal opportunity for debriefing, connecting the IR theories, the UN reform debates, and simulation outcomes.

Debriefing, Reflection, and Assessment

Debriefing, reflection, and assessment are integral parts to simulations as a signature pedagogy. Asal (2005) proposes several methods or stages of debriefing and reflection, including oral debriefing, written debriefing, and as cases to be referenced in examinations. Kollars and Rosen (2013) argue that simulations themselves can be used as active assessment in place of examinations. I adapt these two models to combine debriefing, reflection, and assessment strategies. To review the simulation interactions and outcomes, I begin with an online survey questionnaire or a short reflection paper, followed by group and whole-class oral debriefing. Exams or long essays or papers are effective tools to assess student knowledge of theories and concepts that can be applied to explain the simulation outcomes. Finally, a series of self- and peer-evaluation surveys are conducted following each simulation and at the end of the semester to complement instructor observation. Inspired by student feedback, I have implemented some changes in simulation design, including allowing students to rotate their country and team roles, creating a clearer division of labor within teams, and experimenting alternative voting structures.

Before students leave the classroom after a simulation, I give them a reflection prompt or a link to an online survey, with an identical list of questions. I frequently switch between these two methods because they provide valuable feedback in different ways. Students take the online survey anonymously and therefore are more candid about their personal feelings and opinions. The cost of this approach is that it cannot be graded, and students often do not elaborate on their thoughts. A written reflection paper can give students the flexibility to prioritize certain questions and more space for them to elaborate. However, it does not allow the same anonymity and comprehensiveness an online survey can offer. Students can complete the survey online or submit the reflection via the course management system (CMS) 24 hours before next class. Survey questions include:

- Were the rules and structures of the simulation clear to you?
- What were the simulation outcomes? Do they meet your expectations? Why or why not?
- If this is not the first simulation, what are some key similarities and differences between this simulation and previous ones?
- How do changes in the decision-making rules affect the simulation outcomes?
- Were you and your teammates in character? How about others?
- How do you feel during and after the simulation? Describe your emotions.
- If we are going to have another simulation, is there anything we can do to improve the simulation design?
- If we are going to have another simulation, is there anything you and your team can do to improve your performance?
- If this is the last simulation, what would be your suggestions to students taking this class next semester?

Once students submit their answers, I put together a few slides that highlight the survey results or quotes from reflection papers. The online survey or written reflection therefore allow me to collect student feedback and set the tone for oral debriefing, which occurs during the next class following the simulation. During oral briefing, I ask students to shuffle their seats and find people who are not in their team to form discussion groups. This helps students to more quickly extract from their roles. Student discussion groups then go through the questions one by one before coming back to a whole-class discussion. The open discussion focuses on three themes: how to effectively deal with emotions and feelings, possible confusions and clarifications about simulation design and rules, what improvements I can make in the next simulation experience and for my future classes.

While students frequently express their frustrations with the P5 states and failures to pass resolution within the time constraints, many of them also agree that it helps them learn how difficult it is in reality to achieve meaningful collective action under the current UN structure. This provides a good transition to our next discussion when I ask students to consider the theoretical question: *Which IR theory and level of analysis best explains this particular simulation outcome? How about previous iterations? Why?* To help students connect the theories to their analysis, I provide a review sheet of key assumptions and arguments of each IR theory. Student first work in groups to make a list of potential evidence for each IR theory, then complete a short, written individual reflection. This is part of the active learning sequence following each game and simulation played in the classroom. The recursive theory exercises help students prepare for relevant exam questions and final essay or written papers where they elaborate on their arguments.

Treating simulations as standalone assessments in addition to the exams and policy papers can incentivize active participation and reduce test anxiety. That said, assessing simulations can be difficult when they are team-based, not individual-based. To address issues of free-riding and unequal contribution, it is important to separate individual efforts from overall team performance. First, I ask students to mark individual authorship or contribution in the written position statements and draft clauses. Second, I make my own observations during each simulation session and take notes of in-class performance. Finally, I use student self-evaluation and peer assessment to complement my instructor observation. Each simulation is followed by a self-evaluation on a ten-point scale. For peer evaluations, I ask students to assign an average of ten points to their teammates, with some differentiation in the ratings. For example, students can give 12 points to teammate A who contributed more, and eight points to teammate B who contributed less. The highest score a person can receive is 15 points and the lowest score zero. The final grading rubric therefore integrates instructor observation, self-evaluation, and peer assessment, and creates a comprehensive score for each student's simulation performance. Both instructor and peer feedback comments are provided to each student to help them improve in future simulations.

Conclusion

This chapter explores ways to use simulations as a signature pedagogy in an introductory or survey IR class. Rather than introducing students to formalized MUN as a standalone exercise, I developed a series of small, in-class simulations in combination with games, case studies, and discussion groups to create recursive and active learning sequences. This strategy helps reduce the potential time dedicated to standalone simulations and allows for a more balanced approach between lecture content and active learning components. In particular, simulations as a signature pedagogy help students grasp threshold concepts in IR, such as anarchy and sovereignty, empirically examine the interactions among states and non-state actors, and apply competing theoretical perspectives to explain patterns of conflict and cooperation.

When applying this approach to an IR class, several potential limitations or challenges should be considered. First, by prioritizing the UN simulation, students may develop some hidden assumptions about who are the primary actors in IR and the power dynamics among them. Non-state actors, for example, are not introduced until later iterations of the UN simulation to reduce the complexity of the first simulation. Depending on whether it is based on UNSC or UNGA, students may also develop competing interpretations of how the UN works without an in-depth understanding of the other institutions within the UN. Furthermore, while the P5 countries dominate the UNSC, the power dynamics can be slightly or significantly different in other IGOs and regional institutions. It is possible, though, to review and discuss these hidden assumptions during the debriefing stage and complement the UN simulations with case studies of other IGOs and NGOs across issue areas.

Even short simulations can be time-consuming. Although the actual simulations are timed, the time spent on preparation and debriefing can be less predictable. Typically, the first simulation requires more time for in-class preparation and debriefing in comparison with later iterations. Sometimes the instructor may have to let go of some lecture content to allow students to fully reflect on the simulation experience. In other words, there is a tradeoff between deep learning and breadth of knowledge. By integrating simulations into an introductory class, the instructor needs to carefully review their learning objectives and make sure that simulations complement, rather than compete with, lectures in meeting the objectives.

The instructor also needs to actively pay attention to potential issues of equity and inclusion in simulations. Not all students like simulations, and there are always students who would prefer to sit in the back and not participate. Some students prefer lectures over any type of active learning. Other students do not like work in teams or their teammates may not contribute fairly, which may undermine their team and individual performance. For those students, simulation experiences can be confusing and challenging rather than empowering. Instructors therefore need to diversify their pedagogy portfolios and assessment strategies to the extent possible, rather than solely relying on lectures or simulations. Furthermore, simulations themselves can create unequal power dynamics and feelings of exclusion at times. A UNSC simulation almost always makes student teams who represent non-P5 countries feel less important. Within each team, the ambassador or representative almost always has more visibility in comparison with their teammates. The instructors need to be conscious of these issues and make active adjustments in instructor observations and grading rubrics. They can also ask teams and students to rotate roles, despite the potential cost of giving up their in-depth knowledge about a specific country or expertise developed based on division of labor.

Building on the burgeoning literature of IR simulations and student feedback, I plan to incorporate or experiment with some potential changes in future replications of UN simulations. For example, for assessment purposes, it may be important to develop a pool of standardized questions for pre- and post-test on students' knowledge of the UN and IR theories. This set of questions can be used standalone or included as a subset of the general course assessment questions. Gasglow (2014) also discusses the importance of engaging students more actively in the design of simulations by asking them to help craft the rules early in the semester. Another potential strategy is to incorporate some experiment design, as discussed by Lohmann (2019), which allows students to discuss alternative issue scenarios and how they can respond under each circumstance. This may also apply to voting mechanisms, which allow students to compare simulation outcomes while controlling for issue-specific factors.

References

Asal, Victor. 2005. "Playing Games with International Relations." *International Studies Perspectives* 6 (3): 359–73. https://doi.org/10.1111/j.1528-3577.2005.00213.x.

Asal, Victor, and Elizabeth Blake. 2006. "Creating Simulations for Political Science Education." *Journal of Political Science Education* 2 (January): 1–18. https://doi.org/10.1080/15512160500484119.

Asal, Victor, and Jayson Kratoville. 2013. "Constructing International Relations Simulations: Examining the Pedagogy of IR Simulations Through a Constructivist Learning Theory Lens." *Journal of Political Science Education: Thematic Issue: Simulations in Political Science* 9 (2): 132–43. https://doi.org/10.1080/15512169.2013.770982.

Baker, Trish, and Jill Clark. 2010. "Cooperative Learning – a Double-edged Sword: A Cooperative Learning Model for Use with Diverse Student Groups." *Intercultural Education* 21 (3): 257–68. https://doi.org/10.1080/14675981003760440.

Boyer, Mark A. 2011. "Simulation in International Studies." *Simulation & Gaming* 42 (6): 685–89. https://doi.org/10.1177/1046878111429765.

Burch, Kurt. 2000. "A Primer on Problem-Based Learning for International Relations Courses." *International Studies Perspectives* 1 (1): 31–44. https://doi.org/10.1111/1528-3577.00003.

Dacombe, Rod, and Elizabeth A. Morrow. 2017. "Developing Immersive Simulations: The Potential of Theater in Teaching and Learning in Political Studies." *PS: Political Science & Politics* 50 (1): 209–13. https://doi.org/10.1017/S1049096516002456.

Ellington, Henry, and Shirley Earl. 1998. *Using Games, Simulations and Interactive Case Studies: A Practical Guide for Tertiary-Level Teachers*. Staff and Educational Development Association.

Engel, Susan, Josh Pallas, and Sarah Lambert. 2017. "Model United Nations and Deep Learning: Theoretical and Professional Learning." *Journal of Political Science Education* 13 (2): 171–84. https://doi.org/10.1080/15512169.2016.1250644.

Fischer, Beth A. 2019. "Fact or Fiction? Designing Stories for Active Learning Exercises." *Journal of Political Science Education* 15 (2): 179–90. https://doi.org/10.1080/15512169.2018.1447947.

Glasgow, Sara M. 2014. "Stimulating Learning by Simulating Politics: Teaching Simulation Design in the Undergraduate Context." *International Studies Perspectives* 15 (4): 525–37. https://doi.org/10.1111/j.1528-3585.2012.00501.x.

Hammond, Augustine, and Craig Douglas Albert. 2019. "Learning by Experiencing: Improving Student Learning Through a Model United Nations Simulation." *Journal of Political Science Education*, 1–18. https://doi.org/10.1080/15512169.2018.1548967.

Horn, Laura, Olivier Rubin, and Laust Schouenborg. 2016. "Undead Pedagogy: How a Zombie Simulation Can Contribute to Teaching International Relations 1." *International Studies Perspectives* 17 (2): 187–201. https://doi.org/10.1111/insp.12103.

Kollars, Nina A., and Amanda M. Rosen. 2013. "Simulations as Active Assessment?: Typologizing by Purpose and Source." *Journal of Political Science Education* 9 (2): 144–56. https://doi.org/10.1080/15512169.2013.770983.

Lamy, Steven L. 2007. "Challenging Hegemonic Paradigms and Practices: Critical Thinking and Active Learning Strategies for International Relations." *PS: Political Science & Politics* 40 (1): 112–16. https://doi.org/10.1017/S1049096507250279.

Leib, Julia, and Samantha Ruppel. 2020. "The Learning Effects of United Nations Simulations in Political Science Classrooms." *European Political Science*. https://doi.org/10.1057/s41304-020-00260-3.

Lohmann, Robert. 2019. "Taking a Glimpse Into the Future by Playing?" Simulation & Gaming 50 (3): 377–92. https://doi.org/10.1177/1046878119848133.

Lüdert, Jan. 2016. "Signature Pedagogies in International Relations." E-International Relations. https://www.e-ir.info/2016/06/18/signature-pedagogies-in-international-relations/

Lüdert, Jan. 2019. "Signature Pedagogies and Threshold Concepts in International Relations.". Pasadena, CA: International Studies Association (ISA) West.

McCarthy, Mary M. 2014. "The Role of Games and Simulations to Teach Abstract Concepts of Anarchy, Cooperation, and Conflict in World Politics." *Journal of Political Science Education* 10 (4): 400–413. https://doi.org/10.1080/15512169.2014.947417.

McIntosh, Daniel. 2001. "The Uses and Limits of the Model United Nations in an International Relations Classroom." *International Studies Perspectives* 2 (3): 269–80. https://doi.org/10.1111/1528-3577.00057.

Meyer, Jan, Rey Land, and Jan Smith. 2008. *Threshold Concepts within the Disciplines*. Sense publisher. https://doi.org/10.1163/9789460911477.

Michelsen, Niall, and Alan Goggins. "Teaching World Politics With Zombies." In *Annual Convention of the American Political Science Association*, Washington, DC, September, vol. 2. 2010.

Obendorf, Simon, and Claire Randerson. 2012. "The Model United Nations Simulation and the Student as Producer Agenda." *Enhancing Learning in the Social Sciences* 4 (3): 1–15. https://doi.org/10.11120/elss.2012.04030007.

Sasley, Brent E. 2010. "Teaching Students How to Fail: Simulations as Tools of Explanation." *International Studies Perspectives* 11 (1): 61–74. https://doi.org/10.1111/j.1528-3585.2009.00393.x.

Sharan, Yael. 2010. "Cooperative Learning: A Diversified Pedagogy for Diverse Classrooms." *Intercultural Education* 21 (3): 195–203. https://doi.org/10.1080/14675981003760390.

Starkey, Brigid A., and Elizabeth L. Blake. 2001. "Simulation in International Relations Education." *Simulation & Gaming* 32 (4): 537–51. https://doi.org/10.1177/104687810103200409.

Taylor, Kirsten. 2013. "Simulations Inside and Outside the IR Classroom: A Comparative Analysis." *International Studies Perspectives* 14 (2): 134–49. https://doi.org/10.1111/j.1528-3585.2012.00477.x.

Wakelee, Daniel. n.d. "Short Duration Political Science Simulations." Rapid Intellect Group.

Wheeler, Sarah M. 2006. "Role-Playing Games and Simulations for International Issues Courses." *Journal of Political Science Education* 2 (3): 331–47. https://doi.org/10.1080/15512160600840814.

Youatt, June, and Kim Wilcox. 2008. "Intentional and Integrated Learning in a New Cognitive Age: A Signature Pedagogy for Undergraduate Education in the Twenty-First Century." *Michigan State University* 10 (4): 24–26.

13

Teaching International Relations in the Undergraduate Classroom: The Use of Metaphors, Simulations, and Games

ISMAIL ERKAM SULA

This chapter discusses signature pedagogies in International Relations (IR) and introduces three alternative techniques to active learning, which are used to teach challenging topics in the undergraduate classroom. The first technique is the strategy game, which is designed to encourage students' active participation and help them grasp key concepts. The second technique is a simulation that aims to let students experience a hypothetical international crisis as representatives of states and understand difficulties in conflict resolution scenarios. Simulations are generally inspired from certain real-life crisis and developed with a touch of entertainment. The third technique is the use of metaphors or stories. It aims to explain the literature on "sciences" and "methods" in the IR as a discipline via a fictional story and the use of certain metaphors. The chapter first reviews existing teaching techniques in the academic literature. It lists and discusses various "game/simulation designs" built by scholars in the field. Second, it introduces the three techniques as part of my signature pedagogy with examples from previously applied cases. This part details the design of each technique in a step-by-step format to make them replicable for readers. Third, the chapter discusses the applicability of each technique. Combined, these three approaches give fruitful results especially when applied to undergraduate students of politics and IR. The chapter ends with a set of recommendations on when, with whom, and how to utilize each technique.

IR is a content-rich discipline with no clear-cut disciplinary boundaries. This variation and breadth make it a challenging task to decide on what an IR signature pedagogy should look like. There are certainly many similarities as well as divergences on how IR is taught as a profession across the world. Like most social science disciplines, IR education also has conventional or traditional pedagogical techniques. After summarizing my take on the traditional ways of teaching IR, this chapter delves into recent and innovative techniques. The chapter analyzes active learning and other alternative practices in IR education and assesses the capacity of those techniques to inform my signature pedagogy.

The chapter first looks at the definition of signature pedagogy to discuss how an IR signature pedagogy may look. Here, I emphasize that what we teach as IR and how we teach it are closely related. The section argues that these two questions need to be considered together when thinking about IR as a profession. Accordingly, while making an assessment of the former question of what we teach as IR, the first section connects it with the latter question of how we teach IR. The section discusses both conventional and non-conventional techniques that are used in IR education and provides examples from the academic literature on participatory learning practices employed by IR educators across the world. The second section discusses the use of three alternative education techniques: (1) strategy games, (2) simulations, and (3) storification. The second section also shares my own teaching and learning experiences, as well as suggestions on the use of each alternative technique. The chapter also evaluates existing active learning practices by discussing the advantages of each technique while providing suggestions for overcoming certain disadvantages. It concludes with a discussion of how my teaching approaches can contribute to an IR signature pedagogy more broadly. By doing so, this chapter aims to add to existing ways of teaching IR as a profession.

Signature Pedagogies and IR Education

The IR discipline is quite rich in content. Accordingly, the curricula of IR degree programs contain a variety of topics and courses. The tendency in most IR undergraduate programs is to start with certain core introductory social and political science courses in the first years of study and then delve into field-specific ones for the final years. IR-specific courses include various forms of theoretical, historical, and methodological topics to equip students with a toolbox to analyze world politics. After the knowledge-base is set up with required courses, students are offered a selection of issue-specific courses depending on the expertise of professors in respective departments. Required courses are mostly similar in many departments across the world, yet the extensive scope of the term IR usually results in a picturesque scene of various elective courses in different IR departments. There are no clear-cut boundaries of the IR discipline. Indeed, everyone understands that the discipline has boundaries, but most of them are unsure about where those boundaries are or how to set them. This unbounded (or multi-, inter-, trans-disciplinary) nature of IR provides an important maneuvering capacity to educators in their task of teaching IR. This maneuvering capacity affects both what we teach as IR and how we teach it; hence, both direct us to open up a discussion on signature pedagogies.

Signature pedagogies are "types of teaching that organize the fundamental ways in which future practitioners are educated for their new professions… These are the forms of instruction that leap to mind when we first think about the preparation of members of particular professions" (Shulman 2005, 52). Each field develops signature pedagogies that educators use to teach what they think are fundamental requirements of their specific profession. Indeed, every profession has its own signature pedagogy where "novices are instructed in critical aspects of the three fundamental dimensions of professional work – to *think*, to *perform*, and to *act with integrity*" (Shulman 2005, 52). These fundamental dimensions are closely associated with what we teach and how we teach the concepts and content we want to teach. In the IR discipline, an important aspect that educators need to think about are the skills and knowledge to transfer in the class to get students ready their careers. This requires us to decide what IR as a profession means. Here, the above-mentioned characteristics of the discipline complicates things as graduates of IR degree programs are not directed towards a single profession. What we do, instead of directing students towards a single profession, is generally to transfer main and core topics as a toolbox and leave it up to students to decide their area of expertise. What we teach at the core and beyond becomes quite important as we let the student construct their profession at the end. Regarding signature pedagogies, what we teach is followed by how we teach it. Indeed, as has been noted, signature pedagogies are more concerned with how educators transfer knowledge rather than what content they teach (Lüdert 2016, 1).

IR education, like most of the other social science disciplines, contains traditional methods of course design, evaluation, and in-class activities. Traditional methods generally follow similar routines:

> 1. Design a syllabus that contains essential information about the course.
> 2. Develop a weekly course plan including required readings (textbook chapters or articles).
> 3. Deliver regular lectures in-class based on these readings.

4. Add some student participation component (attendance, single or group presentations).
5. Evaluate performance through exams and written paper assignments.

In this traditional approach, the degree of knowledge and skill transfer in the class is dependent on the educator's performance and her/his skill in using classroom technology. Indeed, education techniques are abundant and are usually based on the creativity of the educator. New and innovative approaches have also been developed over time. Especially as technological capabilities have increased, scholars have started to look for alternative ways of transferring knowledge and skills to students. One aim of these innovative approaches has been increasing student participation and designing more interactive in-class and off-class routines. Here, the topics are taught through a set of activities to train students via active participation. Active learning techniques have increasingly become an important component of signature pedagogies in IR.

Active learning is defined as "an education process that takes place through student engagement with the content through different types of activities that encourage reflection, in order to promote active thinking" (Alves, Silva, and Barbosa 2019, 1). The educator uses novel approaches, including simulations, games, case studies, and other innovative techniques to encourage and monitor student participatory learning. The process shifts the educator from being mere lecturer towards a learning coordinator. Of course, the balance of this shift between lecturer and coordinator is determined by the educator's own preference and teaching style, creativity, skills, and institutional and technical capabilities. The most common technique is the use of simulations in the classroom. The academic literature offers abundant examples of the application on simulations (Shaw and Switky 2018; Shaw 2004; Asal and Blake 2006; Asal and Kratoville 2013; de Freitas 2006; Wedig 2010). Simulations have been used in teaching various IR topics, including international human rights (Killie 2002), peacekeeping (Shaw 2004), diplomacy and the UN (Chasek 2005), international law (Ambrosio 2006), theories of international political economy (Boyer, Trumbore, and Fricke 2006), international negotiations (Shaw 2006), international trade (Switky and Avilés 2007), humanitarian intervention (Switky 2014), the European Union (Elias 2014), and decision-making (DiCicco 2014).[1] Particularly, Killie (2002, 271–272) asks students to prepare a draft international human rights treaty to simulate international negotiations and encourage student interest on various IR concepts, including

---

[1]   See also various other simulation, problem based learning and active learning examples: Switky (2014); Horn, Rubin, and Schouenborg (2016); Zappile, Beers, and Raymond (2017); Kempston and Thomas (2014); and Thomas (2002).

"diplomacy, two-level games, international law, human rights, and group decision making." Chasek (2005) offers a crisis simulation based on multi-lateral diplomacy, where participants try to resolve a hypothetical UN Security Council crisis. Similarly, Switky (2014) uses a crisis simulation to let students experience the difficulties of decision-making in "humanitarian intervention." Ambrosio (2006, 159–160) utilizes "Problem Based Learning (PBL)" techniques to teach international law, "in which students assumed roles in a mock war crimes trial." In the mock trial, the author uses a real-life case and designs a hypothetical trial to (1) deepen student understanding of the material, (2) give "hands-on experience in the difficulties associated with interpreting and applying international law," and (3) bolster student interest in the topic (Ambrosio 2006, 160). Boyer, Trumbore, and Fricke (2006) use a family card game "Pit," to help students understand abstract theories and concepts of international political economy and increase their interest in course material.

Scholars also use in-class games (Alves, Silva, and Barbosa 2019), mock trials (Ambrosio 2006), zombie simulations (Horn, Rubin, and Schouenborg 2016; Drezner 2014), fiction (Boaz 2020) and novels, series, and popular movies like the Lord of the Rings (Ruane and James 2008; 2012), Harry Potter (Nexon and Neumann 2006), Game of Thrones (Young and Ko 2019), Star Trek and Star Wars (Dyson 2015; Campbell and Gokcek 2019), and others (Weber 2014; 2010; 2001). Through such approaches, IR educators both aim to encourage student participation and make it easier for students to understand challenging topics in IR.

Teaching Challenging IR Topics: Three Alternatives

Active learning tools are utilized by educators to (1) let student participate in crisis-like situations and have them experience the practical side of the profession and (2) help student understand abstract theoretical and philosophical topics through metaphors and real-life examples. Each technique, as will be outlined in this section, has advantages and disadvantages. Here, I find it useful to group these techniques into three teaching approaches: (1) strategy games, (2) crisis simulations, and (3) storification. These techniques assist educators in teaching a variety of complex topics. For instance, as part of my own signature pedagogy, I have actively used strategy games to teach about collective action dilemmas, security dilemmas, and theories of IR, crisis simulations to let students experience certain international political crises that require skills in negotiation, conflict resolution, and coordinating summit meetings, and storification to teach philosophy of science debates in IR theory.

The first technique, strategy games, has a specific purpose: to learn and teach IR in an entertaining manner (See, for instance, Thomas 2002; Freitas 2006; Boyer, Trumbore, and Fricke 2006). A strategy game can be defined as a teaching technique that is used to explain and introduce fundamental concepts in IR, such as security and foreign policy, in a smooth and swift manner. It is smooth as the alternative actions, turns of the game, and number of actors are all predetermined and controlled by the instructor. It is swift because the waiting time between the turns in limited, and the games end in approximately 40 minutes. These games are especially useful as icebreakers (to introduce participants to each other) and as short, entertaining breaks between lecture weeks in course design and syllabi. In my classes, I generally prefer an adjusted version of the "Isle of Ted Simulation" designed by Glen Dale Thomas (2002). Isle of Ted is a turn-based game-like simulation where participants represent certain actors and interact with each other according to pre-determined rules. After letting participants play this turn-based interactive game, the educator can cover a variety of topics in IR, such as independence and sovereignty, complex interdependence, security dilemma, collective action dilemma, and others. An important aspect here is to monitor how the participants interact with each other throughout the turns of the game as each specific round of the game with different participants uncovers interesting points for discussion and lessons for reflection.

Strategy games have certain, specific characteristics. First, these games are designed to finish in a relatively short amount of time. Since there is a limited number of decision and action alternatives for the participants, the game will start to repeat itself after several turns, which diminishes the entertainment factor for both participants and the educator. Second, unlike simulations, in strategy games the educator's role is more active as she/he must keep participants on the move and active because of the time-limit. Third, the application of these games should be carefully designed to make it both engaging and easy to grasp. It should be designed practically and not require advanced prior knowledge, long readings, or lectures to prepare the participants. Last but not the least, the strategy game should be adjusted in creative and imaginative ways to be relevant to the student population. For example, the educator may change currency denominations to "York Liras" (rather than dollars or euros), include chance moves in the game (like dice-rolling or coin-flipping to decide faith), or may use imaginary country names, such as "Kolombistan, Tartartolia" (rather than real country names). Adjusting the game in these ways helps keep students actively engaged rather than focused on being overly realistic and stale.

Strategy games are highly useful in teaching key concepts of IR (e.g., anarchy, collective action dilemma, conflict vs. cooperation, absolute vs. relative gains) and the existence of multiple actors in IR (e.g., states, non-governmental organizations [NGOs], intergovernmental organizations [IGOs]). As such, they are more suitable to use as complementary educating techniques to support lectures throughout the semester. Depending on the preferences of the educator, strategy games may be used as icebreakers in the first weeks of any class or might be applied occasionally throughout the semester to consolidate and evaluate what knowledge has been transferred to the students. According to my experience, they serve as great icebreakers, increasing the self-confidence of the students by letting them know each other and feel more comfortable to participate in in-class activities throughout the semester. This technique is more suitable to early-period, junior students, who do not have preliminary knowledge of the field or topics to be covered.

The second technique, crisis simulation, is usually based on a replay of a real-life crisis (see Chasek 2005; Ambrosio 2006; Switky 2014, among others). A crisis simulation in IR is a pedagogical technique based on a scenario to create a situation inspired from real life, which is used to train, give experience to, and inform participants of the probable behavior alternatives to resolve international political crises and conflicts. It is very useful, as there are many cases in IR that can be simulated in this technique (the Cold War, the First and Second World War, the Abkhazia Crisis between Russia and Georgia, the Economic Crisis of Greece and the European Union, the establishment of the European Union, etc.). The scenario is often created by an educator who is an expert in this area of research. Real-life crises are employed (1) to teach specific topic areas, such as causes and reasons for war and conflict, and (2) to illustrate and let participants experience how difficult it may become for practitioners in the field (state leaders, diplomats, politicians, IGOs and NGOs, civil society) to resolve conflicts on the ground. In this sense, crisis simulations differ from strategy games. In simulations, participation is made as realistic as possible and entertainment is not necessarily a consideration. However, in strategy games there is a careful balance between teaching and entertainment, which requires more imagination and creativity. In addition, simulations aim to transfer experience to the participants through illustrating the process of crisis management while strategy games mostly aim to teach fundamental concepts. Simulations have their own strict rules, but they are not carved in stone. For instance, if the simulation is prepared to resolve conflict, participants may not have the option to resort to violence (declare war) until a certain turn comes. However, these rules are not as mechanical as those of the strategy games. Since simulations take longer (ranging from half a day, a whole day, a couple of days, and even longer), the educator may let participants decide how to deal with the situation through diplomacy and other measures. In strategy games however, there is a time limit, and rules are typically stricter and less fluid. Indeed, in simulations the result of crisis-management or conflict-resolution processes are left to the participants to decide. For instance, in one of the cases, I was expecting the participants to come to a summit and resolve their differences there. However, it was a surprise for me to see the participants revealed that they signed a secret treaty instead of using open discussion channels. This turned out to be an interesting example on what can be achieved by leaving some space for the creativity of the participants. I took it as an encouragement for increasing students' participation during the flow of the simulation and for leaving more space to the participants by letting them to come up with alternative more creative courses of action. Compared to strategy games, I think simulations give the educator an increased maneuvering capacity both in terms of content and encouraging participants involvement.

Typically, simulations are based on a common design that includes:

1. Creating teams according to the class size and number of participants
2. Determining the number of turns and length based on the allocated time
3. Establishing a communication platform, such as a roundtable that participants use as a summit to discuss their differences
4. Preparing and distributing a strategy document for each team at the beginning of the game that the participants use a guideline
5. Establishing an international media team through which participants receive news about each other
6. Starting the simulation, monitoring the turn-based flow, and letting the participants resolve the conflict

The educator generally gives information to the participants before the simulation starts, monitors the flow of the simulation, assesses the simulation at the end, and covers relevant topics afterwards. Once the details of this simulation design are established by the educator, it becomes easier to write an IR crisis simulation on any topic in international politics. While scenarios and minor details change across different simulations, there are certain common characteristics as well. First, simulations usually take longer than other techniques. Since the alternatives are not constant for participants, the simulations do not fall into repetition after a couple of turns like those in strategy games. Second, the main aim of simulations is to create a realistic scenario.

Crisis simulations are not games, they are intentionally designed with the aim of transferring realistic experiences from the IR profession. Last but not least, crisis simulations need substantial preparation and prior knowledge of the topic. Educators often need to assign selective readings to participants, explain rules in detail, and allocate sufficient time for participants to prepare for the simulation.

Simulations require a longer time for preparation and are best used to educate senior students who have prior knowledge of the key concepts in IR and the case at hand. Compared to strategy games, I recommend that simulations be used with relatively more experienced IR students. However, the educator may prefer to prepare more detailed instructions and allocate more time for preparation. Crisis simulations are great ways to let students experience IR as a profession through diverse perspectives. Students experience many aspects of IR as a profession at different stages of the simulation, including, but not limited to the difficulties of reaching consensus in international negotiations, the effort needed to reach a common ground in diplomacy, the challenges in the process of peaceful resolution of disputes, the alternative ways of representing a state as a diplomat, the importance and role of communication and international media, and the role of international institutions in world politics. The educator needs to follow the simulation carefully and take notes of the topics to evaluate at the end of the simulation. The evaluation at the end of the simulation is of key importance since the educator makes a final assessment to connect her/his observations during the simulation with the knowledge she/he intends to transfer to the students.

Finally, storification, is a technique that I use to teach science and methods in IR to undergraduate students with no prior knowledge (see Ruane and James 2008; 2012; Nexon and Neumann 2006; Young and Ko 2019 among others). I invented a story titled "The Tale of Two Villages: Rationalia and Reflectia" with the goal of explaining to students and helping them understand the so-called great theoretical debates and rationalist-reflectivist divide in IR (Luleci and Sula 2016; Sula and Luleci 2015; Sula 2019a; 2019b). The story is about people living in two distinct neighborhoods, their different lifestyles and the events happening after their first encounter. The story starts by describing life in Rationalia. Residents of Rationalia have quite similar lifestyles and daily routines where they construct and live in very similar buildings and houses. Then the story continues with residents of Reflectia, who live in very different conditions. Reflectians do not have similar houses, routines, or priorities but enjoy uniqueness in the lives of each resident. The story continues with the first encounter of Rationalians and Reflectians and with how Rationalians try to keep Reflectians out of their life. Rationalians even build huge walls, put gatekeepers to stop Reflectians from entering their sacred territories until a certain natural disaster (an earthquake) destroys their walls. After telling this short story, I ask the students to speculate and discuss the metaphors in the story. For instance, the towers of Rationalia representing the rationalist research programs, the huge wall-representing disciplinary boundaries in IR, the earthquake representing the end of the Cold War, and other metaphors that I inject into the story. When this technique is combined with creativity, and prior readings on the topic, it helps the student understand and remember the discussions made in the classroom. Just like the use of popular series, movies, and novels, the use of storification and metaphors also has the potential to help educators simplify the topics and transfer knowledge to their students.

I use this technique to transfer knowledge of complex theoretical topics in IR to students through simplifying and using metaphors. Storification highly depends on the creativity of the educator. I suggest that, before creating a story, the educator think whether the metaphors she/he uses in the story truly represent the knowledge she/he intends to transfer to the students. Based on the feedback that I get from the students, on certain occasions I realized that I have been telling "The Tale of Two Villages: Rationalia and Reflectia" in a way that directs the students to support one side of the debate more than the other. Since that was not my intent, I had had to explain the students that I do not support any of those theoretical positions more than the other. This feedback required me to readjust and think about the ways I tell the story in the classroom. Hence, carefully assessing what knowledge has been transferred to the students is an important aspect of this technique. If the course has reading material on complex theoretical topics, the instructor may ask the students to read the material before telling the story; then, after telling the story in class, give students additional time to think about the reading and assess the transfer of knowledge through discussion of the metaphors used in the story. Thereby, the educator can assess the degree of knowledge transfer and check if she/he transferred any unintended positions to the students.

Conclusion

The abundance of alternative pedagogical techniques helps educators formulate innovative, participatory, and efficient ways of teaching IR as a profession. Indeed, the usefulness of each technique depends on how the educator designs her/his education profile and what she/he understands as IR signature pedagogy. My experience is that each approach has advantages and disadvantages in teaching and learning IR. One of the shared aims of the approaches discussed above is to transfer knowledge and experience to the participant through a simplified and entertaining process.

There are a couple of important aspects to remember while utilizing these techniques: (1) the educator may miss some important details of the topic that she/he wants to cover while trying to use these techniques, and (2) maybe more importantly, the educator may transfer the wrong message to the participants. Both aspects require the educator to carefully assess the degree of knowledge and experience transferred to the participant and fill in the gaps and correct information if identified. My experience is that the educator may quite easily transfer unintended messages to participants turning them into fanatic supporters of a specific way of thinking in IR (realists, liberals, rationalists, etc.) or nationalist supporters of one of the countries in the simulations. This is especially so when the participant does not have prior knowledge of the topic. Therefore, I prefer using these techniques after letting students understand the basics of the course (usually after a couple of lecture weeks throughout the semester).

Specifically, strategy games are great icebreakers in the undergraduate classroom, letting students know each other before continuing the course throughout the semester. Other two techniques are more suitable for explaining certain topics in detail. Since crisis simulations require prior training, it is better to use them towards the final weeks of the semester. They may even be used as exams to assess and evaluate student knowledge and experience at the end of the course. Storification can be spread throughout the course depending on the creativity of the educator. I use stories and metaphors as discussion starters just after lectures and other times when necessary.

The education techniques discussed in this chapter are quite useful, as their structure is open for adjustment, their design can be updated, and their application is open to variation. However, while these techniques encourage active participation, it is the educator that puts the signature at the end. What the educator teaches and how she/he teaches it determines the definition of IR as a profession. Regarding the abundance of alternative education techniques in the current state of the literature, it is a great time to start discussing signature pedagogies in IR.

References

Alves, Elia Elisa Cia, Ana Paula Maielo Silva, and Gabriela Gonçalves Barbosa. 2019. "A Framework for Active Learning in International Relations: The Case of the Challenge Game." *Journal of Political Science Education* Published (May): 1–16. https://doi.org/10.1080/15512169.2019.1612755.

Ambrosio, Thomas. 2006. "Trying Saddam Hussein: Teaching International Law Through an Undergraduate Mock Trial." *International Studies Perspectives* 7: 159–71.

Asal, Victor, and Elizabeth L. Blake. 2006. "Creating Simulations for Political Science Education." *Journal of Political Science Education* 2 (1): 1–18. https://doi.org/10.1080/15512160500484119.

Asal, Victor, and Jayson Kratoville. 2013. "Constructing International Relations Simulations: Examining the Pedagogy of IR Simulations Through a Constructivist Learning Theory Lens." *Journal of Political Science Education* 9 (2): 132–43. https://doi.org/10.1080/15512169.2013.770982.

Boaz, Cynthia. 2020. "How Speculative Fiction Can Teach about Gender and Power in International Politics: A Pedagogical Overview." *International Studies Perspectives* 21 (3): 240–57. https://doi.org/10.1093/isp/ekz020.

Boyer, Mark A., Peter Trumbore, and David O. Fricke. 2006. "Teaching Theories of International Political Economy from the Pit: A Simple In-Class Simulation." *International Studies Perspectives* 7: 67–76.

Campbell, Joel R., and Gigi Gokcek. 2019. *The Final Frontier: International Relations and Politics through Star Trek and Star Wars*. London: Rowman & Littlefield Pub.

Chasek, Pamela S. 2005. "Power Politics, Diplomacy and Role Playing: Simulating the UN Security Council's Response to Terrorism." *International Studies Perspectives* 6: 1–19.

DiCicco, Jonathan M. 2014. "National Security Council: Simulating Decision-Making Dilemmas in Real Time." *International Studies Perspectives* 15 (4): 438–58. https://doi.org/10.1111/insp.12018.

Drezner, Daniel W. 2014. *Theories of International Politics and Zombies. Theories of International Politics and Zombies: Revived Edition*. New Jersey: Princeton University Press. https://doi.org/10.2307/j.ctt7zvcg0.

Dyson, Stephen Benedict. 2015. *Otherworldly Politics: The International Relations of Star Trek, Game of Thrones, and Battlestar Galactica*. Baltimore: Johns Hopkins University Press.

Elias, Anwen. 2014. "Simulating the European Union: Reflections on Module Design." *International Studies Perspectives* 15 (4): 407–22. https://doi.org/10.1111/insp.12009.

Freitas, Sara I. de. 2006. "Using Games and Simulations for Supporting Learning." *Learning, Media and Technology* 31 (4): 343–58. https://doi.org/10.1080/17439880601021967.

Horn, Laura, Olivier Rubin, and Laust Schouenborg. 2016. "Undead Pedagogy: How a Zombie Simulation Can Contribute to Teaching International Relations." *International Studies Perspectives* 17 (February): 187–201. https://doi.org/10.1111/insp.12103.

Kempston, Tanya, and Nicholas Thomas. 2014. "The Drama of International Relations: A South China Sea Simulation." *International Studies Perspectives* 15 (4): 459–76. https://doi.org/10.1111/insp.12045.

Killie, Kent J. 2002. "Simulating the Creation of a New International Human Rights Treaty: Active Learning in the International Studies Classroom." *International Studies Perspectives* 3: 271–90.

Lüdert, Jan. 2016. "Signature Pedagogies in International Relations." *E-International Relations*. 18 June. https://www.e-ir.info/2016/06/18/signature-pedagogies-in-international-relations/

Luleci, Cagla, and Ismail Erkam Sula. 2016. "Survival 'Beyond Positivism?' The Debate on Rationalism and Reflectivism in International Relations Theory." *Politikon: IAPSS Journal of Political Science* 30 (July): 43–55. https://doi.org/10.22151/politikon.30.3.

Nexon, Daniel H, and Iver B Neumann, eds. 2006. *Harry Potter and International Relations. Harry Potter and International Relations*. London: Rowman & Littlefield.

Ruane, Abigail E., and Patrick James. 2008. "The International Relations of Middle-Earth: Learning from The Lord of the Rings." *International Studies Perspectives* 9 (4): 377–94. https://doi.org/10.1111/j.1528-3585.2008.00343.x.

Ruane, Abigail E., and Patrick James. 2012. *The International Relations of Middle-Earth*. Ann Arbor, MI: University of Michigan Press. https://doi.org/10.3998/mpub.590468.

Shaw, Carolyn M. 2004. "Using Role-Play Scenarios in the IR Classroom: An Examination OfExercises on Peacekeeping Operations and Foreign Policy Decision Making." *International Studies Perspectives* 5: 1–22.

Shaw, Carolyn M. 2006. "Simulating Negotiations in a Three-Way Civil War." *Journal of Political Science Education* 2 (1): 51–71. https://doi.org/10.1080/15512160500484150.

Shaw, Carolyn M., and Bob Switky. 2018. "Designing and Using Simulations in the International Relations Classroom." *Journal of Political Science Education* 14 (4): 523–34. https://doi.org/10.1080/15512169.2018.1433543.

Shulman, Lee S. 2005. "Signature Pedagogies in the Professions." *Dædalus* 134 (3): 52–59.

Sula, Ismail Erkam. 2019a. "An Innovative Approach to Teach International Relations: The Use of Metaphors, Simulations & Games in the Undergraduate Classroom." In *60th ISA Annual Convention*. Toronto, CA.

Sula, Ismail Erkam. 2019b. "Uluslararası İlişkiler Eğitiminde Alternatif Uygulamalar: Oyun, Simülasyon ve Hikayeleştirme (Alternative Applications in International Relations Education: Games, Simuations, Storification)." Küresel Çalışmalar Platformu (Global Studies Platform). 2019. https://kureselcalismalar.com/uluslararasi-iliskiler-egitiminde-alternatif-uygulamalar-oyun-simulasyon-ve-hikayelestirme/

Sula, Ismail Erkam, and Cagla Luleci. 2015. "A Tale of Two Villages: Rationalia and Reflectia." In *The 56th ISA Annual Convention*. New Orleans, USA.

Switky, Bob. 2014. "Simulating a Foreign Policy Dilemma: Considering US Humanitarian Intervention." *PS: Political Science & Politics* 47 (3): 682–86. https://doi.org/10.1017/S1049096514000833.

Switky, Bob, and William Avilés. 2007. "Simulating the Free Trade Area of the Americas." *PS - Political Science and Politics*. https://doi.org/10.1017/S1049096507070631.

Thomas, G. Dale. 2002. "The Isle of Ted Simulation: Teaching Collective Action in International Relations and Organization." *Political Science & Politics* 35 (03): 555–59. https://doi.org/10.1017/S1049096502000835.

Weber, Cynthia. 2001. "The Highs and Lows of Teaching IR Theory: Using Popular Films for Theoretical Critique." *International Studies Perspectives* 2 (3): 281–87. https://doi.org/10.1111/1528-3577.00058.

Weber, Cynthia. 2010. "International Relations Theory: A Critical Introduction By Cynthia Weber." *Global Discourse* 1 (2): 217–20. https://doi.org/10.1080/23269995.2010.10707872.

Weber, Cynthia. 2014. *International Relations Theory: A Critical Introduction*. New York: Routledge.

Wedig, Timothy. 2010. "Getting the Most from Classroom Simulations: Strategies for Maximizing Learning Outcomes." *PS - Political Science and Politics*. https://doi.org/10.1017/S104909651000079X.

Young, Laura D, and Ñusta Carranza Ko. 2019. *Game of Thrones and Theories of International Relations*. Lanham, MD.: Lexington Books.

Zappile, Tina M., Daniel J. Beers, and Chad Raymond. 2017. "Promoting Global Empathy and Engagement through Real-Time Problem-Based Simulations." *International Studies Perspectives* 18 (February): 194–210. https://doi.org/10.1093/isp/ekv024.

14

Enhancing Creativity and Communication Skills Through IR Signature Pedagogies

XIRA RUIZ-CAMPILLO, KATTYA CASCANTE HERNÁNDEZ AND
ANTONIO MORENO CANTANO

Graduated students in International Relations (IR) have a broad number of jobs at their reach depending on their interests, from working in international organizations, governments, and the international departments of companies to working as analysts and advocators of human rights, gender, or the environment, in think tanks or non-governmental organizations (NGOs) of all sizes. But what skills should a student of IR master? A broad survey of IR programs worldwide shows part of the skills students must have to maximize their opportunities once they have finished their studies. We could all agree that communication and language skills, cross-cultural management skills, the ability to write clearly and concisely, flexibility, teamwork, organizational, analytical, and negotiation abilities, as well as autonomy would be some of the multiple skills we expect from IR graduates and that we can easily promote these through our IR signature pedagogies.

As pointed out by some authors (Delors 1996; Martín del Peso et al. 2013), universities play a fundamental role in generating new knowledge through the development of innovative procedures and in offering specialized training adapted to economic and social needs. Thus, teaching plays a fundamental role in which students are educated for their future professional careers, and it is important that students can create routines and actively engage in their own learning during their years of university studies (Shulman 2005, 52–59). Moreover, over recent years, "universities have increasingly recognized the importance of engaging students in active learning, relating that learning to students' lived experiences, and helping them recognize that they are creators of knowledge rather than mere recipients of learned truths" (Hunter et al. 2008, 42).

The aim of this chapter is to focus on signature pedagogies used by its authors with the goal of enhancing the above skills. Although all of these skills are relevant, an internal analysis undertaken by members of the Department of International Relations at the Complutense University of Madrid highlighted that placements where students have undertaken internships rated our IR students' creativity, written and oral communication skills as good yet not excellent. The chapter seeks therefore to share tools that could help improve creativity, written and oral communication skills, in IR degrees, all of them critical abilities in a challenging global landscape where graduates will have to show their expertise to get a job.

Although authors link creativity to divergent thinking, creativity also requires students to evaluate in creative ways and, above all, a great deal of domain knowledge and skills (Baer and Garrett 2010, 7). The purpose of promoting creativity or communication skills among students can by no means be done at the expense of knowledge transfer; what evidence suggests instead is that content knowledge is essential for improving students' thinking in any given domain (Baer and Garrett 2010, 9). Therefore, the use of policy memos or graphic novels, as it will be shown below, would be considered tools to foster basic knowledge using an alternative pedagogy.

Creativity has been portrayed as a tool that provides us with the ability to adapt and resort to imagination or fiction to escape from our immediate environment in a way that can be useful (Runco 2010, 15). Creativity has been also recognized as a skill that often leads to beneficial advances in art and literature, science, medicine, engineering, manufacturing, business, and other areas, and as a way of bringing vitality, meaning, and novelty into our lives (Kaufman and Baer 2004, xiv; Cropley 2010, 1; Lundin 2009, xiii). Moreover, there are authors that find creativity and innovation essential skills for meeting the challenges of the early twenty-first century arising from technological advances, social change, globalization, and competitiveness (Cropley 2010, 3; Florida 2004; Nakano and Wechsler 2018) and therefore an ability that must be cultivated in education (Florida 2004; Buzan 2009, xi; Soriano de Alencar, Fleith and Pereira 2017), especially in IR students who, by the nature of their future jobs, will have to face and solve numerous challenges and complex problems along their careers as future leaders, policy makers, managers of NGO, or analysts in a wide variety of institutions. Despite this recognition, universities may not be providing students with the necessary training to face and deal with these complexities. Indeed, surveys reveal that up to three-quarters of recent graduates, regardless of their discipline of study, were considered by employers as unsuitable for employment due to deficiencies in creativity, problem solving, and critical and independent thinking (Cropley 2014; Soriano de Alencar, Fleith and Pereira 2017, 555).

Any improvement in training university students must be based on the development of their communication skills. In the university environment, there are teachers with extraordinary memory skills and hundreds of publications, but when it comes to their performance during the lessons, they may not receive the best scores. The diagnosis is simple: they do not express or transmit their expertise and knowledge effectively to students. Studies such as Haji's et al. (2012), through a mixed method analysis of nearly a thousand Malaysian university students, demonstrate students' limited capacity to respond to what is transmitted to them verbally. This situation is a direct consequence of adopting signature pedagogies that prioritize master classes, in which students assist as passive agents who do not get involved or engage in dialogue during their learning. This lack of engagement is inevitably translated into the students' oral presentations, who often conceal difficulties by resorting to camouflage via innovative and eye-catching digital presentations while avoiding discussing content with depth and subject relevance. At the opposite pole are forms of written communication, such as essays and research papers, which, due to tradition and frequent use, reaches a higher state of development in most students. Without the interaction between the oral and the written, as Avedaño and Moretti (2007) point out, this communicative process is not carried out adequately. Because of these realities, we claim here that it is essential to give meaning to what is transmitted. In fact, innovative IR signature pedagogies present opportunities for IR lecturers to enhance students' education and training through a focus on meaning-making. As we propose in this chapter, the teacher can innovate IR signature pedagogies by designing strategies for translating ideas they assimilate in IR degrees not only via written and oral communication, but also visually—through graphic novels or the use of posters. This way, students would get additional skills to communicate and analyze international events using more visual approaches.

With this in mind, the chapter examines how the use of policy memos, graphic novels, academic posters, and simulations can be an effective tool to increase the knowledge of different IR subjects (e.g., global environmental challenges, international cooperation and conflict, human rights) while concurrently building creativity and communication skills for IR students in an appealing way (Bustos et al. 2017; Moreno Cantano 2019; Ruiz-Campillo 2019; Herman 2012; Fernández de Arriba 2016; Kaplan 2019). All of the above tools would fall into the "student as researchers" approach (Walkington 2015) and are good examples of signature pedagogies that Calder (2006,

1361) describes as "ways of being taught that require them to do, think, and value what practitioners in the field are doing, thinking, and valuing." All of them, at the same time, are approaches through which students can learn basic content, but most importantly, the ability to understand and practice disciplinary ways of thinking or habits of mind (Chick, Haynie, and Gurung 2009, 2). Following Jackson (2006, 12) and Soriano de Alencar, Fleith, and Pereira (2017), the tools described in this chapter promise to enhance creativity in higher education through offering students situations for learning where there are no right answers; providing activities that are meaningful to them; offering opportunities for collaborative working and discussion; challenging them with real, demanding, and exciting work; diversifying the teaching strategies used in the classroom; affording learning situations that are both fun and challenging; and encouraging students to pursue topics that most interest them.

Graphic Novels: Reading and Visual Learning

There is a vast literature on the educational powers that the use of graphic novels can bring to students, from secondary to higher education. Studies, among others, by Saitua (2018), in reference to historical themes; by Fernández de Arriba (2016) in relation to IR, by Rocamora-Pérez et al. (2017) in the field of physiotherapy, or by Hecke (2011) in reference to foreign languages, highlight graphic novels' multiple applications. Underlying this line of research are a number of elements that underscore their contribution to communication skills and blended learning (Garrison and Kanuka 2004), such as their permeability to transmit values; their capacity to bring other social and cultural realities closer to the student; their accessibility; the possibilities of promoting cooperative work through multiple readings of the same text; or their motivational format, favored by the interaction between images and text.

In our signature pedagogies, the graphic novel, as detailed by Marie-Crane (2008, 13), allows students to "train" and "develop" their visual culture, giving greater weight to images in the study of IR, and increasing students' emotions and empathy to such international tragedies as humanitarian crises or natural disasters. The use of this format in the university classroom or the creation of their own comics for the study of international issues facilitates, from a critical and constructive point of view, and reaffirms the relationship between the textual and the visual (Mannay 2017, 11).

Throughout several courses, we chose two ways to exploit the use of graphic novels in the university classroom, focusing on building students' creativity, capacity for synthesis, and empathy. Firstly, one of the compulsory practices established in the subject of international cultural relations has been the creation of a digital comic book on an international problem, whether it be a war or a humanitarian crisis. The use of the free online program COMIC LIFE was indicated, since it allows the handling of all kinds of images and elements typical of the visual language of comics in a simple way (e.g., text boxes, snacks, thought clouds). In this activity, students must demonstrate their ability and resources when summarizing a large amount of information and highlighting it in a brief and direct manner in a visual format, combining creativity with rigor. Graded evaluations considered the following as obligatory items: capacity for synthesis and textual summary of the event; visual variety; use of explanatory tables, dialogues, thoughts; and diversity of bibliographical sources and images.

At first, students showed reluctance to undertake an activity that departs from the more standardized and traditional IR practices and were more inclined to read academic texts and analyze written documents. However, while going deeper into it and sharing advice and experiences with each other, the final results were surprising and very positive. For instance, students were impressed by how graphic novels were able to capture a documentation of an event while summarizing its complexities in a few strips, or how they could resort to humor without losing accuracy in the data used.

Secondly, it must be highlighted that this implementation of a workshop on graphic novels related to the subject of international cultural relations and Spanish foreign affairs, with topics as diverse and heterogeneous as the persecution of the Rohingyas in Myanmar, the genocide in Rwanda, the Syrian refugee crisis, the Israeli-Palestinian conflict, and the influence of foreign powers in the Spanish Civil War. The implementation of this exercise requires professors to ensure that students can access learning materials in advance. For that reason, months beforehand, a request was made to the faculty's library to provide them with a complete list of graphic novels. Afterwards, a date was set for students—either individually or in pairs—to carry out their case study readings. After a first iteration to this format, students were asked to cover titles and author, with a brief outline of the format; general subject matter; contextualization; analysis through images of the most relevant elements of the comic's narrative and its relationship with the embodied conflict. It was also designed to learn about the students' own assessment of the methodological potential of this format, namely: is the graphic novel a useful tool for the study of IR? Through this type of engagement and reflection, a number of conclusions were reached: participants in this workshop considered the graphic novel as a valid way to study an international conflict, not only because of the detailed documentation behind them, but also because they appeal to engage students in affective learning and empathy. The use of images generates interest and greater awareness in the reader, thanks to the use of secondary plots (love, loss, incomprehension) in a global narrative framework (wars, peace processes, conflict resolution). In general, workshop participants agreed on the need to use this format, as well as all others that favor enhanced interaction between students and our international reality through *serious games* (Robinson 2015; Hayden, Lee, and Shirkey 2017).

Academic Posters: Learning to Communicate Concisely and Effectively

Researchers examined how the use of posters can contribute to improvements in students' communication skills (El-Sakran and Prescott 2013; Gobind and Ukpere 2014). Indeed, to communicate effectively is a basic ability that all students should be encouraged to develop during their university education. Another important competency informing communication skills is the ability to locate and critically analyze information. Traditional IR signature pedagogies tend to resort to essay-writing as the main tool to assess whether students acquire certain knowledge (mainly finding and transmitting information). The essay, depending on the professor, has a length that usually goes from a few pages up to twenty and can be a good way for students to learn about a specific topic more deeply. Despite its usefulness, professors tend to give students the same types of assignment, which risks turning essay-writing into a mechanical, dull, and repetitive task for students. Academic posters, on the other hand, demand research and analytical rigor from students while also developing their specific communication styles to conveys ideas clearly and succinctly (Hensley 2013, 121) and introducing a level of creativity ranging from poster layout and its display.

Posters give students the opportunity to focus on countless topics of their interest. For instance, and to name a few, the comparison between IR theories through the analysis of one and the same topic (e.g., the Syrian civil war seen from realist, liberal, or constructivist approaches; the impact of climate change in fast fashion; the role of the United Nations in the empowerment of women; links between capitalism and globalization, European Union crisis management, and conflict prevention tools).

It is advisable that professors give students the freedom to choose their own area of interest and examples of how a poster may look along with basic information and minimum requirements (e.g., the size of the poster, the need to include an introduction, a methodology, discussion of results, and conclusions together with the mandatory use of references, all of them presented in an appealing and attractive way). Typically, students choose their topic, obtain approval from the professor and then engage in research. Ideally, they receive feedback on the first draft of their poster before it is handed in for grading.

Both the freedom of choosing the layout and the specific topic (e.g., the rights of girls in country X) within a global subject area (e.g., human rights) are a way of demanding creativity from students (Jackson 2006, 12; Soriano de Alencar, Fleith and Pereira 2017). In addition, asking them to work in teams opens opportunities to learn from each other; exploring weaknesses and strengths in their arguments, deciding through reaching common ground, negotiating how to handle disagreements on a specific issue; or distributing tasks among team members. Depending on the poster requirements, students use a range of communications skills, such as internet search, sending emails, writing formal letters, meeting with experts and academics, as well as giving PowerPoint (or similar) presentations, oral presentations, and submitting final research reports (El-Sakran and Prescott 2013, 76).

Students will give their most in their poster assignment if they are asked to share their work voluntarily with other students, either by exhibiting posters in the department hallways, classrooms, or in widely accessible spaces, such as libraries. Students communicate when displaying posters and making them available for the wider community. Another source of motivation for students is the prospect of recommending the best posters to be displayed at a conference, which can be an extraordinary opportunity for students to participate in academia and research (Hensley 2013, 120). In all cases, asking them to share their own work shifts the nature of student work from cautionary and reactive to reflective and proactive, apart from gaining additional knowledge on issues, such as open access, author rights, and copyright (Davis-Kahl 2012, 213). Thus, posters are an excellent tool for students to develop a wide variety of abilities they will have at their disposal as future professionals.

Simulations: Practicing for Future Professional Positions

Over the past few years, numerous simulations of the United Nations (UN) General Assembly and Security Council, debates on how to address poverty and inequality or increase the visibility of women around the world have been held in our classrooms and with excellent results (Ruiz-Campillo 2019). These, as part of our IR signature pedagogies, will serve as a basis for sharing and developing best practices.

Simulations have a long history in political science as a means of achieving higher order educational goals (Boocock and Schild 1968; Dewey 1938; Heitzmann 1974; Walcott 1980). They have proven to be an effective way of putting students in the role of a political actor, getting them to consider the actor's objectives and the means by which the objectives can be achieved, as well as the possible movements of others in the situation. Ideally, simulations should enable students to gain a deeper understanding of the complex interests and concerns, the way in which decisions are made, the consequences of those decisions, the basics of persuasion mechanisms, agenda-setting and framing of international negotiations, as well as building affective empathy (Lüdert and Stewart, 2017).

Simulations take a global perspective, allowing students to play the roles of countries in the UN General Assembly, the Security Council, or other international institutions. In these simulations, students navigate divergent objectives of these countries as they attempt to forge a consensus. Through the simulation, students are exposed to the complexities of international cooperation and develop their analytical and argumentation skills, and gain abilities to synthesize and present information by interacting with other actors (Bustos et al. 2017, 5; Bernstein 2012). Materials for simulations that the professor can share with students include case study background content, research materials, and assessments adapted to the international agency in question.[1] These types of materials make easier both for the student to start looking for specific information on their role in the simulation and to familiarize themselves with how real actors behave when convening an international meeting, thus helping students model behaviors that directly translate into their careers.

Depending on the IR subject (human rights, climate change, women, conflicts), simulations can be organized not only around the UN General Assembly or the Security Council, but also other international institutions, such as the European Union, the Organization for Security and Co-operation in Europe (OSCE), the North Atlantic Treaty Organization (NATO), the Association of Southeast Asian Nations (ASEAN), or the African Union (AU). In all of them, students can be divided into teams to represent the delegation of states or the institutions they will be role-playing (e.g., secretariat members, chairpersons, the President of the General Assembly). Moreover, simulations can be organized in class, creating a situation where students have to solve an existing or imaginary crisis, and decide how to deploy staff in the field or how distribute funds to alleviate suffering or solve a global problem. In such scenarios, students can be assigned additional roles of international emergency organizations, intergovernmental organizations (civil and military), local and insurgency actors, and others.

Simulations allow IR students to explore existing functions of multilateral negotiations, according to the enabling and constraining legal-political

---

[1]   Some cases of model diplomacy and case studies can be found on sites such as that of the European Council on Foreign Relations, which offers hypothetical cases in different parts of the world with the aim of increasing students' knowledge and skills, and broadening their perspectives. See European Council on Foreign Relations, Model Diplomacy at https://modeldiplomacy.cfr.org/

parameters of the respective international organizations. In the face of conflicting interests with no possible agreement, simulations highlight the importance of negotiation as options for cooperation and that are beneficial for the majority of actors. Moreover, studies show how mediation must be performed not only between national partners, but also between state interests, which will require a renewed understanding of what diplomacy can do (Stanzel 2018). The fact that the students must logically order their arguments and expose them with determination, allows them to see the reactions of their opponents and force them to adapt their messages to the circumstances.

Understanding a conflict from the need to reach an agreement helps students contemplate other perspectives in their analysis and offer opportunities to cooperate, which will be of value in their future careers. These abilities and skills are essential for work in multilateral organizations, transnational companies, development agencies, and private sector organizations, clear objectives for the future work of International Relations students. As Bernstein (2012, 87–88) remarks, this type of pedagogy allows students to be more engaged in the subject matter, increase their understanding of the course material, and get a stronger sense of their ability to understand the discipline and participate in politics when they are motivated to do so.

Policy Memos: Facilitating Essential Information to Decision-Makers

While something should not be defined for what it is not, allow an exception to be made in this case. A policy memo is not an academic work. However, IR students are trained to produce quality academic works that follow a specific format and a specific structure. That is why it is useful to define a policy memo starting from what it is not: it is not a piece of standard academic work. A policy memo is substantially different from the assignments students typically produce. However, it is one of the most in-demand pieces of writing for politicians, lobbyists, NGOs, community leaders, and public initiatives. At its most fundamental level, a policy memo "aims to communicate essential information to decision-makers quickly and clearly" (Herman 2012, 2).

We claim that drafting policy memos challenges students' creativity in at least three ways. The first is to provoke a change in the student's approach to a topic. Developing a policy memo requires students to change the direction of the information being transmitted towards decision-makers, not to academic colleagues. This means that only the most relevant information has to be presented in the first paragraph of the memo, using the remainder of the document to justify the initial statements made in the first paragraph. Also, the closing part, where political recommendations are typically presented link back to that first paragraph. For the student, this means a radical change in how they are asked to structure writing content, succinctly presenting information of interest in a quick and almost intuitive manner.

The second challenge concerns the type of language and the extensions of the text. Writing policy memos is most successful the more specific and concise its content is. This often means to craft writing that is simple, direct, and free of adjectives. If the author of a policy memo aims to help a busy politician make a decision based on the information it contains, it should not exceed three pages. To be effective, the concepts and references used in a policy memo should match the political and technical jargon usually employed in the sector addressed.

The third challenge has to do with the purpose of the policy memo. A good policy memo may contain valuable unpublished and primary information, which can be overlooked if it fails to reach the person responsible for making decisions. The goals of a policy memo make it imperative to associate it from minute one to a communications strategy that allows its effective diss-emination and overall impact. While standard communication channels in academic work are specialized journals and academic conferences, a policy memo differs and employs a wide range of strategies to reach decision makers; these range from organizing roundtables that integrate all types of actors relevant to the issue, to the creation of databases listing the most relevant actors to be invited to public events where information will be shared and subsequently turned into a policy memo. Without a doubt, this implies having corresponding communication skills and knowledge on using effective media and dissemination channels.

We argue that these three challenges allow for the development of other important capacities, mainly the ability to relate to all stakeholders without excluding ideas, people, or alternative policy preferences. Also, the capacity to have access to the communities where real policies are made helps validate acquired knowledge as useful and applied. It is also an opportunity to actively participate in decisions that allow for the design and implementation of more equitable and less ideological public policies. In fact, higher education institutions like Harvard University's Kennedy School (2020) draw on precise guides of how to write a policy memo. Following a simple, three-step process: think, write and format, and revise, IR students will be able to craft policy memos on a wide variety of topics (e.g., the 2030 Agenda, international crisis, pandemics, election integrity, human rights in a specific country or context) and put themselves in the shoes of multiple actors (e.g., analysts at think tanks, NGOs, military and political advisors, public officers, private companies, etc.). Among others, written communication at the higher education level in particular should, in our view, involve critical and reflective engagement with other's ideas, development and support of one's own thinking, and skills in producing compelling arguments directed to an audience (Sparks, Song, Brantley and Liu 2014, 45). Thanks to the use of policy memos as teaching and learning vehicles in the IR, students can develop essential abilities, which are in-demand in professional settings, as are the ability to define and identify a problem, design policy solutions, and justify these through elaboration and recommendations.

Conclusions

The authors of this chapter contribute to the emergence of new IR signature pedagogies by sketching how graphic novels, simulations, posters, and policy memos support twenty-first century IR teaching. This century, perhaps more than ever, increases the complexities of events and requires IR students to be trained to face problems through creativity, good communication and cross-cultural skills, and the ability to negotiate effectively. The first two decades of the century indeed have included global events, such as the 9/11 attacks and the subsequent global war on terror, conflicts in Iraq, Afghanistan, Syria, Yemen, and, most recently, global pandemics. All these events give us an awesome responsibility as trainers and educators of future decision-makers. More important than ever, this means that IR academics need to adapt and adopt signature pedagogies that can help spark the interest of our students in the study of IR. Undoubtedly, uncertainty will be part of this type of teaching, transforming the classroom into a space that may become unpredictable and surprising (Lüdert 2016, 1) both for students and professors, as certainly are the times we live in. But providing students with greater space for practicing creativity also gives them the opportunity to strengthen their leadership capacities and develop creative problem-solving skills with novelty, uniqueness, and unusualness to approach reality (Mumford 2004, 218; Runco, 2010, 17).

Giving students a chance to develop their analytical and oral skills in an environment that engages, and puts students in the shoes of policy makers and IR practitioners, ought to be a mandatory requirement in every university in this century.

References

Avedaño, F., M. L. Miretti. 2007. *El desarrollo de la lengua oral en el aula.* Sevilla: MAD.

Baer, J., Garrett, T. 2010. "Teaching for Creativity in an Era of Content Standards and Accountability." In R. Beghetto, J. Kaufman (eds.) *Nurturing Creativity in the Classroom*. Cambridge: Cambridge University Press.

Bernstein, J. 2012. "Signature Pedagogies in Political Science. Teaching Students How Political Actors Behave", in A. Haynie, N. Chick, R. Gurung (eds) *Exploring More Signature Pedagogies: Approaches to Teaching Disciplinary Habits of Mind*. Sterlyn, Virginia: Stylus Pub.

Bustos, R.; K. Cascante; R. Ferrero; A. González; M. Guinea; P. Rodríguez. y X. Ruiz. 2017. *Guía de Simulaciones en Negociaciones Internacionales Multilaterales (SINIM)*, UCM. Madrid. https://eprints.ucm.es/44898/7/ GU%C3%8DA%20SINIM%20FINAL.pdf

Buzan, T. 2009. "Foreword", in S. Lundin, *Cats.The nine lives of innovation*. New York: McGraw Hill.

Calder, L. 2006. "Uncoverage: Toward a signature pedagogy for the history survey". *Journal of American History* 92 :1359–1369.

Chick, N., A. Haynie, and R. Gurung. 2009. "From generic to signature pedagogies", in A. Haynie, N. Chick, R. Gurung (eds) *Exploring Signature Pedagogies: Approaches to Teaching Disciplinary Habits of Mind*. Sterlyn, VA: Stylus Pub.

Council on Foreign Relations. *Model Diplomacy - A free interactive program that uses role-play to demonstrate the challenges of shaping United States foreign policy in an interconnected world.* Accessed 28 July 2020. https:// modeldiplomacy.cfr.org/case-library

Cropley, A. 2014. "Neglect of Creativity in Education: A Moral Issue.", in S. Moran, D. Cropley, J. Kaufman (eds). *The Ethics of Creativity*. Springer.

Davis-Kahl, S. 2012. "Engaging Undergraduates in Scholarly Communication: outreach education and advocacy." *C&RL News*, Vol. 73, no. 4.

Delors, J. 1996. *Learning: the treasure within; report to UNESCO of the International Commission on Education for the Twenty-first Century (highlights)*. Paris. UNESCO Publishing. https://unesdoc.unesco.org/ ark:/48223/pf0000109590

El-Sakran, T., D. Prescott. 2013. "Poster presentations improve engineering students' communication skills." *International Journal of Education and Practice*, vol. 1, no. 7: 75–86.

Fernández de Arriba, D. 2016. *"Las Relaciones Internacionales en la novela gráfica. Una aproximación,"* Cuco. Cuadernos de cómic 6: 62–79.

Florida, R. 2004. 'America's looming creativity crisis.' *Harvard Business Review*, 82(10): 122–136.

Garrison, R., H. Kanuka. 2004. "Blended learning: Uncovering its transformative potential in higher education". *Internet and Higher Education*, 7: 95–105.

Gobind, J, W. Ukpere. 2014. "The use of posters in disseminating HIV/AIDS awareness information within higher education institutions". *Mediterranean Journal of Social Sciences*. Vol. 5 no. 20: 739–747.

Haji, Z., Zakaria, E.; T. MohdMeerah et al. 2012. "Communication skills among university students." *Procedia-Social and Behavioural Sciences* 50: 71–76.

Harvard Kennedy School. 2020. *How to Write a Policy Memo.* Communications Program. Available at: https://projects.iq.harvard.edu/files/ hks-communications-program/files/lb_how_to_write_pol_mem_9_08_17.pdf

Hayden, C. "The Procedural Rhetorics of Mass Effect: Video Games As Argumentation in International Relations." *International Studies Perspectives*, 18 (2017): 175–193.

Hecke, C. "Graphic Novels as a Teaching Tool in High School and University English as a Foreign Language (EFL) Classroom." *Amerikastudien / American Studies*, Vol. 56, No. 4, (2011): 653–668.

Hensley, M. 2013. "The poster session as a vehicle for teaching the scholarly communication process", in S. Davis-Kahl and M. Kensley (eds.) *Common ground at the nexus of information literacy and scholarly communication.* Chicago: Association of College and Research Libraries. http://www.ala.org/ acrl/sites/ala.org.acrl/files/content/publications/booksanddigitalresources/ digital/commonground_oa.pdf

Herman, L. 2012. *Policy Memo*. Shorenstein Center on Media, Politics and Public Policy.

Hunter, G. 2008. "Interrogating the university, one archival entry at a time". *Change: The Magazine of Higher Learning* 40, no. 5: 40–45.

Jackson, N. 2006. "Developing and Valuing Student's Creativity: a new role for personal development planning?" *Working Paper*. http://www. normanjackson.co.uk/uploads/1/0/8/4/10842717/creativity_and_pdp.pdf

Kaplan, A. 2019. *Writing for Public Policy. A guide for writing public policy memos*. http://commons.trincoll.edu/115vernon/files/2019/03/Writing-Public-Policy-Memos-by-Alex-Kaplan-2018.pdf

Kaufman, J., Baer, J. 2004. "Introduction: How people think, work and act creatively in diverse domain", in J. Kaufman and J. Baer, *Creativity across domains: faces of the muse*. Abingdon: Taylor & Francis Group.

Lee, M. & Z. Shirkey. 2017. "Going Beyond the Existing Consensus: The Use of Games in International Relations Education". *PS: Political Science & Politics*, 50 (2): 571–575.

Lundin, S. 2009. *Cats: The nine lives of innovation*. New York: McGraw Hill.

Lüdert, J. 2016. 'Signature Pedagogies in International Relations'. *E-International Relations*. 18 June. https://www.e-ir.info/2016/06/18/signature-pedagogies-in-international-relations/

Lüdert, J. & K. Stewart. 2017. 'Nurturing Cognitive and Affective Empathy: The Benefits of Perspective-Taking'. 19 November. *E-International Relations*. https://www.e-ir.info/2017/11/19/nurturing-cognitive-and-affective-empathy-the-benefits-of-perspective-taking/

Mannay, D. 2017. *Métodos visuales, narrativos y creativos en investigación cualitativa*. Madrid: Narcea Ediciones.

Marie-Crane, R. 2008. "Image, Text, and Story: Comics and Graphic Novels in the Classroom". *Art education*, November, 13–19.

Martín del Peso, M.; A. B. Rabadán; J. Hernández. 2013. *Desajustes entre formación y empleo en el ámbito de las Enseñanzas Técnicas universitarias: la visión de los empleadores de la Comunidad de Madrid. Revista de Educación, 360.* Enero-abril.

Moreno, A. 2019. *Novelas gráficas y aprendizaje de Relaciones Internacionales: guía didáctica*, UCM. Madrid. https://eprints.ucm.es/58132/

Mumford, M., J. Strange, G. Scott, B. Gaddis. 2004. "Creative Problem-Solving Skills in Leadership: Direction, Actions, and Reactions", in. J. Kaufman and J. Baer, Introduction: How people think, work and act creatively in diverse domain. In J. Kaufman and J. Baer. *Creativity across domains: faces of the muse.* Abingdon: Taylor & Francis Group.

Nakano, T., S. Wechsler, S. 2008. "Creativity and innovation: Skills for the 21st Century." *Estudos de Psicologia (Campinas),* 35(3): 237–246.

Robinson, N. 2015. "Videogames and IR: Playing at Method", in F. Caso and C. Hamilton, *Popular Culture and World Politics: Theories.* E-International Relations Publishing.

Rocamora-Pérez, P. et al. 2017. "The Graphic Novel as an Innovative Teaching Methodology in Higher Education: Experience in the Physiotherapy Degree Program at the University of Almeria." *Procedia - Social and Behavioral Sciences*, 237: 1119–1124.

Ruiz-Campillo, X. 2019. "La realización de prácticas y su relación con la motivación del alumnado de Relaciones Internacionales." (*Exploring new fields through the scholarship of teaching and learning* III EuroSoTL Conference, Bilbao-Spain) (pp. 728–730). https://cutt.ly/JcwaH5

Runco, M. 2010. "Creativity Has No Dark Side", in D. Cropley, A. Cropley, J. Kaufman, M. Runco, *The Dark Side of Creativity.* Cambridge: Cambridge University Press.

Saitua, I. 2018. "La enseñanza de la Historia a través de la novela gráfica: una estrategia de aprendizaje emergente." *Didácticasespecíficas*(18): 65–87.

Shulman, L. 2005. "Signature Pedagogies in the Professions". *Daedalus* 134, no. 3, 52 – 59.

Soriano de Alencar, E., D. Fleith, N. Pereira, N. 2017. "Creativity in Higher Education: Challenges and Facilitating Factors." *Trends in Psychology*, Vol. 25, no. 2: 553–561.

Sparks, J., Y. Song, W. Brantley, O. Liu. 2014. "Assessing written communication in higher education: Review and recommendations for next-generation assessments." *ETS Research Report Series*: 1–52.

Stanzel, V. (ed.). 2018. "New Realities in Foreign Affairs: Diplomacy in the 21st Century". SWP Research Paper 11, November. *German Institute for International and Security Affairs*. https://www.swp-berlin.org/fileadmin/contents/products/research_papers/2018RP11_sze.pdf

Walkington, H. 2015. "Students as researchers: Supporting undergraduate research in the disciplines in higher education". *The Higher Education Academy*. https://www.heacademy.ac.uk/system/files/resources/Students%20as%20researchers_1.pdf

Note on Indexing

Our publications do not feature indexes. If you are reading this book in paperback and want to find a particular word or phrase you can do so by downloading a free PDF version of this book from the E-International Relations website.

View the e-book in any standard PDF reader such as Adobe Acrobat Reader (pc) or Preview (mac) and enter your search terms in the search box. You can then navigate through the search results and find what you are looking for. In practice, this method can prove much more targeted and effective than consulting an index.

If you are using apps (or devices) to read our e-books, you should also find word search functionality in those.

You can find all of our e-books at: http://www.e-ir.info/publications

www.ingramcontent.com/pod-product-compliance
Lightning Source LLC
Chambersburg PA
CBHW070928030426
42336CB00014BA/2580